FOR 2007 RETURNS

ZONDERVAN | 2008

Church and Nonprofit
Tax & Financial Guide

Dan Busby
CPA

ZONDERVAN.com/
AUTHORTRACKER
follow your favorite authors

We want to hear from you. Please send your comments about this book to us in care of zreview@zondervan.com. Thank you.

The Zondervan Church and Nonprofit Tax & Financial Guide: 2008 Edition
Copyright © 2007 by Dan Busby

Requests for information should be addressed to:

Zondervan, *Grand Rapids, Michigan* 49530

ISBN-10: 0-310-26185-6
ISBN-13: 978-0-310-26185-8

Publisher's note: This guide is published in recognition of the need for clarification of tax and other laws for churches and nonprofit organizations. Every effort has been made to publish timely, accurate, and authoritative guide. The publisher, author, and reviewers do not assume any legal responsibility for the accuracy of the text or any other contents.

Readers are cautioned that this book is sold with the understanding that the publisher is not rendering legal, accounting, or other professional service. Organizations with specific tax problems should seek the professional advice of a tax accountant or lawyer.

References to IRS forms and tax rates are derived from preliminary proofs of 2007 forms or 2006 forms. Some adaptation for changes may be necessary. These materials should be used solely as a guide in filling out 2007 tax and information returns. To obtain the final forms, schedules, and tables for filing returns and forms, contact the IRS or a public librar

All rights reserved. With the exception of the sample board resolutions, checklists, charts, and procedures, no part of this publication may be reproduced, stored in a retrieval system, or transmitted in any form or by any means—electronic, mechanical, photocopy, recording, or any other—except for brief quotations in printed reviews, without the prior permission of the publishe.

Printed in the United States of America

07 08 09 10 • 10 9 8 7 6 5 4 3 2 1

Contents...

Special Index for Church Treasurers	v
Introduction	viii
■ Recent Developments	1
■ 1 Financial Accountability	11
• Accountability to an independent board	12
• Accountability to donors	19
■ 2 Tax Exemption	25
• Advantages and limitations of tax exemption	25
• Tax exemption for churches	27
• Starting a church or other nonprofit organization	28
• Unrelated business income	32
• Private benefit and private inurement	39
• Filing federal returns	42
• Postal regulations	50
• State taxes and fees	50
• Political activity	53
■ 3 Compensating Employees	55
• Reasonable compensation	55
• Housing and the housing allowance	56
• Deferred compensation	61
• Maximizing fringe benefits	63
• Nondiscrimination rules	74
• Paying employee expenses	75
■ 4 Employer Reporting	85
• The classification of workers	85
• Reporting compensation	89
• Payroll tax withholding	89
• Depositing withheld payroll taxes	93
• Filing the quarterly payroll tax forms	94
• Filing the annual payroll tax forms	97

5 Information Reporting 107
- General filing requirements 107
- Reporting on the receipt of funds 109
- Reporting on the payment of funds 109
- Summary of payment reporting requirements 117

6 Financial Records 119
- Handling incoming funds 119
- Handling outgoing funds 124
- Accounting records 127
- Financial reports 132
- Budgeting 143
- Audits, reviews, and compilations 143

7 Charitable Gifts 151
- Charitable gift options 155
- Percentage limitations 158
- Gifts that may not qualify as contributions 159
- Charitable gift timing 161
- Acknowledging and reporting charitable gifts 162
- Quid pro quo disclosure requirements 175
- Deputized fund-raising 181
- Short-term mission trips 184
- Other special charitable contribution issues 192

Citations 207

Index 210

10 Biggest Tax and Financial Mistakes Made by Churches and Nonprofits 213

10 Tax and Finance Questions Most Frequently Asked by Churches and Nonprofits 214

SPECIAL INDEX
FOR CHURCH TREASURERS
A guide within a guide

Unrelated business income 32

Political activity 53

Employee compensation
    COBRA 67
    Deferred compensation 61
    Dependent care assistance plan 65
    Disability insurance 69
    Expense reimbursements 75
    403(b) plans 61
    Health insurance 66
    Housing allowances 56
    Loans to employees 70
    Medical expense reimbursement 68
    Moving expenses 71
    Overtime and minimum pay 73
    Property transfers 71
    Social security reimbursement 70
    Vehicles provided to employees 63
    Workers' Compensation 72

Workers at the church
    Are ministers employees or independent contractors? 88
    Assignment of ministers 88
    Depositing withheld payroll taxes 93
    Filing quarterly payroll tax returns 94
    Filing Form W-2 97
    Special tax provisions for ministers 89
    Withholding FICA taxes 89
    Withholding federal income taxes 90

Information return filings
    Interest payments 109
    Payments to nonresident aliens 111

Payment for services **112**
Payments to volunteers **114**
Payment of moving expenses **114**
Receipt of mortgage interest **109**

Financial records of the church

Budgeting **143**
Cash disbursements **124**
Cash receipts **119**
Chart of accounts **138**
Church management software systems **133**
Financial reports **132**
Guidelines for handling offerings **120**
Internal audit guidelines **145**
Petty cash system **127**

Charitable contributions

Contributions to support: specific workers or missionaries **181**
                               employees of a charity **193**
                               individuals other than staff members or the needy **194**
                               the needy **194**
                               short-term mission trips **184**
Contributions by volunteers **197**
Donor privacy **201**
Gifts that may not qualify as contributions **159**
Granting of scholarships **196**
Letter to noncash donors **164**
Quid pro quo disclosures **175**
Private schools **192**
Receipting charitable contributions **162**
Refunding gifts or sending contributions to another charity **200**
Reporting gifts to the IRS **162**

Insurance for the church

Disability **69**
Health **66**
Workers' Compensation **72**

Key laws that apply to churches

Fair Labor Standards Act **73**
Immigration control **115**

SPECIAL INDEX FOR CHURCH TREASURERS

Sample Board Resolutions, Checklists, Charts, and Procedures

Accountable expense reimbursement plan	77
Assignment of a minister	88
Benevolence fund	195
Chart of accounts	138
Compensation for a disqualified person	40
Conflict of interest	16-17
Credit cards	82-83
Donor privacy	202
401(k) and 403(b) plans compared	62
Handling church offerings	120-23
Housing allowance	57
Internal audit guidelines	145-49
Providing assistance to or for adoptive parents	205
Receipts issued other than to the remitter of the funds	201
Records retention	130
Travel and other expense reimbursement	78-81
Unrelated business income	34

Caution: You may need to consult with a tax or legal professional before adapting these materials to the specific needs of your organization.

Sample Charitable Contribution Letters and Forms

Letter to donors of noncash gift	164
Letter to volunteers	198
Receipts for gifts when goods or services *were* provided in exchange for the gift:	
• Periodic or annual receipt for all gifts whether over or under $250	179
Receipts for gifts when *no* goods or services were provided in exchange for the gift:	
• Periodic or annual receipt for all gifts whether over or under $250	163
Short-term mission trip letter, forms, and check	188-91

INTRODUCTION

The 18th annual edition of this guide is designed to help church and parachurch leaders understand what is required by and how to comply with federal and state laws. But it is much more!

Last year brought a fresh round of tax changes that are integrated throughout the text. For the first time, a page of IntegrityPoints is included at the end of each chapter. I believe these key points are worth the price of the book.

The voluminous laws and regulations that apply to churches and other nonprofits are mind-boggling. Yet this book is extremely readable and understandable—defying the complexity of the topics covered. Even more sample policies and resolutions have been added to the 2008 edition. The ease of use of this product is what sets it apart from any other book covering these topics.

This Guide challenges those who lead these organizations not just to meet the minimum requirements of the law or to meet fundamental ethical levels but to strive for levels of integrity far beyond the basics.

This book includes the basic rules for reporting to the IRS, handling charitable contributions, compensation to nonprofit employees, and much more. It also highlights issues raised in workshops where I have been the presenter in 38 states and in the hundreds of emails and telephone calls I receive from church and other nonprofit leaders each year! It is a veritable one-stop resource for answers to the tax and finance issues most frequently asked by churches and other nonprofits.

Proper understanding and treatment of the issues addressed in this guide are essential if Christ-centered organizations are to earn the public's trust by practicing accountability and God-honoring ethical practices.

Dan Busby

Recent Developments

IRS releases draft of new Form 990 for comments

The IRS has released a draft of the new proposed Form 990, which could be effective as early as 2008. The proposed changes are partially in response to increased scrutiny on organizations abusing their exempt status. Lois Lerner, Director of the Exempt Organizations Division of the Internal Revenue Service, stated that the redrafting was guided by the following three goals: to enhance transparency in reporting to provide a clearer picture of an organization's operations and a basis for comparison; to promote IRS reporting compliance; and to minimize the burden on organizations to file the Form 990.

With these goals in mind, the new form is formatted to be more readily understood and now has a 10-page core form to be completed by all filers. Additionally, there are now 15 separate schedules, which organizations will be required to file only if the particular schedules apply to the organization.

Some of the major changes include:

- A summary page providing the organization's identifying information and a snapshot of the organization's key financial, compensation, governance, and operational information.
- Reporting of certain governance information including composition of the board, and certain other governance and financial statement practices.
- Increased reporting of foreign transactions.
- Increased transparency in director, officer, and key employee compensation.
- Revenues calculated as a percentage of Total Revenue and Expenses as a percentage of Net Income.
- A new streamlined appearance to the form.

The proposed Schedule F—Statement of Activities Outside the U.S. raises concerns for many charities. The responses to Schedule F will be publically disclosed as mandated under certain subparagraphs of Internal Revenue Code 6104 and available worldwide on the Internet. This availability of the detailed information required by Schedule F will endanger personnel related to U.S. charities, both U.S. citizens and non-U.S. citizens, and the work in which they are engaged. The safety and security of charity-related personnel and the continuity of their usually unpublicized work outweighs the limited public interest for this information.

A legislative solution is being sought which would redact the information on Schedule F from public disclosure. The redaction of data would be a similar approach that applies to contribution data on Form 990, Schedule B.

Classification of workers

In May 2007, the General Accounting Office (GAO) presented a report on the impact of employee misclassification. They estimate that $4.7 billion was not paid in income taxes last year because of misclassification.

The report indicated that when employees are misclassified as independent contractors, they may be excluded from coverage under key laws designed to protect workers and may not have access to employer-provided health insurance coverage and pension plans. Moreover, misclassification of employees can affect the administration of many federal and state programs, such as payment of taxes and payments into state workers' compensation and unemployment insurance programs.

Some of the key laws designed to protect workers but that only apply to "employees" include the following:

- **Fair Labor Standards Act**—establishes minimum wage, overtime, and child labor standards;
- **Family and Medical Leave Act**—requires employers to allow employees to take up to 12 weeks of unpaid, job-protected leave for medical reasons related to a family member's or the employee's own health;
- **Occupational Safety and Health Act**—requires employers to maintain a safe and healthy workplace for their employees and requires employers and employees to comply with all federal occupational health and safety standards;
- **Unemployment Insurance**—pays benefits to workers in covered jobs who become unemployed and meet state-established eligibility rules; and
- **Workers' Compensation**—provides benefits to injured workers while limiting employers' liability strictly to workers' compensation payments.

Minimum wage rate increased

For the first time in 10 years, the federal minimum wage rate has been increased. The increases are effective in three steps: to $5.85 per hour effective July 24, 2007; to $6.55 per hour effective July 24, 2008; and to $7.25 per hour effective July 24, 2009.

The minimum wage rate in about 12 states exceed the new federal rates. Additionally, the minimum wage rate in 18 states has increased:

RECENT DEVELOPMENTS

- The minimum wage in the following states increased to $5.85 per hour on July 24, 2007 because their rates are tied to the federal rates: Georgia, Idaho, Indiana, New Mexico, North Dakota, Oklahoma, Texas, Utah, Virginia, and Wyoming.

- Kentucky and South Dakota passed legislation requiring employers to pay $5.85 per hour effective July 1, 2007.

- Kansas has a minimum wage law lower than the federal level ($2.65) which means the new federal rate applies to all employees covered by the FLSA.

- The new federal rate also applies to Alabama, Louisiana, Mississippi, South Carolina, and Tennessee, which have no minimum wage laws.

- In New Hampshire, effective September 1, 2007, the state minimum wage is $6.50 per hour.

IRS updates family of 941 forms for 2008

The Form 941c won't have to be filed much longer. It will be replaced with the new stand-alone Form 941x starting the first quarter of 2008.

With the new Form 941x, you will be able to submit one quarter amendment per form, file the form independently of the Form 941, and assign overpayments to your next 941 liability, or request a refund.

The primary changes to the 2008 941 include the deletion of Lines 7d, 7e, 7f, and 7g. Line 7a, 7b, and 7c remain.

Social Security Administration (SSA) upgrades social security number verification process

Verifying employees' social security numbers (SSNs) throughout the year, as they're hired, can help year-end run smoother. You'll avoid those IRS mismatch letters and W-2cs should employees find an SSN error when filing their taxes.

It is easier to figure out if every SSN submitted to SSAs Social Security Number Verification Service (SSNVS) is confirmed. In the past, SSA only returned numbers that couldn't be verified. Starting August 25, 2007, SSA will return results on all SSNs in your file.

SSA will also start using a 16-digit confirmation number for all the files submitted to SSNVS for verification. That will be instead of the usual eight-position tracking number that allows you to view results and request your file status.

Donor-advised funds investigation

The IRS continues to investigate donor-advised funds and donors to them. They have identified more than 200 donors for examination and are investigating 11 donor-advised funds that "account for a significant portion of the assets and income in the donor-advised fund universe."

The IRS has proposed that two large national donor-advised fund operators lose their tax-exempt status because they allegedly have been using some of their funds for donors' personal benefit, such as reimbursing donors for their expenses or to pay college-tuition bills of their children.

As part of the Pension Protection Act of 2006, Congress ordered the Treasury Department to investigate donor-advised funds and recommend potential ways to ensure they are providing appropriate benefits to charitable causes.

Form 990-N required for small charities

Beginning in 2008, small tax-exempt organizations who previously were not required to file a return with the Internal Revenue Service (IRS) may now be required to file an annual electronic notice, Form 990-N, Electronic Notice (e-Postcard) for Tax-Exempt Organizations not Required to File Form 990 or 990-EZ.

Who must file? Small tax-exempt organizations whose gross receipts are normally $25,000 or less and who therefore do not file an IRS Form 990 or 990-EZ are required to file the new 990-N. Failure to make such filing could jeopardize the organization's exempt status.

Exceptions to this filling requirement:

- Religious organizations already exempted from filling Form 990 for reasons other than the income restriction
- Organizations who are included in a group return
- Private foundations required to file IRS Form 990-PF
- Section 509(a)(3) supporting organizations required to file IRS Form 990 or 900-EZ

What must be filed? The following information will be required in order to complete the online form:

- Organization's name
- Any other names your organization uses
- Organization's mailing address
- Organization's website address (if applicable)
- Organization's federal employer identification number (FEIN)
- Name and address of a principal officer of your organization
- Organization's annual tax period
- A statement that your organization's annual gross receipts are still normally $25,000 or less
- If applicable, indicate if your organization is dissolving

When must the Form 990-N be filed? This filing requirement applies to tax periods beginning after December 31, 2006. Thus beginning in 2008, the e-Postcard will be due every year by the 15th day of the fifth month after the close of your tax period. For example, if your tax period ends on December 31, 2007, the e-Postcard is due May 15, 2008.

Where must the Form 990-N be filed? The 990-N must be filed electronically therefore there will not be any paper forms available. The IRS has not released the final details of how this will be accomplished, but instructions are anticipated to be released in the near future. The IRS has indicated that this will be an internet based form that will not require the purchase of any software or services. Therefore this return can be completed from any computer that has Internet access, such as at a local library.

IRS reiterates its position on cellular telephones

The IRS has stated that "an employer can exclude an employee's use of an employer-provided cell phone from the employee's gross income, if the employer has some method of requiring the employee to keep records that distinguish business from personal phone charges. If the employee uses the telephone exclusively for business, all use is excludable from income (as a working condition fringe benefit). The employer must include the value of any personal use of the cell phone in the employee's wages. Personal use includes individual personal calls, as well as a prorate share of monthly service charges.

To ensure that an employee's business use of an employer-provided cell phone is excludable from gross income, the employee should keep a record of each call and its business purposes. If calls are itemized on a monthly statement, the employee should identify each call as personal or business. The employee should submit this information to the employer, who must maintain these records to support the exclusion of the phone use from the employee's wages. If the employee does not sue the cell phone to make personal calls, or has only minimal personal use of the cell phone, the business use of the phone is not taxable to the employee." INFO 2007-0025

IRS determines mission agency is not a church

A nondenominational mission agency did not qualify as a church because it failed to satisfy most of the criteria established by the IRS and courts to be classified as a church.

The mission agency's primarily activities involve the establishment of new churches and performance of missionary activities in Spanish-speaking countries. The agency did not hold itself out publicly as a church, but sought reclassification as a church. The Court said the agency did not satisfy the IRS's 14 point test for classification as a church. Specifically, it lacked an established congregation served by an organized ministry. It failed to provide regular worship services and it lacked a formal code of doctrine and discipline. It also failed to meet other criteria, such as ordaining ministers, having a distinct ecclesiastical government, possessing an established place of worship, or a membership not associated with other churches or denominations. PLR 200727021

IRS releases an initial report on Nonprofit Executive Compensation

On March 1, 2007, the IRS issued its initial report on its executive compensation project—involving some 2,000 nonprofit organizations. A summary of the finding follows:

➤ Significant reporting issues exist – Over 30% of compliance check recipients amended their Forms 990. Fifteen percent (15%) of the compliance check recipients were selected for examination.

➤ Examinations completed to date do not evidence widespread concerns other than reporting. However, as this was not a statistical sample, no definitive statement can yet be made concerning the compliance level in this area. Continued work in the area of executive compensation is warranted.

➤ Where problems were found, significant dollars are being assessed (25 examinations have resulted in proposed excise tax assessments under Chapter 42, aggregating in excess of $21 million, against 40 disqualified persons or organization managers).

➤ Although high compensation amounts were found in many cases, generally they were substantiated based on appropriate comparability data.

➤ Additional education and guidance, as well as training for agents, are needed in the areas of reporting requirements, and the "rebuttable presumption" procedure that may be relied upon by public charities to establish appropriate compensation.

➤ Changes in the Form 990 series are necessary to reduce errors in reporting and provide sufficient information to enable the IRS to identify compensation issues.

➤ Part I and Part II utilized new compliance contact techniques, which have since been refined in later projects such as Credit Counseling and Down Payment Assistance.

➤ Using those refined techniques and concentrating on particular industries, demographics and governance practices in future efforts should allow us to better assess and understand compliance levels and enable us to identify and concentrate our efforts on noncompliant taxpayers.

The report cites the following lessons learned and recommendations:

1. The size of the Project and the diverse universe created logistical difficulties. Future initiatives involving a similarly large number of organizations should consider breaking the project into components such as separating public charities and private foundations.

2. Using correspondence as the exclusive method of conducting single issue examinations for factually sensitive and complicated issues, such as self-dealing and excess benefit transactions, should be reconsidered.

   Although it is appropriate to use broad contacts to identify cases to be examined, an upfront field visit or other contact with the examined organization might substantially reduce the volume of records needed to be reviewed and the time spent on the examination.

3. Compliance check questions must be clear and focused in order to produce responses that can be readily analyzed and can enable the Service to select appropriate cases for examination.

4. Form 990 compensation reporting needs to be revised to facilitate accurate and complete reporting. The Form 990 redesign project should focus on reducing the number of places the same information is reported on the form, providing clearer instructions regarding what needs to be reported, and requesting specific information to identify potential noncompliance areas such as loans to officers and directors.

5. Nonprofits need to revisit the issue of when penalties should be assessed for filing an incomplete Form 990 or 990-PF.

6. Nonprofits should communicate to the public the most common return preparation errors identified during the compliance checks and examinations.

7. Nonprofits should further educate the public charity sector about the section 4958 rebuttable presumption and how to satisfy the requirements of the presumption.

8. Future initiatives should focus on the correlation between satisfaction of the rebuttable presumption by an organization and the reasonableness of compensation paid to its disqualified persons by such an organization.

9. Nonprofits should change its process for monitoring excise taxes collected for excessive compensation to better distinguish between the different types of excise taxes collected from public charities and private foundations.

10. The relatively small percentage of corrections made by disqualified persons before contact by nonprofits illustrates the need for a continued enforcement presence in this area. Nonprofits should continue to review compensation issues in more focused projects and should pursue baselining general compliance with the compensation rules. The full report may be found at: http://www.irs.gov/pub/irs-tege/exec._comp._final.pdf.

Tax Relief and Health Care Act impacts charitable remainder trusts

Prior to the enactment of the Tax Relief and Health Care Act of 2006, charitable remainder trusts (*e.g.*, charitable remainder annuity or unitrusts) lost their tax exemption for any year in which the trust has any unrelated business income.

Under the new law charitable remainder trusts with unrelated business income retain their tax-exempt status but are subject to a 100-percent excise tax on their unrelated business taxable income.

Legislation to expand and make permanent IRA charitable rollovers is pending

Senators Byron Dorgan (D-ND) and Olympia Snowe (R-ME) and Representatives Earl Pomeroy (D-ND) and Wally Herger (R-CA) have introduced the "Public Good IRA

Rollover Act of 2007" in the House (H.R. 1419) and Senate (S. 819).

Currently, the IRA rollover permits individuals age 70½ and above to make charitable donations of up to $100,000 from Individual Retirement Accounts (IRAs) and Roth IRAs without having to count the distributions as taxable income. The "Public Good IRA Rollover Act of 2007" would be permanent, would remove the $100,000 annual limit on donations, and would provide IRA owners with a planned giving option starting at age 59½. The IRA Charitable Rollover provision included in the Pension Protection Act of 2006 allows individuals age 70½ and older to make charitable donations of up to $100,000 from Individual Retirement Accounts (IRAs) and Roth IRAs without having to count the distributions as taxable income. That provision is set to expire in December.

The existing IRA Rollover, though limited, has already led Americans to make millions of dollars in new charitable donations from their IRAs. Initial reports to the National Committee on Planned Giving already show that during the first four months the provision was in effect, Americans made more than $50 million in contributions to nonprofits through the IRA rollover.

IRS issues regulations on informal church retirement plans

Many churches have established informal retirement arrangements for ministers, often a founding pastor or a pastor who served the congregation for many years. These arrangements are often made when the payments to a qualified retirement pan were not substantial during the minister's service to the congregation.

Examples of informal retirement plans include:

➤ A church agrees to make payments for 15 years (or another specific number of years) after the minister leaves the church.

➤ A church agrees to make monthly payments to a retiring minister (or surviving spouse) for the minister's life.

Section 409A of the Internal Revenue Code has applied to informal church retirement arrangements since 2005. On April 10, 2007, the IRS issued Final Regulations, effective in 2008, to provide clarity to the requirements. The deadline for document compliance was to be December 31, 2007. However, on September 10, 2007 (IR-2007-157), the IRS extended the document compliance deadline to December 31, 2007 but it did not extend the January 1, 2008, effective date of the final regulations.

Section 409A requires a written document which meets specific requirements. Failure to comply with the Section 409A operational or plan documentation requirements can result in significant tax penalties for participants in deferred compensation arrangements, including a 20% federal penalty tax, plus interest and penalties, on the participant. Certain states also have adopted similar tax provisions. For example, California imposes an additional 20 percent state tax, interest, and penalties.

> RECENT DEVELOPMENTS

Plans established before October 3, 2004 are not subject to Section 409A if the plans are not materially modified after October 3, 2004. Congregations with plans established before October 3, 2004 should determine if the plans can operate without any further modifications or benefit accrual.

All congregations should:

> **Identify arrangements subject to Section 409A.** A crucial first step is to understand the congregation's arrangements that potentially are subject to Section 409A.

> *Consider changing payment elections. If participants in arrangements wish to make changes in the time or form of payment of nonqualified deferred compensation, those changes must be made and documented by December 31, 2007. Notice 2007-78 does not extend this transition relief.*

> **Ensure operational compliance.** Deferred compensation arrangements must be operated in compliance with the final Section 409A regulations, even if such compliance is not yet documented in writing.

Certain tax-favored vehicles such as 401(k) and 403(b) plans are exempt from 409A and the related regulations.

Key Federal Tax Limits, Rates, and Other Data

	2006	2007	2008
Social security:			
SECA (OASDI & Medicare) rate	15.3%	15.3%	15.3%
FICA (OASDI & Medicare) rate	7.65%	7.65%	7.65%
OASDI maximum compensation base	$94,200	$97,500	$102,000
Benefits and contributions:			
Maximum annual contribution to defined contribution plan	$44,000	$45,000	$46,000
Maximum salary deduction for 401(k)/403(b)	$15,000	$15,500	$15,500
401(k) & 403(b) over 50 "catch up" limit	$5,000	$5,000	$5,000
Maximum income exclusion for nonqualified plans in 501(c)(3) organizations (IRC 457)	$15,000	$15,500	$15,500
IRA contribution limit – age 49 and below	$4,000	$4,000	
IRA contribution limit – age 50 and above	$1,000	$1,000	
Highly compensated employee limit	$100,000	$100,000	$105,000

	2006	2007	2008
Per diem and mileage rates and other transportation:			
Standard per diem: Lowest rates in continental USA	Lodging $60 Meals & Incidentals $39	Lodging $60 Meals & Incidentals $39	
IRS high/low substitute per diem system (Effective October 1)	High $226 Low $141	High $246 Low $148	
Business auto mileage rate:	44.5 cents per mile (entire year)	48.5 cents per mile (entire year)	
Moving & medical auto mileage rate	18 cents per mile (entire year)	20 cents per mile (entire year)	
Charitable auto mileage rate	14 cents per mile	14 cents per mile	
Motorcycle mileage rate (1)		30.5 cents per mile	
Airplane mileage rate (1)		$1.07 per mile	
Maximum value of reimbursement of business expenses (other than lodging) without receipt	$75	$75	
Luxury automobile value (limit on use of cents-per-mile valuation of company automobile)	$15,000	$15,100	
Monthly limit on free parking		$205	$215
Transit passes/token — monthly tax-free limit	$105	$110	$110
Form 990/990-T/990-N and 1099-MISC threshold:			
Threshold for required filing Form 990 (if not otherwise exempt)	$25,000 in annual gross receipts	$25,000 in annual gross receipts	$25,000 in annual gross receipts
Threshold for filing Form 990 electronically	$10 million in total assets	$10 million in total assets	$10 million in total assets
Threshold for required filing Form 990-N	N/A	N/A	Under $25,000 in annual gross receipts
Threshold for required filing Form 990-T	$1,000 annual gross UBI	$1,000 annual gross UBI	$1,000 annual gross UBI
Threshold for required filing of Form 1099-MISC (payment for most personal services)	$600	$600	$600
Quid pro quo:			
Minimum contribution and maximum cost of token	Minimum gift: $43 Maximum cost: $8.60	Minimum gift: $44.50 Maximum cost: $8.90	
Maximum value of de minimus benefit	2% of gift, but not more than $86	2% of gift, but not more than $89	
Other:			
Federal minimum wage per hour	$5.15	$5.85 effective 7/24/07	$6.55 effective 7/24/08 and $7.25 effective 7/24/09
Sec. 179 expensing limit	$108,000	$125,000	$128,000
Gift tax annual exclusion	$12,000	$12,000	$12,000
Unified estate and gift tax exception	$2,000,000	$2,000,000	$2,000,000

CHAPTER ONE
Financial Accountability

In This Chapter
- Accountability to an independent board
- Accountability to donors

The public has high expectations of churches and other religious organizations. Day after day, thousands in the nonprofit community work tirelessly and selflessly to address physical and spiritual needs worldwide, only to find the public casting a wary eye on them due to the highly publicized misdeeds of a few. Donors recognize that enormous needs exist, and they want to respond generously to those needs. But they also want to be sure that optimum use of their sacrificial gifts is employed by the charities they support. There is no acceptable alternative to accountability.

For some nonprofit organizations, accountability issues may relate to complex issues of private inurement or conflicts of interest. Charities receiving significant contributions in the aftermath of a disaster may face the challenge of spending donations within donor expectations. In other organizations, the issues may be as basic as whether to accept a gift that appears to be a pass-through contribution for the personal benefit of a designated individual.

Financial accountability is based on the principle of stewardship. A steward-manager exercises responsible care over entrusted funds. Good stewardship rarely occurs outside a system of accountability.

Financial accountability is the natural outgrowth of proper organizational leadership. Providing clear, basic explanations of financial activity starts with the detailed record of transactions and evolves to adequate reporting to donors and boards.

Being accountable to an organization that promotes stewardship principles often enhances accountability. The organization that provides leadership in the area of financial accountability to the most Christian organizations is the Evangelical Council for Financial Accountability (ECFA). With over 1,250 members, ECFA has established standards relating to proper accounting, an independent and responsible volunteer board of directors, full disclosure of finances, and fair treatment for donors (see pages 22-23). Its program of random site visits of 15 percent of its memebers each year adds credibility to its accountability process.

Accountability to an Independent Board

Board governance

The importance of an independent board cannot be overemphasized. Even minor board neglect, left unchecked, can eventually intrude upon the accountability and effectiveness of the ministry. In contrast, the independent board will hold to the mission, protect the integrity of ministry objectives, establish adequate board policies, and ensure consistent adherence to these policies.

Finding a proper balance between the staff leadership of a church or other nonprofit organization and the board is fundamental. Any charity with too powerful or too weak a leader is a charity in trouble. When the top leader is too strong, it may be difficult for the board to provide adequate governance over the charity. Conversely, where the top leader is weak, boards or one or more board members often inappropriately move in and take over.

Can your organization's leadership be challenged and voted down? Are the board members permissive and passive or involved and active? Are your values and policies clearly articulated? Are they operative in the organization daily? Are annual evaluations, based on predetermined goals, made of the pastor(s) or the nonprofit chief executive officer, president, or director?

> **Key Issue**
>
> Boards should develop a cyclical pattern of self-evaluation. The purpose of self-assessment is to individually and collectively improve board performance. It can take a variety of formats, from soliciting feedback from individual board members about their contributions to the board's performance, to evaluating the effectiveness of time spent together as a board.

A board should generally meet at least semiannually and many boards will meet more frequently. Each board should determine the appropriate number of meetings based on the nature of the organization and the number and structure of committees the board has created to assist it in overseeing the organization's business. However, meetings held too frequently often result in the inappropriate involvement by the board in management issues. Meetings should be more than listening to the a leader's report and rubber-stamping a series of resolutions prepared by the top leader.

A board should generally consist of at least five individuals. A majority of the board must be other than employees or staff, or those related by blood or marriage, to ensure independence. Even when employee membership on the board is slightly less than a majority, the independence of the board may be jeopardized. Employees often lack independence and objectivity in dealing with many board-level matters. While the organization's top leader is often a member of an organization's board of directors, department heads are generally not members of the board.

Recording board actions

The actions of an organization's board and its committees should be recorded by written minutes, including the signature of the secretary, prepared within a few days after the meeting concludes. The minute books of some charities are almost nonexistent. Minutes of the most recent board meeting often appear to be placed in proper written form on the eve of the succeeding board meeting. Such lack of organization can be indicative of weak board governance and may leave a poor paper trail to document the board's actions.

The actions of an organization's board often include the approval and revision of policies. These policies should be reflected in the board policy manual, with the manual updated as appropriate.

Financial audit, review, or compilation

Many churches and nonprofit organizations have an independent annual audit, review, or compilation (see pages 143-44) prepared by an independent certified public accountant (CPA).

Here is what to look for from your CPA firm:

- A firm thoroughly knowledgeable about current accounting standards and one that understands your segment of Christian nonprofits.
- A firm that routinely prepares value-added management letters for its audit clients.
- A firm that helps you reduce your audit fee.
- A firm that understands your accounting system.

> **Remember**
>
> Independence is the cornerstone of the auditing profession. The independent auditor should have no ties to management and no responsibility for governance or finance. The public can place faith in the audit function because an auditor is impartial and recognizes an obligation of fairness.

When an organization has an external audit, review, or compilation, the board or a committee consisting of a majority of independent members should review the annual audit and maintain direct communication between the board and the independent CPA.

If a charity does not have an annual external audit, an internal audit should be performed using written procedures (see pages 145-49). The largest charities often choose to have both annual external and internal audits.

Compensation review

An annual review of the minister's or nonprofit organization executive's compensation package is vital. The review should focus on all elements of pay, taxable and nontaxable, in addition to reviewing performance and establishing performance objectives and criteria.

Pay and fringe benefit packages should be determined by an objective evaluation of responsibilities, goals reached, and available resources. A comparison with positions in other organizations may be helpful. National salary surveys may provide meaningful data;

ECFA provides salary data at no cost at www.ECFA.org. The approved compensation package should be documented in board and/or subcommittee minutes.

With increased scrutiny of nonprofit salaries (see chapter 3), it is important that compensation amounts be accurately stated. Gross pay may include the following elements (some taxable and some tax-free or tax-deferred):

- Cash salary
- Fair rental value of a house, including utilities, provided by the organization
- Cash housing or furnishings allowance
- Tax-deferred payments
- Value of the personal use of organization-owned aircraft or vehicle
- Value of noncash goods and services
- Cash bonuses

> **Caution**
>
> Reasonable salary and fringe benefits, especially for the highest paid employees of a charity, should be carefully documented. The intermediate sanction regulations provide penalties for "excess benefit transactions." Examples of such transactions include unreasonable salaries or bonuses to key employees and excessive travel expenses or other perks.

Budget process

The organization should prepare an annual budget consistent with the major classifications in the financial statements and approved by the board. The budget should allow meaningful comparison with the previous year's financial statements. A capital budget (including anticipated purchases of property and equipment) and a cash budget (to reflect the ebb and flow of cash received and expended) is often helpful to organizations.

Responsibility for budgetary performance should be clearly assigned to management as appropriate (for example, department heads, field directors, and so on). The chief financial officer or treasurer of an organization is normally responsible for budgetary enforcement and reporting. For more information on the budgeting process, see page 143.

Conflicts of interest and related-party transactions

Fairness in decision making is more likely to occur in an impartial environment. Conflicts of interest and related-party transactions are often confused. However, they are clearly different concepts.

The potential for a conflict of interest arises in situations in which a person is responsible for promoting one interest at the same time he or she is involved in a competing interest. If this person exercises the competing interest over the fiduciary interest, he or she is guilty of conflict of interest. Always avoid conflicts of interest.

Related-party transactions occur between two or more parties with interlinking relationships. These transactions should be disclosed to the governing board and evaluated to ensure they are made on a sound economic basis. The organization may decide to pursue any related-party transactions that are clearly advantageous to the organization.

Undertake transactions with related parties only in the following situations:

- The audited financial statements of the organization fully disclose material related-party transactions.
- Related parties are excluded from the discussion and approval of related-party transactions.
- There are competitive bids or comparable valuations.
- The organization's board approves the transaction as one that is in the best interest of the organization.

Caution

Integrity requires that a board member or other insider disclose a potential conflict of interest to the board. The individual should refrain from voting on the transactions involving a related issue, not be included in the quorum for the meeting when the matter is considered, and not be present during the voting.

Example 1: An organization purchases insurance coverage through a firm owned by a board member. This is a related-party transaction. If the cost of the insurance is disclosed, the purchase is subject to proper approvals, the price is below the competition's, the purchase is in the best interests of the organization, and the related party is not present at the meeting when the decision is made, the transaction does not constitute a conflict of interest but qualifies as a related-party transaction.

Warning

Information concerning prospective and current board members may reveal potential conflicts that will disqualify the individual. If a conflict is sufficiently limited, the individual may simply need to abstain from voting on certain issues. If the conflict of interest is material, the election or reelection of the individual may be inappropriate.

Example 2: The CEO and several employees are members of the board. When the resolution on salary and fringe-benefit adjustments comes to the board, should those affected by the resolution discuss and vote on the matter? No. The CEO and employees not only should avoid discussing and voting on such matters, but also should absent themselves from the meeting to avoid even the appearance of a conflict of interest.

Example 3: A nonprofit board considers a significant loan to a company in which a board member has a material ownership interest. Should this loan even be considered? Yes, but only if it is in the best interest of the nonprofit organization, is allowed under its bylaws, and is allowed under state laws.

Sample Conflict of Interest Policy Statement

All trustees, officers, agents, and employees of this organization shall disclose all real or apparent conflicts of interest that they discover or that have been brought to their attention in connection with this organization's activities. "Disclosure" shall mean providing properly, to the appropriate person, a written description of the facts comprising the real or apparent conflict of interest. An annual disclosure statement shall be circulated to trustees, officers, and certain identified agents and employees to assist them in considering such disclosures, but disclosure is appropriate and required whenever conflicts of interest may occur. The written notices of disclosures shall be filed with the board chair or such other person designated by the board chair to receive such notifications. At the meeting of the top governing body, all disclosures of real or apparent conflicts of interest shall be noted for the record in the minutes.

An individual trustee, officer, agent, or employee who believes that he or she or an immediate member of his or her immediate family might have a real or apparent conflict of interest, in addition to filing a notice of disclosure, must abstain from

(1) participating in discussions or deliberations with respect to the subject of the conflict (other than to present factual information or to answer questions),

(2) using his or her personal influence to affect deliberations,

(3) making motions,

(4) voting,

(5) executing agreements, or

(6) taking similar actions on behalf of the organizations where the conflict of interest might pertain by law, agreement, or otherwise.

At the discretion of the top governing body or a committee thereof, a person with a real or apparent conflict of interest may be excused from all or any portion of discussion or deliberations with respect to the subject of the conflict.

A member of the top governing body or a committee thereof, who, having disclosed a conflict of interest, nevertheless shall be counted in determining the existence of a quorum at any meeting in which the subject of the conflict is discussed. The minutes of the meeting shall reflect the individual's disclosure, the vote thereon, and the individual's abstention from participation and voting.

The board chair shall ensure that all trustees, officers, agents, employees, and independent contractors of the organization are made aware of the organization's policy with respect to conflicts of interest.

Sample Conflict of Interest Disclosure Annual Reporting Statement

Certification

I have read and understand the Conflict of Interest Policy. I hereby declare and certify the following real or apparent conflict of interest:

Disclosure Statement

_____
_____
_____
_____
_____
_____
_____

(If necessary, attach additional documentation.)

I agree to promptly inform the board upon the occurrence of each event that could potentially result in my involvement in (or implication in) a conflict of interest.

_____   _____
Date   Signature

                                         _____
                                         Title

Honoraria

When a board member or an employee of an organization speaks at a function related to the organization or speaks on behalf of the organization and receives an honorarium, a related-party transaction has occurred. While the facts and circumstances may assist in determining whether a conflict of interest has occurred, it is often helpful for the organization to adopt a policy regarding the ownership of honoraria received in these situations.

Proper treatment of intellectual properties

General copyright law provides that the employer is considered the author of a "work made for hire" and "owns all of the rights comprised in the copyright," unless the employer and employee "have expressly agreed otherwise in a written instrument signed by them." A "work made for hire" is "a work prepared by an employee within the scope of his or her employment." Such rights may pertain to books, articles, sermons, music, and other materials.

Accordingly, organizations should affirm corporate ownership of all such rights in personnel policies and manuals, and should retain signed acknowledgment by employees of this provision.

However, if an individual rather than the organization owns the rights, care should be taken to

➤ Assure that work on the product containing the rights is performed outside the time and duties of employment with the organization, and that compensation is appropriately reduced if the work infringes upon the employee's time and duties.

➤ Assure that the organization is reimbursed for any organizational resources used in the production of work owned by individuals (*e.g.,* equipment, secretarial help, proofreading, recording, etc.) at fair value. This is true even if the organization supports the "ministry" of the works as good or worthwhile. Alternatively, if a board agrees to absorb support cost as in the best interest of the organization, then the fair value of the work must be added to the employee's taxable income.

In cases where intellectual property rights are owned by the employer and subsequently assigned to an individual, or where duties are concurrent (such as a pastor's sermons), care should be taken to

➤ Consult legal counsel knowledgeable in the specialized area of intellectual property rights.

➤ Establish written agreements approved by the board and signed by the organization and individual.

➤ Consider the fair value of the rights as an element of compensation when establishing reasonable compensation limits and when reporting compensation for tax purposes.

Tax-exempt organizations must take care not to enter into any arrangement with their officers, directors, or other related parties that would constitute "private inurement" or an "excess benefit transaction" under federal tax law. Entering into such an arrangement can subject the parties involved to personal penalties and can expose the organization's tax-exempt status to risk.

> **Example:** An excess benefit transaction or private inurement may occur if an exempt organization transfers something of value to one of its officers without receiving something of at least equal value in exchange.

Due to its complexity, the area of intellectual property ownership in the context of exempt organizations has a heightened risk. Organizations addressing these issues would be well advised to consult competent tax and legal counsel.

Accountability to Donors

When a charity receives charitable contributions, it accepts the responsibility of accountability to its donors. Some of the primary facets of this responsibility include the following:

Donor communication

All statements made by an organization in its fund-raising appeals about the use of a gift must be honored by the organization. The donor's intent may be shaped by both the organization's communication of the appeal and by any donor instructions with the gift.

If a donor responds to a specific appeal, the assumption may be made that the donor's intent is that the funds be used as outlined in the appeal. There is a need for clear communication in the appeal to ensure that the donor understands precisely how the funds will be used. Any note or correspondence accompanying the gift or conversations between the donor and donee representatives may indicate donor intent.

All aspects of a proposed charitable gift should be explained fully, fairly, and accurately to the donor. Any limitations on the use of the gift should be clear and complete both in the response device and the appeal letter. These items should be included in the explanation:

➤ **The charity's proposed use of the gift.** Realistic expectations should be communicated regarding what the donor's gift will do within the programs of the donee organization.

➤ **Representations of fact.** Any description of the financial condition of the organization or narrative about events must be current, complete, and accurate. References to past activities or events should be appropriately dated. There should be no material omissions, exaggerations of fact, use of misleading photographs, or any other communication tending to create a false impression or misunderstanding.

➤ **Valuation issues and procedures.** If an appraisal is required, the donor should fully understand the procedures and who is responsible to pay for the appraisal.

➤ **Tax consequences and reporting requirements.** While tax considerations should not be the primary focus of a gift, the donor should clearly understand the current and future income, estate, and gift tax consequences, and reporting requirements of the proposed gift. A charitable gift should never be represented as a tax shelter.

➤ **Alternative arrangements for making the gift.** The donor should understand the current and deferred gift options that are available.

> **Warning**
>
> Soliciting gifts from elderly donors requires special care. A charity should communicate with the donor's legal counsel to establish that the donor has sufficient information about the charity, to clarify the conditions for the use of the gift, if any, and that counsel has formed an opinion regarding the donor's legal capacity to make a gift.

> **Financial and family implications.** In addition to the tax consequences, the overall financial implications of the proposed gift and the potential impact on family members should be carefully explained.

> **Possible conflicts of interest.** Disclose to the donor all relationships that might constitute, or appear to constitute, conflicts of interest. The disclosure should include how and by whom each party is compensated and any cost of managing the gift.

Fund-raising appeals must not create unrealistic donor expectations of what a donor's gift will actually accomplish within the limits of the organization's ministry.

Accounting for restricted gifts

Donors often place temporary or permanent restrictions on gifts that limit their use to certain purposes. These stipulations may specify a use for a contributed asset that is more specific than broad limits relating to the nature of the organization, the environment in which it operates, and the purposes specified in its articles of incorporation or bylaws or comparable documents for unincorporated entities. A restricted gift generally results whenever a donor selects a giving option on a response device other than "unrestricted" or "where needed most."

> **Warning**
>
> A caveat statement used on all offering envelopes at a church, on all direct mail appeals, or on the screen for television offering appeals is rarely appropriate. If donors believe their money is going for a certain project but much of it is used for the general fund or for some other project, truthfulness in communication is an issue.

Projects unrelated to an organization's primary purpose

A nonprofit sometimes receives funds for programs that are not part of its present or prospective ministry but are proper according to its exempt purpose (*i.e.*, one of the exempt purposes under the Internal Revenue Code). In these instances the organization must either treat them as restricted funds and channel them through an organization that can carry out the donor's intent, or return the funds to the donor.

Reporting for incentives and premiums

Fund-raising appeals may offer premiums or incentives in exchange for a contribution. If the value of the premiums or incentives is not insubstantial, the donee organization generally must advise the donor of the fair market value of the premium or incentive and clarify that the value is not deductible for tax purposes (see page 186 for more detailed information).

Reporting to donors and the public

As a demonstration of transparency, a charity should provide a copy of its current financial statements upon written request. Additionally, many nonprofit organizations are subject to the public disclosure rules requiring charities to provide copies of annual information returns (Form 990) and certain other documents when requested to do so (see pages 42 and 48).

Compensation of gift planners

Payment of finders' fees, commissions, or other fees on a percentage basis by a donee organization to an outside gift planner or to an organization's own employees as a condition for delivery of a gift is never appropriate. Competency-based pay is acceptable when paid to employees responsible for an organization's general fund-raising program and includes a modest component for achieving broad fund-raising goals.

Every effort must be made to keep donor trust. Donor attitudes can be unalterably damaged in reaction to undue pressure and the awareness that a direct commission will be paid to a fund-raiser from his or her gift, thus compromising the trust on which charity relies.

Tax-deductible gifts for a named recipient's personal benefit

According to the Internal Revenue Code and other laws and regulations governing tax-exempt organizations, tax-deductible gifts may not be used to pass money or benefits to any named individual for personal use. The intent of the donor ordinarily determines whether a transfer should be characterized as a tax-deductible contribution to a ministry or a nondeductible transfer to an individual. Did the donor intend to make a contribution to the ministry or only to benefit the designated individual (using the ministry as an intermediary in order to obtain a tax deduction for an otherwise nondeductible gift)? The fact that the payment was made to a tax-exempt organization is not controlling, since taxpayers can document a deduction merely by funneling a payment through a charity. As the IRS often asserts, it is the substance, not the form, of a transaction that is controlling.

Acting in the interest of the donor

Every effort should be made to avoid accepting a gift from or entering into a contract with a prospective donor that would knowingly place a hardship on the donor or place the donor's future well-being in jeopardy.

Fund-raisers should recognize that it is almost impossible to properly represent the full interests of the donor and the charitable organization simultaneously. When dealing with persons regarding commitments on major estate assets, gift planners should seek to guide and advise donors so that they may adequately consider the broad interests of the family and the various organizations they are currently supporting before they make a final decision. Donors should be encouraged to discuss the proposed gift with competent and independent attorneys, accountants, or other professional advisors.

Evangelical Council for Financial Accountability
www.ECFA.org • 1-800-323-9473
Standards of Responsible Stewardship

A higher standard. A higher purpose.

The ECFA Standards of Responsible Stewardship required for membership:

- **Standard 1 – Doctrinal Statement**: Every member shall subscribe to a written statement of faith clearly affirming its commitment to the evangelical Christian faith and shall conduct its financial and other operations in a manner which reflects those generally accepted biblical truths and practices.
- **Standard 2 – Board of Directors and Financial Oversight**: Every member shall be governed by a responsible board of not less than five individuals, a majority of whom shall be independent, which shall meet at least semiannually to establish policy and review its accomplishments. The board or a committee consisting of a majority of independent members shall review the annual financial statements and maintain direct communication between the board and the independent certified public accountants.
- **Standard 3 – Financial Statements**: Each member is required to submit complete and accurate financial statements. Accredited members must submit an annual audit performed by an independent certified public accounting firm in accordance with U.S. generally accepted auditing standards (GAAS) with its financial statement prepared in accordance with U.S. generally accepted accounting principles (GAAP). ECFA policies may allow for an alternate category of membership that does not require audited financial statements, in which case the member must submit financial statements (with disclosures) prepared either in conformity with U.S. GAAP or the modified cash basis of accounting in which financial statements are either compiled or reviewed by an independent certified public accounting firm.
- **Standard 4 – Use of Resources**: Every member shall exercise the management and financial controls necessary to provide reasonable assurance that all resources are used (nationally and internationally), in conformity with applicable federal and state laws and regulations, to accomplish the exempt purposes for which they are intended.
- **Standard 5 – Financial Disclosure**: Every member shall provide a copy of its current financial statements upon written request and provide other disclosures as the law may require. If audited financial statements are required to comply with Standard 3, they must be disclosed under this Standard. A member must provide a report, upon written request, including financial information, on any specific project for which it is soliciting gifts.
- **Standard 6 – Conflicts of Interest**: Every member shall avoid conflicts of interest. Transactions with related parties may be undertaken only if all of the following are observed: 1) a material transaction is fully disclosed in the audited financial statements of the member; 2) the related party is excluded from the discussion and approval of such transaction; 3) a competitive bid or comparable valuation exists; and 4) the member's board has acted upon and demonstrated that the transaction is in the best interest of the member.
- **Standard 7 – Fund-Raising**: Every member shall comply with each of the ECFA Standards for Fund-Raising:

- **7.1: Truthfulness in Communication**: All representations of fact, description of the financial condition of the member, or narrative about events must be current, complete and accurate. References to past activities or events must be appropriately dated. There must be no material omissions or exaggerations of fact or use of misleading photographs or any other communication which would tend to create a false impression or misunderstanding.
- **7.2: Communication and Donor Expectations**: Fund-raising appeals must not create unrealistic donor expectations of what a donor's gift will actually accomplish within the limits of the member's ministry.
- **7.3: Communication and Donor Intent**: All statements made by the member in its fund-raising appeals about the use of the gift must be honored by the member. The donor's intent is related both to what was communicated in the appeal and to any donor instructions accompanying the gift. The member should be aware that communications made in fund-raising appeals may create a legally binding restriction.
- **7.4: Projects Unrelated to a Ministry's Primary Purpose**: A member raising or receiving funds for programs that are not part of its present or prospective ministry, but are proper in accordance with its exempt purpose, must either treat them as restricted funds and channel them through an organization that can carry out the donor's intent or return the funds to the donor.
- **7.5: Incentives and Premiums**: Members making fund-raising appeals which, in exchange for a contribution, offer premiums or incentives (the value of which is not insubstantial, but is significant in relation to the amount of the donation) must advise the donor of the fair market value of the premium or incentive and that the value is not deductible for tax purposes.
- **7.6: Financial Advice**: The representative of the member, when dealing with persons regarding commitments on major estate assets, must seek to guide and advise donors so they have adequately considered the broad interests of the family and the various ministries they are currently supporting before they make final decisions. Donors should be encouraged to use the services of their attorneys, accountants, or other professional advisors.
- **7.7: Percentage Compensation for Fund-Raisers**: Compensation of outside fund-raising consultants or a member's own employees based directly or indirectly on a percentage of charitable contributions raised is not allowed.
- **7.8: Tax-Deductible Gifts for a Named Recipient's Personal Benefit**: Tax-deductible gifts may not be used to pass money or benefits to any named individual for personal use.
- **7.9: Conflict of Interest on Royalties**: An officer, director, or other principal of the member must not receive royalties for any product that the member uses for fund-raising or promotional purposes.
- **7.10: Acknowledgement of Gifts-in-Kind**: Property or gifts-in-kind received by a member should be acknowledged describing the property or gift accurately *without* a statement of the gift's market value. It is the responsibility of the donor to determine the fair market value of the property for tax purposes. The member may be required to provide additional information for gifts of motor vehicles, boats, and airplanes.
- **7.11: Acting in the Interest of the Donor**: A member must make every effort to avoid accepting a gift from or entering into a contract with a prospective donor which would knowingly place a hardship on the donor, or place the donor's future well-being in jeopardy.

Integrity Points

- **Setting the tone at the top.** Financial accountability starts with the organization's board and top leadership and permeates down through the staff. If the organization is a church, the accountability tone starts with the senior pastor. If it is a parachurch organization, it starts with the president, CEO, executive director, or other leadership position.

- **The importance of an independent board.** A majority of independent board members (not staff members or relatives of staff or board members) is vital to ensure the board's action is done without partiality, undue influence, or conflict of interest. An independent board is equally important for churches and parachurch organizations.

- **Accountability to donors heightens with gift restrictions.** When a donor makes an unrestricted gift, the donee charity has a general accountability for the funds. However, when a donor places a purpose or time restriction on a gift, the donee charity accepts the responsibility to expend the funds within the donor's limitations.

    Although the courts are often hesitant to enforce donors' gift restrictions, integrity requires a charity's use of the gift as the donor intended.

- **The importance of the work of an independent CPA and/or internal audits.** Churches and other nonprofit organizations of a significant size (annual revenue of $500,000 is often considered a proper threshold to obtain these services) should annually utilize the services of an independent CPA. Large organizations should always have an annual audit. For smaller organizations, an annual review or compilation by an independent CPA may be sufficient. One of the most overlooked CPA services is an "agreed upon procedures" engagement whereby the CPA only focuses on certain issues, *e.g.,* bank reconciliations, expense reimbursements, or another area that is often troublesome for an organization.

CHAPTER TWO
Tax Exemption

In This Chapter

- Advantages and limitations of tax exemption
- Tax exemption for churches
- Starting a nonprofit organization
- Unrelated business income
- Private benefit and private inurement
- Filing federal returns
- Postal regulations
- State taxes and fees
- Political activity

Qualifying tax-exempt organizations have many advantages. One of the most important benefits is the eligibility to attract deductible charitable contributions from individual and corporate donors. The potential exemption from tax liability, primarily income, sales, and property tax, is also important. There are many exceptions to these exemptions.

The term "nonprofit organization" covers a broad range of entities such as churches, colleges, universities, healthcare providers, business leagues, veterans groups, political parties, country clubs, and united-giving campaigns. The most common type of nonprofits is the charitable organization.

The nonprofit organization concept is basically a state law creation. But tax-exempt organizations are based primarily on federal law. The Internal Revenue Code does not use the word "nonprofit." The Code refers to nonprofits as exempt organizations. Certain state statutes use the term "not-for-profit." A not-for-profit organization under state law may or may not be tax-exempt under federal law. In this book, the term "nonprofit" refers to nonprofit organizations that are exempt from federal income tax.

Advantages and Limitations of Tax Exemption

Upon approval by the IRS, tax exemption is available to organizations that meet the requirements of the tax code. This exemption provides relief from federal income tax. This income tax exemption may or may not extend to local and state income taxes. Even if an organization receives tax-exempt status, certain federal taxes may still be imposed. There may be tax due on the unrelated business income, tax on certain "political" activities, and tax on excessive legislative activities.

Tax exemption advantages

Besides the basic exemption from federal income and excise taxes, an organization that is recognized as a charitable organization under the Internal Revenue Code enjoys several advantages:

➤ Its donors can be offered the benefit of a deduction for contributions.

➤ It can benefit from using special standard nonprofit mail rates.

➤ It is in a favored position to seek funding from foundations and other philanthropic entities, many of which will not support organizations other than those recognized as tax-exempt organizations under 501(c)(3).

➤ It is eligible for government grants available only to entities exempt under 501(c)(3).

➤ It often qualifies for exemption not only from state and local income taxes but from property taxes (for property used directly for its exempt function) and certain sales and use taxes as well.

Remember

A tax-exempt organization usually means the entity is exempt, in whole or in part, from federal income taxes. The entity may still be subject to social security taxes and certain excise taxes. Nonprofit organizations may be subject to taxes at the state level on income, franchise, sales, use, tangible property, intangible property, and real property.

➤ It may qualify for exemption from the Federal Unemployment Tax Act in certain situations.

➤ Its employees may participate in 403(b) tax-sheltered annuities.

➤ It is an exclusive beneficiary of free radio and television public service announcements (PSAs) provided by local media outlets.

➤ If it is a church or a qualified church-controlled organization, it may exclude compensation to employees from the FICA social security base. The organization must be opposed on religious grounds to the payment of FICA social security taxes. The social security liability shifts to the employees of the electing organizations in the form of SECA social security tax.

Tax exemption limitations

Offsetting the advantages of tax-exempt status are some strict requirements:

➤ An organization must be engaged "primarily" in qualified charitable or educational endeavors.

- There are limitations on the extent to which it can engage in substantial legislative activities or other political activities.
- An organization may not engage in unrelated business activities or commercial activities to an impermissible extent.
- There is a prohibition against private inurement or private benefit.
- Upon dissolution, the organization's assets must be distributed for one or more exempt purposes.

Tax Exemption for Churches

Tax law and IRS regulations do not define "religious." But the courts have defined "religious" broadly. In part, because of these constitutional concerns, some religious organizations are subject to more lenient reporting and auditing requirements under federal tax law.

The "religious" category includes churches, conventions of churches, associations of churches, church-run organizations (such as schools, hospitals, orphanages, nursing homes, publishing entities, broadcasting entities, and cemeteries), religious orders, apostolic groups, integrated auxiliaries of churches, missionary organizations, and Bible and tract societies. IRS regulations define religious worship as follows: "What constitutes conduct of religious worship or the ministration of sacerdotal functions depends on the interests and practices of a particular religious body constituting a church."

Although not stated in the regulations, the IRS applies the following 14 criteria to decide whether a religious organization can qualify as a "church":

- Distinct legal existence
- Recognized creed and form of worship
- Definite and distinct ecclesiastical government
- Formal code of doctrine and discipline
- Distinct religious history
- Membership not associated with any other church or denomination
- Organization of ordained ministers
- Established places of worship
- Literature of its own
- Ordained ministers selected after completing prescribed courses of studies
- Regular congregations

Remember

All churches are religious organizations, but not all religious organizations are churches. While many churches have steeples, the definition of a church for IRS purposes is much broader. The term "church" may include religious schools, publishers, television and radio broadcasters, rescue missions, religious orders, and other organizations.

- Regular religious services
- Sunday schools for religious instruction of the young
- Schools for preparation of its ministers

Churches receive favored status in that they are not required to file either an application for exemption (Form 1023) or an annual report (Form 990) with the IRS. A church is still subject to filing and disclosing an annual report on unrelated business income (Form 990-T) and Form 5578 for private schools as well as payroll tax, sales tax, and other forms, if applicable. Individuals employed by churches qualify more easily for the special ministerial tax treatments, including a housing allowance.

Churches generally avoid audits because of the highly restrictive requirements of the Church Audit Procedures Act. While the IRS may begin a "church tax inquiry" to determine whether a church qualifies for tax-exempt status or is carrying on an unrelated business, the inquiry must be approved by an appropriate high-level IRS official. However, this audit restriction does not apply to a church that is not filing or paying payroll taxes, to criminal investigations, to separately incorporated private schools, or to any inquiry relating to the tax status or liability of persons other than the church, such as ministers or contributors.

Starting a Church or Other Nonprofit Organization

The choice of a nonprofit organizational form is a basic decision. Most churches are unincorporated associations. However, many churches incorporate for the purpose of limiting legal liability. Most other nonprofit organizations are corporations. While incorporation is usually desirable for churches and other nonprofit organizations, it is generally not mandatory.

Organizations using the corporate form need articles of incorporation and bylaws. An unincorporated organization will typically have the same instruments, although the articles may be in the form of a constitution.

Several planning questions should be asked. If the organization is formed for charitable purposes, is public status desired or is a private foundation acceptable? Are any business activities contemplated, and to what degree will the organization be incorporated? Is an attorney competent in nonprofit matters available to help with the preparation of the legal documents? What provisions will the bylaws contain? Who will serve on the board of directors? What name will be used for the organization?

Key Issue

If a church or other nonprofit organization wishes to incorporate, it must file articles of incorporation with the appropriate state. Some states also require the filing of trust documents. Following incorporation, the new entity should conduct an organizational meeting of the initial board of directors, adopt bylaws, and elect officers.

The following materials may provide useful information when starting a church or other nonprofit organization:

Package 1023   Application for

Recognition of Exemption with Instructions

Publication 557   Tax-Exempt Status for Your Organization

Obtaining an employer identification number

All entities, whether exempt from tax or not, must obtain an employer identification number (EIN) by filing IRS Form SS-4. An EIN is required for a church even though churches are not required to file with the IRS for tax-exempt status. This number is not a tax-exempt number, but is simply the organization's unique identifier in the IRS's records, similar to an individual's social security number.

When an organization is approved by the IRS for exemption from federal income tax (not required for churches), it will receive a "determination letter." This letter does not assign the organization a tax-exempt number.

If an organization is a "central organization" that holds a "group exemption letter," the IRS will assign that group a four-digit number, known as its group exemption number (GEN). This number must be supplied with the central organization's annual report to the IRS (updating its list of included subordinate organizations). The number also is inserted on Form 990 (if required) of the central organization and the subordinate organizations included in the group exemption.

When an organization applies for exemption from state or local income, sales, or property taxes, the state or local jurisdiction may provide a certificate or letter of exemption, which, in some jurisdictions, includes a serial number. This number is often called a "tax-exempt number." This number should not be confused with an EIN.

Application for recognition of tax-exempt status

Although a church is not required to apply to the IRS for tax-exempt status under Section 501(c)(3) of the Internal Revenue Code and is exempt from filing Form 990, it may be appropriate to apply for recognition in some situations:

➤ National denominations typically file for group exemption to cover all local congregations. A copy of the national body's IRS determination letter may be used by the local group to provide evidence of tax-exempt status.

Independent local churches that are not a part of a national denominational body often file for tax-exempt status to provide evidence of their status. The local congregation may wish to file for group exemption if it is a parent church of other local congregations or separately organized ministries.

Filing Tip

The filing for tax-exempt status by a parachurch ministry will determine whether the organization will be recognized as tax-exempt, whether it will be eligible to receive deductible charitable contributions (and sometimes to what extent), and whether the organization will be a public charity or a private foundation.

2008 CHURCH AND NONPROFIT TAX & FINANCIAL GUIDE

Form SS-4 (Rev. July 2007)
Department of the Treasury
Internal Revenue Service

Application for Employer Identification Number
(For use by employers, corporations, partnerships, trusts, estates, churches, government agencies, Indian tribal entities, certain individuals, and others.)
▶ See separate instructions for each line. ▶ Keep a copy for your records.

OMB No. 1545-0003
EIN

Type or print clearly.

1. Legal name of entity (or individual) for whom the EIN is being requested
   Lynn Haven Church

2. Trade name of business (if different from name on line 1)

3. Executor, administrator, trustee, "care of" name

4a. Mailing address (room, apt., suite no. and street, or P.O. box)
    PO Box 4382

4b. City, state, and ZIP code (if foreign, see instructions)
    Miami, FL 33168

5a. Street address (if different) (Do not enter a P.O. box.)
    3801 North Florida Avenue

5b. City, state, and ZIP code (if foreign, see instructions)
    Miami, FL 33168

6. County and state where principal business is located
   Dade County, Florida

7a. Name of principal officer, general partner, grantor, owner, or trustor
    Mark Smith, Treasurer

7b. SSN, ITIN, or EIN
    516-03-9091

8a. Is this application for a limited liability company (LLC) or a foreign equivalent? ☐ Yes ☑ No

8b. If 8a is "Yes," enter the number of LLC members ▶

8c. If 8a is "Yes," was the LLC organized in the United States? ☐ Yes ☐ No

9a. Type of entity (check only one box). Caution. If 8a is "Yes," see the instructions for the correct box to check.
    ☐ Sole proprietor (SSN) _____
    ☐ Partnership
    ☐ Corporation (enter form number to be filed) ▶ _____
    ☐ Personal service corporation
    ☑ Church or church-controlled organization
    ☐ Other nonprofit organization (specify) ▶ _____
    ☐ Other (specify) ▶
    ☐ Estate (SSN of decedent) _____
    ☐ Plan administrator (TIN) _____
    ☐ Trust (TIN of grantor) _____
    ☐ National Guard   ☐ State/local government
    ☐ Farmers' cooperative ☐ Federal government/military
    ☐ REMIC   ☐ Indian tribal governments/enterprises
    Group Exemption Number (GEN) if any ▶

9b. If a corporation, name the state or foreign country (if applicable) where incorporated
    State: _____   Foreign country: _____

10. Reason for applying (check only one box)
    ☑ Started new business (specify type) ▶ **Church**
    ☐ Hired employees (Check the box and see line 13.)
    ☐ Compliance with IRS withholding regulations
    ☐ Other (specify) ▶
    ☐ Banking purpose (specify purpose) ▶
    ☐ Changed type of organization (specify new type) ▶
    ☐ Purchased going business
    ☐ Created a trust (specify type) ▶
    ☐ Created a pension plan (specify type) ▶

11. Date business started or acquired (month, day, year). See instructions.
    2-01-06

12. Closing month of accounting year **June**

13. Highest number of employees expected in the next 12 months (enter -0- if none).
    Agricultural | Household | Other
     | | **3**

14. Do you expect your employment tax liability to be $1,000 or less in a full calendar year? ☑ Yes ☐ No (If you expect to pay $4,000 or less in total wages in a full calendar year, you can mark "Yes.")

15. First date wages or annuities were paid (month, day, year). Note. If applicant is a withholding agent, enter date income will first be paid to nonresident alien (month, day, year) ▶ **2-1-06**

16. Check one box that best describes the principal activity of your business.
    ☐ Construction ☐ Rental & leasing ☐ Transportation & warehousing ☐ Health care & social assistance ☐ Wholesale-agent/broker
    ☐ Real estate ☐ Manufacturing ☐ Finance & insurance ☐ Accommodation & food service ☐ Wholesale-other ☐ Retail
    ☑ Other (specify) **Religious Organization**

17. Indicate principal line of merchandise sold, specific construction work done, products produced, or services provided.
    Religious preaching and teaching

18. Has the applicant entity shown on line 1 ever applied for and received an EIN? ☐ Yes ☑ No
    If "Yes," write previous EIN here ▶

Third Party Designee
Designee's name:
Address and ZIP code:
Designee's telephone number (include area code): ( )
Designee's fax number (include area code): ( )

Under penalties of perjury, I declare that I have examined this application, and to the best of my knowledge and belief, it is true, correct, and complete.

Name and title (type or print clearly) ▶ **Mike R. Thomas, Pastor**
Applicant's telephone number (include area code): **(305) 688-7432**
Applicant's fax number (include area code): ( )

Signature ▶ *Mike R. Thomas*   Date ▶ **2-28-07**

For Privacy Act and Paperwork Reduction Act Notice, see separate instructions.   Cat. No. 16055N   Form **SS-4** (Rev. 7-2007)

Nearly every church or other nonprofit organization needs an employer identification number (EIN) obtained by filing this form.

➤ If a local congregation ordains, licenses, or commissions ministers, it may be helpful to apply for tax-exempt status. Ministers that are ordained by a local church may be required to provide evidence that the church is tax-exempt. This could be particularly true if the minister files Form 4361, applying for exemption from self-employment tax.

Organizations desiring recognition of tax-exempt status should submit Form 1023 (see pages 27-28 for churches and filing for tax-exempt status). If approved, the IRS will issue a determination letter describing the category of exemption granted.

The IRS must be notified that the organization is applying for recognition of exemption within 15 months from the end of the month in which it was organized. Applications made after this deadline will not be effective before the date on which the application for recognition of exemption is filed.

Some organizations view the obtaining of an exemption letter from the IRS as an intimidating process. Organizations faced with the process are typically new, with a general mission in mind. The mission is often not fully developed, and therefore it may not be clearly articulated. It may be helpful to have your application reviewed by a CPA or attorney before it is filed.

Organizations that have applied and been approved for tax-exempt status are listed in Publication 78, Cumulative List of Organizations, which identifies organizations to which tax-deductible contributions may be made. However, organizations that do not file Form 990, such as churches, will not be listed.

Determination letter request

A user fee of $750 (with Form 8718) must accompany applications for recognition of tax-exempt status where the applicant has gross receipts that annually exceed $10,000. For an organization that has had annual gross receipts of $10,000 or less during the past four years, the fee is $300. Start-ups may qualify for the reduced fee. Group exemption letter fees are $300 or $900.

Granting tax exemption

Upon approval of the application for exemption, the IRS will provide a determination letter. This letter may be an advance determination or a definitive (or final) determination. The exempt status is usually effective as of the date of formation of the organization, if filing deadlines are met.

An advance determination letter provides tentative guidance regarding status but is a final determination relating to operations and structure of the organization. An advance determination is effective for five years. Before the end of the advance determination period, the organization must show

Key Issue

Approval of tax-exempt status by the IRS is usually effective as of the date of formation of an organization. The effective date determines the date that contributions to the organization are deductible by donors. If an organization is required to alter its activities or substantially amend its charter to qualify, the effective data for tax-exempt purposes will be the date specified in the ruling or determination letter.

31

that it qualifies for nonprivate foundation status. During the advance determination period, contributors may make tax-deductible donations to the organization.

A newly created organization seeking status as a publicly supported organization is entitled to receive, if it so elects, a definitive ruling if it has completed a tax year consisting of eight full months as of the time of filing the application.

A definitive (or final) determination letter represents a determination by the IRS that the organizational and operational plans of the nonprofit entitle it to be classified as exempt.

Group exemption

An affiliated group of organizations under the common control of a central organization can obtain a group exemption letter. Churches that are part of a denomination are not required to file a separate application for exemption if they are covered by the group letter.

The central organization is required to report annually its exempt subordinate organizations to the IRS (the IRS does not provide a particular form for this reporting). The central organization is responsible to evaluate the tax status of its subordinate groups.

Unrelated Business Income

Most Christian ministries are supported primarily from either contributions or revenue from activities directly related to their exempt purposes. Sales of religious books, tuition at schools, and campers' fees at camp are examples of exempt purpose revenue. On the other hand, income from activities not directly related to fulfilling an organization's exempt purposes may be subject to the tax on unrelated business income.

All income of tax-exempt organizations is presumed to be exempt from federal income tax unless the income is generated by an activity that is

> not substantially related to the organization's exempt purpose or function,

> a trade or business, and

> regularly carried on.

Filing Tip

Although churches are exempt from filing Form 990 with the IRS, they are still subject to tax on their unrelated business income. Tax law allows churches and other nonprofit organization to conduct profit-making activities, but it does tax that profit if the income is from an unrelated business activity and none of the exceptions to the tax applies.

Unrelated business income (UBI) is permitted for tax-exempt organizations. However, these organizations may have to pay tax on income derived from activities unrelated to their exempt purpose. UBI must not comprise a substantial part of the organization's operation. There is no specific percentage limitation on how much UBI is "substantial." However, organizations with 50% to 80% of their activities classified as unrelated have faced revocation of their tax-exempt status.

Form 990-T must be completed to report the source(s) of UBI and related expenses and to compute any tax. UBI amounts are also reportable on Form 990 (if the filing of Form 990 is required). Organizations required to file a Form 990-T will generally also be required to make a state filing related to the UBI. The Form 990-T is subject to the public disclosure rules (see page 42).

Although exempt from filing Form 990, churches must file Form 990-T if they have $1,000 or more of gross UBI in a year. There is a specific deduction of $1,000 in computing unrelated business taxable income. This specific deduction applies to a diocese, province of a religious order, or a convention or association of churches with respect to each parish, individual church, district, or other local unit.

Unrelated business income consequences

Some church and nonprofit executives are paranoid about UBI to the point that they feel it must be avoided altogether. Some people equate UBI with the automatic loss of exempt status. A more balanced view is to understand the purpose of the UBI and minimize the UBI tax through proper planning.

The most common adverse result of having UBI is that all or part of it may be taxed. A less frequent, but still possible, result is that the organization will lose its tax exemption. It is possible that the IRS will deny or revoke the tax-exempt status of an organization when it regularly derives over one-half of its annual revenue from unrelated activities.

Congress recognized that some nonprofits may need to engage in unrelated business activities to survive. For example, a nonprofit with unused office space might rent the space to another organization. Also, nonprofits are expected to invest surplus funds to supplement the primary sources of the organization's income.

A trade or business regularly carried on

A trade or business means any activity regularly carried on which produces income from the sale of goods and services and where there is a reasonable expectation of a profit. To decide whether a trade or business is regularly carried on, the IRS considers whether taxable organizations would carry on a business with the same frequency and continuity. Intermittent activities may escape the "regularly carried on" definition.

> **Example 1:** If a church sells sandwiches at an area bazaar for only two weeks, the IRS would not treat this as the regular conduct of a trade or business.
>
> **Example 2:** A one-time sale of property is not an activity that is regularly carried on and therefore does not generate unrelated business income unless the property was used in an unrelated business activity.
>
> **Example 3:** A church is located in the downtown section of a city. Each Saturday, the church parking lot is operated commercially to accommodate

Sample Unrelated Business Income Checklist

Determination of whether an activity produces unrelated business taxable income can be made by answering the questions below:

➤ *Is the activity regularly carried on?*

A specific business activity is regularly carried on if it is conducted with a frequency, continuity, and manner of pursuit comparable to the conduct of the same or similar activity by a taxable organization. An activity is regularly carried on if it is conducted

- intermittently the year round, or
- during a significant portion of the season for a seasonal type of business.

However, an activity is not regularly carried on if it is conducted

- on a very infrequent basis (once or twice a year),
- for only a short period of the year, or
- without competitive or promotional efforts.

➤ *Is the activity substantially related to the exempt purposes of the nonprofit?*

To be substantially related, the business activity must contribute importantly to the accomplishment of a purpose for which the nonprofit was granted tax exemption, other than the mere production of income to support such purpose.

➤ *Is the activity conducted with volunteer services?*

Any business activity in which substantially all (85% or more) of the work is performed by volunteers is specifically exempted from unrelated business income tax.

➤ *Is the activity primarily for the convenience of clients, patients, faculty, staff, students, or visitors?*

So-called "convenience" activities are exempt regardless of their nature. Examples are parking lots, food service, bookstores, laundry, telephone service, and vending machines.

➤ *Is the income derived from debt-financed property?*

Examples of income from debt-financed property are dividends, interest, rents, etc., earned from stocks, bonds, and rental property that have been purchased with borrowed money.

➤ *Is the income from the rental of real property?*

Rental income is generally tax-exempt if it does not relate to debt-financed property. But if significant services, such as setup, cleaning, and laundry service are also provided, then the income is usually taxable.

shoppers. Even though the business activity is carried on for only one day each week on a year-round basis, this constitutes the conduct of a trade or business. It is subject to the unrelated business income tax.

Substantially related

According to the IRS regulations, a trade or business must "contribute importantly to the accomplishment of the exempt purposes of an organization" if it is to be considered "substantially related." Even if all the profits from a business go to support the work of the nonprofit, the profits may still be taxed.

> **Example:** If a church operates a restaurant and devotes all the proceeds to mission work, the church will not escape taxation on the restaurant's income.

Types of income that may be "related" are

- the sale of products made by handicapped individuals as a part of their rehabilitation;
- the sale of homes constructed by students enrolled in a vocational training course; and
- a retail grocery store operated to provide emotional therapy for disturbed adolescents.

Tours conducted by nonprofits usually create UBI. Tours may be exempt from UBI only if they are strongly educationally oriented, with reports, daily lectures, and so on. Tours with substantial recreational or social purposes are not exempt.

The definition of "unrelated trade or business" does not include

- activities in which unpaid volunteers do most of the work for an organization;
- activities provided primarily for the convenience of the organization's members; or
- activities involving the sale of merchandise mostly donated to the organization.

Rental income

Nonprofits often rent facilities, equipment, and other assets for a fee. Rental income usually represents UBI with the following exceptions:

- Renting to another nonprofit may be termed "related" if the rental expressly serves the landlord's exempt purposes.
- Mailing lists produce UBI, with specific exceptions.
- Rental of real estate is excluded from UBI unless the excludable property is acquired or improved with original indebtedness. Rental income from the property becomes UBI to the extent of the ratio of the "average acquisition indebtedness" during the year to the total purchase price. The nonprofit may deduct the same portion of the expenses directly connected with the production of the rental income. Depreciation is allowable using only the straight-line method.

2008 CHURCH AND NONPROFIT TAX & FINANCIAL GUIDE

Form 990-T
Department of the Treasury
Internal Revenue Service (77)

Exempt Organization Business Income Tax Return
(and proxy tax under section 6033(e))

For calendar year 2007 or other tax year beginning _____, 2007, and ending _____, 20 ___. ▶ See separate instructions.

OMB No. 1545-0687

2007

Open to Public Inspection for 501(c)(3) Organizations Only

A ☐ Check box if address changed

B Exempt under section
☑ 501(**C**)(**3**)
☐ 408(e)   ☐ 220(e)
☐ 408A   ☐ 530(a)
☐ 529(a)

Print or Type

Name of organization (☐ Check box if name changed and see instructions.)
Family Bible Crusades

Number, street, and room or suite no. If a P.O. box, see page 9 of instructions.
400 North Sunset Avenue

City or town, state, and ZIP code
Lemon Grove, CA 92045

D Employer identification number
(Employees' trust, see instructions for Block D on page 9.)
35 4427081

E Unrelated business activity codes
(See instructions for Block E on page 9.)

C Book value of all assets at end of year

F Group exemption number (See instructions for Block F on page 9.) ▶

G Check organization type ▶ ☑ 501(c) corporation   ☐ 501(c) trust   ☐ 401(a) trust   ☐ Other trust

H Describe the organization's primary unrelated business activity. ▶

I During the tax year, was the corporation a subsidiary in an affiliated group or a parent-subsidiary controlled group? ▶ ☐ Yes ☑ No
If "Yes," enter the name and identifying number of the parent corporation. ▶

J The books are in care of ▶   Telephone number ▶ (   )

Part I — Unrelated Trade or Business Income

		(A) Income	(B) Expenses	(C) Net
1a	Gross receipts or sales			
b	Less returns and allowances _____ c Balance ▶ 1c			
2	Cost of goods sold (Schedule A, line 7) . . . 2			
3	Gross profit. Subtract line 2 from line 1c . . 3			
4a	Capital gain net income (attach Schedule D) 4a			
b	Net gain (loss) (Form 4797, Part II, line 17) (attach Form 4797) 4b			
c	Capital loss deduction for trusts . . . 4c			
5	Income (loss) from partnerships and S corporations (attach statement) 5			
6	Rent income (Schedule C) . . . 6			
7	Unrelated debt-financed income (Schedule E) . . . 7	79,410	52,301	27,109
8	Interest, annuities, royalties, and rents from controlled organizations (Schedule F) . . . 8			
9	Investment income of a section 501(c)(7), (9), or (17) organization (Schedule G) . . . 9			
10	Exploited exempt activity income (Schedule I) . . . 10			
11	Advertising income (Schedule J) . . . 11			
12	Other income (See page 11 of the instructions; attach schedule.) 12			
13	**Total.** Combine lines 3 through 12 . . . 13	79,410	52,301	27,109

Part II — Deductions Not Taken Elsewhere
(See page 12 of the instructions for limitations on deductions.)
(Except for contributions, deductions must be directly connected with the unrelated business income.)

14	Compensation of officers, directors, and trustees (Schedule K) . . .	14	
15	Salaries and wages . . .	15	
16	Repairs and maintenance . . .	16	
17	Bad debts . . .	17	
18	Interest (attach schedule) . . .	18	
19	Taxes and licenses . . .	19	
20	Charitable contributions (See page 14 of the instructions for limitation rules.) . . .	20	
21	Depreciation (attach Form 4562) . . . 21		
22	Less depreciation claimed on Schedule A and elsewhere on return . . . 22a	22b	
23	Depletion . . .	23	
24	Contributions to deferred compensation plans . . .	24	
25	Employee benefit programs . . .	25	
26	Excess exempt expenses (Schedule I) . . .	26	
27	Excess readership costs (Schedule J) . . .	27	
28	Other deductions (attach schedule) . . .	28	
29	**Total deductions.** Add lines 14 through 28 . . .	29	
30	Unrelated business taxable income before net operating loss deduction. Subtract line 29 from line 13	30	27,109
31	Net operating loss deduction (limited to the amount on line 30) . . .	31	
32	Unrelated business taxable income before specific deduction. Subtract line 31 from line 30	32	27,109
33	Specific deduction (Generally $1,000, but see line 33 instructions for exceptions.) . . .	33	1,000
34	**Unrelated business taxable income.** Subtract line 33 from line 32. If line 33 is greater than line 32, enter the smaller of zero or line 32	34	26,109

For Privacy Act and Paperwork Reduction Act Notice, see instructions.   Cat. No. 11291J   Form **990-T** (2007)

Form 990-T has a total of four pages. Only page one is shown here.

Debt-financed income

To discourage exempt organizations from borrowing money to purchase passive income items, Congress imposed a tax on debt-financed income. An organization may have debt-financed income if

- it incurs debt to purchase or improve an income-producing asset, and
- some of that debt remains within the 12 months prior to when income is received from the asset.

An organization also may have debt-financed income if it accepts gifts or bequests of mortgaged property in some circumstances.

There are exceptions to the debt-financed income rules, including

- use of substantially all (85% or more) of any property for an organization's exempt purposes;
- use of property by a related exempt organization to further its exempt purposes;
- life income contracts, if the remainder interest is payable to an exempt charitable organization;
- neighborhood land rule, if an organization acquires real property in its "neighborhood" (the neighborhood restriction does not apply to churches) mainly to use it for exempt purposes within 10 years (15 years for churches).

> **Remember**
>
> Nonprofits are normally not taxed on income they receive from renting or leasing real estate, even if the rental activity has nothing to do with their exempt purpose. If the property is financed by debt, however, a portion of the otherwise nontaxable income is typically taxed as debt-financed income.

Activities that are not taxed

Income from the following sources is generally not considered UBI:

- **Passive income.** Income earned from most passive investment activities is not UBI unless the underlying property is subject to debt. Types of passive income include
  - dividends, interest, and annuities;
  - capital gains or losses from the sale, exchange, or other disposition of property;
  - rents from real property (some rent is UBI if the rental property was purchased or improved subject to a mortgage);
  - royalties (however, oil and gas working interest income generally constitute UBI).
- **Volunteers.** Any business where volunteers perform most of the work without compensation does not qualify as UBI. To the IRS, "substantially" means at least 85% of total work performed.

Example: A used-clothing store operated by a nonprofit orphanage where volunteers do all the work in the store would likely be exempt.

➤ **Convenience.** A cafeteria, bookstore, or residence operated for the convenience of patients, visitors, employees, or students is not a business. Stores, parking lots, and other facilities may be dually used (part related and part unrelated).

➤ **Donated goods.** The sale of merchandise, mostly received as gifts or contributions, does not qualify as UBI. A justification for this exemption is that contributions of property are merely being converted into cash.

➤ **Low-cost items.** Items (costing no more than $8.90—2007 adjusted amount) distributed incidental to the solicitation of charitable contributions are not subject to UBI. The amounts received are not considered an exchange for the low-cost articles, and therefore they do not create UBI.

Idea

The use of volunteers to conduct an activity is one of the best ways to avoid tax on what would otherwise be a taxable activity. Intermittent activities may also escape the tax. To decide whether a trade or business is regularly carried on, the IRS considers whether taxable organizations would carry on a business with the same frequency and continuity.

➤ **Mailing lists.** Mailing lists exchanged with or rented to another exempt organization are excluded from UBI, although the commercial sale of the lists will generally create UBI. The structuring of the agreement as a royalty arrangement may make the income exempt from UBI treatment.

Calculating the unrelated business income tax

Income tax rules applicable to businesses, such as depreciation method limitations and rates, apply to the UBI computation. Direct and indirect costs, after proration between related and unrelated activities, may be used to offset income. The first $1,000 of annual net unrelated income is exempt from taxation.

For 2007, the corporate tax rates begin at 15% and go up to 38%.

Unrelated business income summary

Be aware of the type of activities that may create UBI in your organization.

➤ Maintain careful records of income and related expenses (both direct and indirect, including depreciation) for any activities that might be considered unrelated to the exempt purpose of your organization. These records should include allocations of salaries and fringe benefits based on time records or, at a minimum, time estimates.

It may be wise to keep a separate set of records on potential unrelated activities. This separate set of records would need to be submitted to the IRS only upon audit.

> Be sure that board minutes, contracts, and other documents reflect the organization's view of relatedness of various activities to the exempt purpose of the entity.

> If the organization has over $1,000 of gross UBI in a given fiscal (tax) year, file Form 990-T.

Private Benefit and Private Inurement

Tax laws and regulations impose prohibitions on nonprofit organizations concerning private benefit and private inurement. Excise taxes are imposed on "excess benefit transactions" between "disqualified persons" and nonprofits. An excess benefit transaction occurs when an economic benefit is provided by an organization, directly or indirectly, to or for the use of a disqualified person, and the value of the economic benefit provided by the organization exceeds the value of the consideration received by the organization in return for providing the benefit. A disqualified person is any person in a position to exercise substantial influence over the affairs of the organization (often referred to as an "insider").

Private benefit

Nonprofit organizations must serve public, and not private, interests. The private benefit prohibition applies to anyone outside the intended charitable class. The law does allow some private benefit if it is incidental to the public benefits involved. It is acceptable if the benefit to the public cannot be achieved without necessarily benefiting private individuals.

Example: The IRS revoked exemption of a charity as having served the commercial purposes and private interests of a professional fund-raiser when the fund-raiser distributed only 3% of the amount collected to the nonprofit organization.

Private inurement

Private inurement is a subset of private benefit. This is an absolute prohibition that generally applies to a distinct class of private interests. These "insiders" may be founders, trustees or directors, officers, managers, or significant donors. Transactions involving these individuals are not necessarily prohibited, but they must be subject to reasonableness, documentation, and applicable reporting to the IRS.

Inurement arises whenever a financial benefit represents a transfer of resources to an individual solely by virtue of the individual's relationship with the organization, without regard to

Remember

The most common example of private inurement is excessive compensation. However, the following transactions between a charity and a private individual are other examples of possible private inurement: (1) sale or exchange, or leasing, of property; (2) lending of money or other extension of credit; or (3) furnishing of goods, services, or facilities.

2008 CHURCH AND NONPROFIT TAX & FINANCIAL GUIDE

Checklist to Document Compensation for a Disqualified Person

1. Name and title: **Frank Basinger, CEO**
2. Effective date of contract: **January 1, 2008**
3. Duration of contract (one year, two years, etc.): **one year**
4. Types of appropriate comparable data relied upon in approving compensation package (check applicable boxes):
   - [X] Compensation paid by similarly situated organizations (taxable and tax exempt)
   - [X] Availability of similar services in the geographical area
   - [ ] Independent compensation surveys
   - [ ] Actual written employment offers from other similar institutions to the disqualified person
5. Explain how comparable data relied upon was obtained: **Surveyed four similar nonprofits in the region and 20 nationally**
6. Annual compensation summary:

	Comparable Data	Approved Compensation
Cash		
• Salary	$ 110,000	$ 95,000
• Bonus or contingent payment (estimate)		5,000
Noncash		
• Deferred compensation	5,000	10,000
• Premiums paid on insurance coverage (life, health, disability, liability, etc.)	20,000	18,000
• Automobile (value of personal use)	4,000	2,000
• Foregone interest on below market loan(s)		
• Other (excluding nontaxable benefits under IRC Sec. 132)	2,000	1,000
Total compensation	$ 141,000	$131,000

7. Members of authorized body present during discussion of compensation package and vote cast:

Present	In Favor	Opposed
18	16	2

8. Members of authorized body having a conflict of interest with respect to the compensation arrangement and how the conflict was handled (*e.g.,* left room during discussions and votes):

Member	Action re: Conflict
William McIlvain	Absent from board meeting for discussion and vote
Hugh Temple	Absent from board meeting for discussion and vote

9. Date compensation package approved: **November 10, 2007**

accomplishing its exempt purposes. When an individual receives something for nothing or less than it is worth, private inurement may have occurred. Excessive, and therefore unreasonable, compensation can also result in prohibited inurement. The IRS may ask the following questions to determine if private inurement exists:

- Did the expenditure further an exempt purpose, and if so, how?
- Was the payment at fair market value, or did it represent reasonable compensation for goods and services?
- Does a low- or no-interest loan to an employee or director fall within a reasonable compensation package?
- On an overseas trip for the nonprofit, did the employee (and perhaps a spouse) stay an additional week for a personal vacation and charge the expenses to the organization?

Example 1: An organization lost its exemption when it engaged in numerous transactions with an insider, including the purchase of a 42-foot boat for the personal use of the insider. The insider also benefitted from several real estate transactions, including donations and sales of real property to the organization that were never reflected on its books.

Example 2: A church lost its tax exemption after it operated commercial businesses and paid substantial private expenses of its founders, including expenses for jewelry and clothing in excess of $30,000 per year. The church also purchased five luxury cars for the founders' personal use. None of these benefits were reported as personal income to the founders.

Example 3: A tax-exempt organization transfers an auto to an employee for $1,000. The transfer was not approved by the board and does not constitute a portion of a reasonable pay package. The fair market value of the auto is $10,000. The net difference of $9,000 is not reported to the IRS as compensation. Private inurement has occurred.

Example 4: Same facts as Example 3, except the transfer was approved by the board and properly constituted a portion of the reasonable pay package, and the $9,000 was added to the employee's Form W-2 as compensation. There is no private inurement.

A two-tiered scheme of penalty taxes is imposed on insiders who improperly benefit from excess benefit transactions and on organization managers who are involved in illegal transactions. Sanctions cannot be imposed on the organizations themselves.

A first-tier penalty tax equal to 25% of the amount of the excess benefit is followed by a tax of 200% if there is no correction of the excess benefit within a certain time period.

Filing Federal Returns

Nearly all nonprofit organizations must file an annual return with the IRS (churches, religious orders, and certain foreign missionary organizations are exempt from filing Form 990). The basic filing requirements are as follows:

Form to Be Filed	Conditions
Form 990-N	Gross annual receipts normally under $25,000
Form 990	Gross annual receipts over $25,000
Form 990-EZ	Gross annual receipts less than $100,000 with total assets of less than $250,000
Form 990-T	Any organization exempt under Sec. 501(a) with $1,000 or more gross income from an unrelated trade or business
Form 1120	Any nonprofit corporation that is not tax-exempt
Form 5500	Pension, profit-sharing, medical benefit, cafeteria, and certain other plans must annually file one of several series 5500 Forms

Remember

Form 990 should generally use the same accounting method as the organization uses to keep its books. If the accrual method is used for the books or the audit, use the accrual method on Form 990.

Public inspection of information returns

IRS regulations require the public disclosure of certain documents:

▶ **Materials made available for public inspection.** Nonprofits, other than private foundations, must provide access to the application for tax exemption (Form 1023) and any supporting documents filed by the organization in support of its application. These also include any letter or other documents issued by the IRS in connection with the application.

Nonprofits must also provide access to their three most recent information returns. This generally includes Forms 990, 990-T, and schedules and attachments filed with the IRS. There is not a requirement to disclose parts of the information returns that identify names and addresses of contributors to the organization.

▶ **Places and times for public inspection.** Specified documents must be made available at the nonprofit's principal, regional, and district

Remember

The law requires certain disclosures of financial information. But a general attitude of transparency serves to deter improper diversions of funds and other misdeeds. It also provides a defense to critics and a witness to both believers and nonbelievers.

CHAPTER 2 ➢ TAX EXEMPTION

Form **990**	**Return of Organization Exempt From Income Tax**	OMB No. 1545-0047
Department of the Treasury Internal Revenue Service (77)	Under section 501(c), 527, or 4947(a)(1) of the Internal Revenue Code (except black lung benefit trust or private foundation) ▶ The organization may have to use a copy of this return to satisfy state reporting requirements.	**2007** Open to Public Inspection

A For the 2007 calendar year, or tax year beginning _____ , 2007, and ending _____ , 20 _____

B Check if applicable: ☐ Address change ☐ Name change ☐ Initial return ☐ Termination ☐ Amended return ☐ Application pending	Please use IRS label or print or type. See Specific Instructions.	**C** Name of organization **Lifeline Ministries** Number and street (or P.O. box if mail is not delivered to street address) Room/suite **1212 South Palo Verde** City or town, state or country, and ZIP + 4 **Phoenix, AZ 85035**	**D** Employer identification number 35 7438041 **E** Telephone number (480) 344-8174 **F** Accounting method: ☐ Cash ☑ Accrual ☐ Other (specify) ▶

• Section 501(c)(3) organizations and 4947(a)(1) nonexempt charitable trusts must attach a completed Schedule A (Form 990 or 990-EZ).

H and **I** are not applicable to section 527 organizations.
H(a) Is this a group return for affiliates? ☐ Yes ☑ No
H(b) If "Yes," enter number of affiliates ▶ _____
H(c) Are all affiliates included? ☐ Yes ☐ No
(If "No," attach a list. See instructions.)
H(d) Is this a separate return filed by an organization covered by a group ruling? ☐ Yes ☐ No
I Group Exemption Number ▶

G Website: ▶ www.lifelinemin.org

J Organization type (check only one) ▶ ☑ 501(c) (3) ◀ (insert no.) ☐ 4947(a)(1) or ☐ 527

K Check here ▶ ☐ if the organization is not a 509(a)(3) supporting organization **and** its gross receipts are normally **not** more than $25,000. A return is not required, but if the organization chooses to file a return, be sure to file a complete return.

M Check ▶ ☐ if the organization is **not** required to attach Sch. B (Form 990, 990-EZ, or 990-PF).

L Gross receipts: Add lines 6b, 8b, 9b, and 10b to line 12 ▶   1,618,911

Part I Revenue, Expenses, and Changes in Net Assets or Fund Balances *(See the instructions.)*

1	Contributions, gifts, grants, and similar amounts received:		
a	Contributions to donor advised funds	1a 1,063,677	
b	Direct public support (not included on line 1a)	1b	
c	Indirect public support (not included on line 1a)	1c	
d	Government contributions (grants) (not included on line 1a)	1d	
e	Total (add lines 1a through 1d) (cash $ 1,037,334 noncash $ 26,543)	1e	1,063,877
2	Program service revenue including government fees and contracts (from Part VII, line 93)	2	498,863
3	Membership dues and assessments	3	
4	Interest on savings and temporary cash investments	4	110
5	Dividends and interest from securities	5	498
6a	Gross rents	6a	
b	Less: rental expenses	6b	
c	Net rental income or (loss). Subtract line 6b from line 6a	6c	
7	Other investment income (describe ▶)	7	
8a	Gross amount from sales of assets other than inventory	(A) Securities 8a (B) Other	
b	Less: cost or other basis and sales expenses.	8b	
c	Gain or (loss) (attach schedule) . . .	8c	
d	Net gain or (loss). Combine line 8c, columns (A) and (B)	8d	-1
9	Special events and activities (attach schedule). If any amount is from **gaming**, check here ▶ ☐		
a	Gross revenue (not including $ _____ of contributions reported on line 1b)	9a 27,416	
b	Less: direct expenses other than fundraising expenses .	9b 18,360	
c	Net income or (loss) from special events. Subtract line 9b from line 9a	9c	9,056
10a	Gross sales of inventory, less returns and allowances . .	10a	
b	Less: cost of goods sold	10b	
c	Gross profit or (loss) from sales of inventory (attach schedule). Subtract line 10b from line 10a . .	10c	
11	Other revenue (from Part VII, line 103)	11	1,288
12	**Total revenue.** Add lines 1e, 2, 3, 4, 5, 6c, 7, 8d, 9c, 10c, and 11	12	1,573,691
13	Program services (from line 44, column (B))	13	1,088,112
14	Management and general (from line 44, column (C))	14	188,159
15	Fundraising (from line 44, column (D))	15	12,716
16	Payments to affiliates (attach schedule)	16	
17	**Total expenses.** Add lines 16 and 44, column (A)	17	1,397,987
18	Excess or (deficit) for the year. Subtract line 17 from line 12	18	175,704
19	Net assets or fund balances at beginning of year (from line 73, column (A))	19	14,631
20	Other changes in net assets or fund balances (attach explanation)	20	
21	Net assets or fund balances at end of year. Combine lines 18, 19, and 20	21	190,335

For Privacy Act and Paperwork Reduction Act Notice, see the separate instructions. Cat. No. 11282Y Form **990** (2007)

Only pages 1, 2 and 5 of Form 990 are reflected on pages 43-45.

43

Form 990 (2007) Page **2**

Part II Statement of Functional Expenses

All organizations must complete column (A). Columns (B), (C), and (D) are required for section 501(c)(3) and (4) organizations and section 4947(a)(1) nonexempt charitable trusts but optional for others. *(See the instructions.)*

Do not include amounts reported on line 6b, 8b, 9b, 10b, or 16 of Part I.

		(A) Total	(B) Program services	(C) Management and general	(D) Fundraising
22a	Grants paid from donor advised funds (attach schedule) (cash $ _____ noncash $ _____) If this amount includes foreign grants, check here ▶ ☐				
22b	Other grants and allocations (attach schedule) (cash $ _____ noncash $ _____) If this amount includes foreign grants, check here ▶ ☐				
23	Specific assistance to individuals (attach schedule)				
24	Benefits paid to or for members (attach schedule)				
25a	Compensation of current officers, directors, key employees, etc. listed in Part V-A	297,198	211,651	31,572	53,975
b	Compensation of former officers, directors, key employees, etc. listed in Part V-B				
c	Compensation and other distributions, not included above, to disqualified persons (as defined under section 4958(f)(1)) and persons described in section 4958(c)(3)(B)				
26	Salaries and wages of employees not included on lines 25a, b, and c	154,156	109,783	16,377	27,996
27	Pension plan contributions not included on lines 25a, b, and c				
28	Employee benefits not included on lines 25a – 27	19,874	11,335	6,333	2,206
29	Payroll taxes	37,560	20,427	14,212	2,921
30	Professional fundraising fees				
31	Accounting fees	13,047	10,438	652	1,957
32	Legal fees				
33	Supplies	11,302	6,408	4,143	751
34	Telephone	10,602	652	9,950	
35	Postage and shipping	26,238	18,301	3,819	4,118
36	Occupancy	50,618	40,494	2,531	7,493
37	Equipment rental and maintenance	173,497	163,905	9,592	
38	Printing and publications	63,102	56,737	1,764	4,601
39	Travel				
40	Conferences, conventions, and meetings	2,747	2,747		
41	Interest	486		486	
42	Depreciation, depletion, etc. (attach schedule)	43,180	34,544	2,159	6,477
43	Other expenses not covered above (itemize):				
a	_____				
b	See Statement #1	494,380	400,690	84,569	9,121
c	_____				
d	_____				
e	_____				
f	_____				
g	_____				
44	**Total functional expenses.** Add lines 22a through 43g. (Organizations completing columns (B)–(D), carry these totals to lines 13–15)	1,397,987	1,088,112	188,1159	121,716

Joint Costs. Check ▶ ☐ if you are following SOP 98-2.
Are any joint costs from a combined educational campaign and fundraising solicitation reported in (B) Program services? ▶ ☐ Yes ☒ No
If "Yes," enter **(i)** the aggregate amount of these joint costs $ _____ ; **(ii)** the amount allocated to Program services $ _____ ;
(iii) the amount allocated to Management and general $ _____ ; and **(iv)** the amount allocated to Fundraising $ _____

Form **990** (2007)

Form 990 (2007) Page **5**

Part IV-A Reconciliation of Revenue per Audited Financial Statements With Revenue per Return *(See the instructions.)*

a	Total revenue, gains, and other support per audited financial statements		a	1,579,432
b	Amounts included on line **a** but not on Part I, line 12:			
1	Net unrealized gains on investments	b1		
2	Donated services and use of facilities	b2	5,741	
3	Recoveries of prior year grants	b3		
4	Other (specify): _____	b4		
	Add lines **b1** through **b4**		b	5,741
c	Subtract line **b** from line **a**		c	1,573,691
d	Amounts included on Part I, line 12, but not on line **a**:			
1	Investment expenses not included on Part I, line 6b	d1		
2	Other (specify): _____	d2		
	Add lines **d1** and **d2**		d	
e	**Total revenue** (Part I, line 12). Add lines **c** and **d** ▶		e	1,573,691

Part IV-B Reconciliation of Expenses per Audited Financial Statements With Expenses per Return

a	Total expenses and losses per audited financial statements		a	1,403,728
b	Amounts included on line **a** but not on Part I, line 17:			
1	Donated services and use of facilities	b1	5,741	
2	Prior year adjustments reported on Part I, line 20	b2		
3	Losses reported on Part I, line 20	b3		
4	Other (specify): _____	b4		
	Add lines **b1** through **b4**		b	5,741
c	Subtract line **b** from line **a**		c	1,397,987
d	Amounts included on Part I, line 17, but not on line **a**:			
1	Investment expenses not included on Part I, line 6b	d1		
2	Other (specify): _____	d2		
	Add lines **d1** and **d2**		d	
e	**Total expenses** (Part I, line 17). Add lines **c** and **d** ▶		e	1,397,987

Part V-A Current Officers, Directors, Trustees, and Key Employees (List each person who was an officer, director, trustee, or key employee at any time during the year even if they were not compensated.) *(See the instructions.)*

(A) Name and address	(B) Title and average hours per week devoted to position	(C) Compensation (If not paid, enter -0-.)	(D) Contributions to employee benefit plans & deferred compensation plans	(E) Expense account and other allowances
Harold Vinson 1212 S Palo Verde, Phoenix, AZ 85035	Exec. Dir. - 40	75,000	10,000	
Bill Horner 1212 S Palo Verde, Phoenix, AZ 85035	Chairman - 10	0	0	
Alice Waymire 1212 S Palo Verde, Phoenix, AZ 85035	Director - 1	0	0	
Fred Patela 1212 S Palo Verde, Phoenix, AZ 85035	Director - 1	0	0	
Mary Vaughn 1212 S Palo Verde, Phoenix, AZ 85035	Director - 1	0	0	
Frank Bristol 1212 S Palo Verde, Phoenix, AZ 85035	Director - 1	0	0	

Form **990** (2007)

Common Problems in Completing Form 990

➤ **Page 1—General Information**

Cash or accrual. You should generally use the same accounting method on the return as you use to keep your books and records. For example, if you keep your books on the accrual method, or convert to accrual at year end, you should generally prepare your Form 990 on the accrual basis.

Item M. This box must be checked if you aren't attaching Schedule B (Schedule of Contributors).

➤ **Page 1—Part I**

Line 1 – Contributions. Report all contributions received on Line 1. Do not net fund-raising expenses against the contributions.

Noncash contributions (other than gifts of services or use of facilities) are shown on Line 1d.

The gift portion of special event revenue is reported on Line 1a. See example under Line 9 explanation below.

Line 1c – Government contributions (grants). Report government grants on this line that enable the donee to provide a service for the direct benefit of the public.

Line 2 – Program service revenue including government fees and contracts. Report grants on this line if they are primarily for the benefit of the organization. This includes anything that is essentially a payment for a service or product. Also report rental income related to exempt purposes and all rental income from affiliated organizations on this line.

Line 9 – Special events and activities. Report activities on this line that only incidentally accomplish an exempt purpose. Their sole purpose is to raise noncontribution funds to finance the organization's activities.

Example: A friend of the ministry attends a fund-raising dinner for which tickets were sold at $20 each. The market value of a similar meal is $12 and the direct cost of the meal to the charity is $9. The $8 difference between the market value and price paid is a contribution (Line 1a). The $12 is reported as special events gross revenue on Line 9a, and the direct cost of the meal of $9 is reported as direct expenses on Line 9b.

Line 20 – Other changes in net assets or fund balances. Use this line to report unrealized gains and losses and prior period corrections.

Line 21 – Net assets or fund balances at end of year. The ending net assets on your balance sheet should agree with Line 21.

CHAPTER 2 › TAX EXEMPTION

➤ **Page 2—Part II**

Columns A, B, C, D. The data in these columns should agree, or reconcile by using the adjustments reported on page 5, Part IV-A and B, with your audited financial statements (if you have an audit).

Lines 41 and 42 – Interest and depreciation expense. Interest and depreciation expense should be functionally allocated unless they are immaterial.

➤ **Page 3—Part III**

Statement of program service accomplishments. This portion of the form is an opportunity to fully explain the programs and accomplishments of the organization. You are not limited by the space on page 2. Attach schedules as you desire.

➤ **Page 5—Part IV-A and B**

This section is only to be completed if your organization has an audit.

Part IV, Line b(1) – Net unrealized gains on investments. Enter the amount of unrealized gains on investments as reported on your audit.

Part IV-A, Line b(2) and Part IV-B, Line b(1) – Donated services and use of facilities. Enter the donated services and use of facilities as reported on your audit.

➤ **Page 5—Part V-A**

All officers, directors, trustees, and key employees must be listed here whether or not they received any compensation.

A "key employee" is any person having responsibilities or powers similar to those of officers, directors, or trustees. Included are

- chief management and administration officials (CEO, Executive Director, President, Senior Pastor, COO, vice presidents)
- CFO and officer in charge of administration or program operations; these qualify if they have the authority to control the organization's activities or finances or both.

It is acceptable to use the charity's address for each officer, director, trustee, or key employee.

➤ **Schedule B Schedule of Contributors**

When Schedule B is distributed to anyone other than the IRS, the names of the donors should be redacted as well as the description of the contribution if it could reveal the identity of the donor.

offices during normal business hours. An office is considered a regional or district office only if (1) it has three or more paid, full-time employees or (2) the aggregate hours per week worked by its paid employees (either full-time or part-time) are 120 or more.

▶ **Responding to requests.** If a person requests copies in person, the request generally must be fulfilled on the day of the request. In unusual circumstances, an organization will be permitted to furnish the copies on the next business day. When the request is made in writing, the organization must provide the requested copies within 30 days. If the organization requires advance payment for reasonable copying and mailing fees, it can provide copies within 30 days of the date it is paid, instead of the date of the request.

▶ **Fees for providing copies.** Reasonable fees may be charged by nonprofits for copying and mailing documents. The fees cannot exceed the amounts charged by the IRS—currently, $1 for the first page and 15 cents for each subsequent page—plus actual mailing costs. An organization can require payment in advance. The IRS protects requesters from unexpected fees by requiring an organization that receives a request in writing without advance payment to obtain consent before providing copies that will result in fees of more than $20.

▶ **Documents widely available.** A nonprofit organization does not have to comply with requests for copies if it has made the appropriate materials widely available. This requirement is satisfied if the document is posted on the organization's web page on the Internet or in another database of similar materials.

> **Filing Tip**
>
> As with all tax returns, nonprofits are required by law to provide complete and accurate information on these annual returns. The IRS makes all Forms 990 available to a nonprofit organization, Philanthropic Research, which posts them at www.guidestar.org.

Reporting substantial organizational changes

An organization's tax-exempt status remains in effect if there are no material changes in the organization's character, purposes, or methods of operation. Significant changes should be reported by letter to the IRS soon after the changes occur.

> **Example:** An organization received tax-exempt status for the operation of a religious radio ministry. Several years later, the organization decided to add a facility for homeless children. This change would likely be considered to be material and should be reported to the IRS.

Change in accounting methods

A nonprofit organization may adopt any reasonable method of accounting to keep its financial records that clearly reflects income. These methods include the cash receipts and disbursements method; the accrual method; or any other method (including a combination of methods) that clearly reflects income.

An organization that wishes to change from one method of accounting to another generally must secure the consent of the IRS to make that change. Consent must be obtained both for a general change of method and for any change of method with respect to one or more particular items. Thus, a nonprofit organization that generally uses the cash method, but uses the accrual method with respect to publications for which it maintains inventories, may change its method of accounting by adopting the accrual method for all purposes. But the organization must secure the IRS's consent to do so.

To obtain the consent of the IRS to change an accounting method, the organization should file IRS Form 3115, Application for Change in Accounting Method. The form must be filed within 180 days after the beginning of the tax year in which the change is made. There is a more expeditious consent for a change from the cash to accrual method filed under Revenue Procedure 85-37.

Change of fiscal years

Generally, an exempt organization may change its fiscal year simply by timely filing Form 990 with the appropriate Internal Revenue Service Center for the "short year." The return for the short year should indicate at the top of page 1 that a change of accounting period is being made. It should be filed not later than the 15th day of the fifth month following the close of the short year.

If neither Form 990 nor Form 990-T must be filed, the ministry is not required to notify the IRS of a change in the fiscal year, with one exception. The exception applies to exempt organizations that have changed their fiscal years within the previous ten calendar years. For this exception, Form 1128 must be filed with the IRS.

Other

- **Form 5578.** Form 5578 (see page 115) may be completed and furnished to the IRS to provide information regarding nondiscrimination policies of private schools instead of completing the information at item 31 of Form 990, Schedule A. If Form 990 is not required to be filed, Form 5578 should be submitted, if applicable. Form 5578 must be filed for schools operated by a church, including preschools.

- **Forms 8717 and 8718.** Nonprofits wishing IRS private letter rulings on exempt organization information or on employee plans must include new Form 8717 or 8718, respectively, with the appropriate fees.

- **Form 8282.** If a nonprofit donee sells or otherwise disposes of gift property for which an appraisal summary is required on Form 8283 within two years after receipt of the property, it generally must file Form 8282 with the IRS. See chapter 7 for more information on these reporting rules.

- **Employee and nonemployee payments.** As an employer, a nonprofit organization must file federal and state forms concerning payment of compensation and the withholding of payroll taxes. Payments to nonemployees may require the filing of information returns. See chapters 4 and 5 for more coverage of these requirements.

Postal Regulations

Churches and other nonprofits may qualify to mail at special standard nonprofit mail rates (formerly called bulk third-class). The application (Form 3624) is available at the post office where you wish to deposit the mail (see page 51 for a sample of Form 3624). The following information must be provided (some items apply only if the organization is incorporated):

➤ description of the organization's primary purpose, which may be found in the articles of incorporation or bylaws;

➤ evidence that the organization is nonprofit, such as a federal (and state) tax exemption determination letter; and

➤ materials showing how the organization actually operated in the previous 6 to 12 months, such as program literature, newsletters, bulletins, and any other promotional materials.

The U.S. Postal Service offers rate incentives to nonprofit mailers that provide automation-compatible mail. Automated mail must be readable by an Optical Character Reader (OCR). Contact your local post office for more information.

State Taxes and Fees

Separate filings are often necessary to obtain exemption from state income tax. The requirements vary from state to state. In some states it is also possible to obtain exemption from licensing fees and sales, use, franchise, and property taxes.

A nonprofit organization may be required to report to one or more states in relation to its exemption from or compliance with state income, sales, use, or property taxation. Many states accept a copy of Form 990 as adequate annual reporting for tax-exempt status purposes. Annual reporting to the state in which the organization is incorporated is normally required even if there is no requirement to file Form 990 with the IRS. Check with the offices of the secretary of state and attorney general to determine required filings.

> **Caution**
>
> Do not send a list of major contributors to the state unless it is specifically required. While this list is not open to public inspection with respect to the federal filing, it may not be confidential for state purposes.

Property taxes

Church property is generally exempt from property tax. Whether real estate of a nonprofit organization is exempt from property tax usually depends on its use and ownership. Many

CHAPTER 2 > TAX EXEMPTION

Application to Mail at Nonprofit Standard Mail® Rates

Section A—Application *(Please read section B on page 2 before completion.)*

Part 1 *(For completion by applicant)*

- All information entered below must be legible so that our records will show the correct information about your organization.
- The complete name of the organization must be shown in item 1. The name shown must agree with the name that appears on all documents submitted to support this application.
- A complete address representing a physical location for the organization must be shown in item 2. If you receive mail through a Post Office™ box, how your street address first and then the box number.

- The applicant named in item 5 must be the individual submitting the application for the organization and must be a responsible official of the organization. Printers and mailing agents may not sign for the organization.
- No additional organization categories may be added in item 6. To be eligible for the Nonprofit Standard Mail rates, the organization must qualify as one of the types listed.
- The applicant must sign the application in item 12.
- The date shown in item 14 must be the date that the application is submitted to the Post Office.

No application fee is required. *(All information must be complete and typewritten or printed legibly.)*

1. Complete Name of Organization *(If voting registration official, include title)*
   Chapel Hill Charity

2. Street Address of Organization *(Include apartment or suite number)*
   300 South Hillcrest Avenue

3. City, State, ZIP+4® Code
   Athens, GA 45701

4. Telephone *(Include area code)*
   614-832-9061

5. Name of Applicant *(Must represent applying organization)*
   Lewis Foster

6. Type of Organization *(Check only one)*

   [✓] (01) Religious   [ ] (03) Scientific   [ ] (05) Agricultural   [ ] (07) Veterans   [ ] (09) Qualified political committee *(Go to item 9)*
   [ ] (02) Educational   [ ] (04) Philanthropic   [ ] (06) Labor   [ ] (08) Fraternal   [ ] (10) Voting registration official *(Go to item 9)*

   Not all nonprofit organizations are eligible for the Nonprofit Standard Mail rates. Domestic Mail Manual® 703.1 lists certain organizations (such as business leagues, chambers of commerce, civic improvement associations, social and hobby clubs, governmental bodies, and others) that, although nonprofit, do not qualify for the Nonprofit Standard Mail rates.

7. Is this a for-profit organization or does any of the net income inure to the benefit of any private stockholder or individual?
   [ ] Yes [✓] No

8. Is this organization exempt from federal income tax? *(If 'Yes,' attach a copy of the exemption issued by the Internal Revenue Service (IRS) that shows the section of the IRS code under which the organization is exempt. Required if exempt. Do not submit State tax exemption information.)*
   [✓] Yes [ ] No

   Has the IRS denied or revoked the organization's federal tax exempt status? *(If 'Yes,' attach a copy of the IRS ruling to this PS Form 3624.)*
   [ ] Yes [✓] No

   From your IRS exemption letter, check off the box corresponding to the section under which the organization is exempt:
   [✓] 501(c)(3)   [ ] 501(c)(5)
   [ ] 501(c)(8)   [ ] 501(c)(19)
   [ ] Other 501(c) (____) *(See statement in item 6 above)*

9. Has this organization previously mailed at the Nonprofit Standard Mail rates? *(If 'Yes,' list the Post Office locations where mailings were most recently deposited at these rates and provide the nonprofit authorization number, if known.)*
   [ ] Yes [✓] No

10. Has your organization had Nonprofit Standard Mail rate mailing privileges denied or revoked? *(If 'Yes,' list the Post Office (city and state) where the application was denied or authorization was revoked and provide the nonprofit authorization number, if known.)*
    [ ] Yes [✓] No

11. Post Office (not a station or branch) where authorization requested and bulk mailings will be made *(City, state, ZIP Code™).*

I certify that the statements made by me are true and complete. I understand that anyone who furnishes false or misleading information on this form or who omits material information requested on the form may be subject to criminal sanctions (including fines and imprisonment) and/or civil sanctions (including multiple damages **and** civil penalties). I further understand that, if this application is approved, a postage refund for the difference between the regular Standard Mail and Nonprofit Standard Mail rates may be made for only mailings entered at regular Standard Mail rates at the Post Office identified above while this application is pending, provided that the conditions set forth in Domestic Mail Manual 703.1 and 703.1.9 are met.

12. Signature of Applicant
    Lewis E. Foster

13. Title
    Manager

14. Date
    1-20-07

Part 2 *(For completion by postmaster at originating office when application filed)*

1. Signature of Postmaster *(Or designated representative)*

2. Date Application Filed With Post Office *(Round stamp)*

PS Form **3624**, February 2007 *(Page 1 of 3)* PSN 7530-02-000-9014   PRIVACY NOTICE: See our privacy policy on www.usps.com

This form is available at www.usps.com/forms.

51

states restrict the exemption of church property to property used for worship. It is also important to note that not all religious organizations are churches. Contact the office of the county tax assessor or collector to determine what property tax exemptions are available.

Parsonages may be exempt from real estate tax in certain jurisdictions. This is true though there may be several ministers on the staff of one church and therefore multiple parsonages. If the pastor owns the parsonage instead of the church, the parsonage is usually subject to property tax.

> **Caution**
>
> An initial (and perhaps annual) registration of the property with the proper state authorities is generally necessary to record exempt property. The initial purchase of real estate with notification of state authorities is usually not sufficient to exempt property from tax.

Church parking lots are usually exempt if properly recorded. It may be possible to obtain an exemption for vacant land. Property tax exemption of church camps and recreation facilities often comes under attack because of income that may be generated through their use. Property partially used for church use and partially leased to a third-party for-profit entity generally results in the proration of the tax exemption.

Sales taxes

There are presently four states with no sales tax law. In some states a nonprofit organization is exempt from sales tax as a purchaser of goods used in ministry. It is generally necessary to obtain recognition of sales tax exemption from the state revenue department. Some states will accept a federal tax exemption as sufficient for a state sales tax exemption.

Even if an organization is exempt from paying sales tax, purchases used for the private benefit of the organization's members or employees are not eligible for exemption.

When a nonprofit organization sells goods to others, a sales tax may or may not be applicable. There are some indications that states may begin a stricter enforcement of laws on the books allowing them to impose sales tax on sales by nonprofit organizations. Occasional dinners and sales of goods at bazaars are typically exempt from sales tax.

Sales by a nonprofit within the state where the nonprofit is located are sometimes taxable. Sales to customers located outside of the state, or interstate sales, may not be subject to sales tax. A 1992 Supreme Court case cleared the way for Congress to decide whether states can require organizations to collect state sales taxes on out-of-state mail-order purchases. Until Congress acts, nonprofits may continue to ship publications and other taxable materials into states where they have no employees or other significant contacts without having to collect taxes.

When a nonprofit organization operates a conference or convention outside of its home state, it is often possible to obtain sales tax exemption for purchases made within the state where the meeting is held. Sales of products at the convention would generally be covered under sales tax laws without an approved exemption.

Political Activity

Churches and other organizations exempt from federal income tax under section 501(c)(3) of the Internal Revenue Code are prohibited from participating or intervening, directly or indirectly, in any political campaign on behalf of or in opposition to any candidate for public office. Even activities that encourage people to vote for or against a particular candidate on the basis of nonpartisan criteria violate the political campaign prohibition of law.

To avoid violating the political campaign provisions of the law:

- Do not use a rating program to evaluate candidates.
- Do not endorse a candidate, or a slate of candidates, directly or indirectly through a sermon, speech, newsletter, or sample ballot.
- Do not publish a candidate's statement.
- Do not publish the names of candidates who agree to adhere to certain practices.
- Do not publish candidate responses to a questionnaire that evidences a bias on certain issues. Classifying particular candidates as too conservative or too liberal is an improper rating system.
- Do not publish responses to an unbiased questionnaire focused on a narrow range of issues.
- Do not raise funds for a candidate or provide support to a political party.
- Do not provide volunteers, mailing lists, publicity, or free use of facilities unless all parties and candidates in the community receive the same services.
- Do not pay campaign expenses for a candidate.
- Do not publish or distribute printed or oral statements about candidates.
- Do not display campaign literature on the organization's premises.

Warning

If a church or 501(c)(3) organization participates in even one political campaign activity (no matter how small the occasion), it can potentially lose its tax-exempt status. The organization must not be involved or participate in the campaign of the individual seeking public office. This is based on the date the candidacy is announced.

If the IRS finds that an organization has engaged in these activities, the organization could lose its exempt status. Also, the IRS may assess an excise tax on the amount of the funds spent on the activity.

Forums or debates may be conducted to educate voters at which all candidates are treated equally, or a mailing list may be rented to candidates on the same basis as it is made available to others. Organizations may engage in voter registration or get-out-the-vote activities. However, it is wise to avoid defining a target group by political or ideological criteria (*e.g.*, encouraging individuals to vote who are "registered Republicans").

IntegrityPoints

- **The church audit potential.** Very few churches are audited each year, perhaps less than 100. The number of churches audited is low because approval of an appropriate high-level IRS official is required to open a church tax inquiry. This is the protection provided in the tax law in recognition of the separation of church and state. However, this audit restriction does not apply to a church that is not filing or paying payroll taxes.

    The danger is for churches to conduct their financial operations beyond the bounds of the law in the belief the church will never be audited. Integrity requires compliance with the law even if the IRS never calls.

- **The danger of "excess benefit transactions."** Excess benefit transactions (as defined on page 41) are often overlooked by churches and other charities. The "insider" involved in the transaction can be subjected to a penalty of up to 225%.

    An excess transaction can be as simple as providing a taxable fringe benefit and not reflecting it as taxable income to a senior pastor, executive director, president CEO or other insider. It could be as easy as transferring equipment from a nonprofit organization to an insider at less than fair market value and failing to treat the amount as taxable income to the recipient.

- **The ever-changing Form 990.** Most charities other than churches must annually file Form 990. The Form 990 has always been a challenging form to file but the proposed Form 990 for 2008, to be filed in 2009, takes the complexity to a new level.

    The staff of very few charities have the ability to accurately file the present and proposed new Form 990. At a minimum, a charity should have the Form 990 reviewed by their external CPA or Attorney. Better yet is to have the Form 990 prepared by an external professional. After the Form 990 is filed with the IRS, it is soon posted (minus Schedule B) on the Internet by GuideStar. So, an improperly prepared Form 990 soon becomes available for anyone in the world to see. A poorly prepared Form 990 reflects negatively on the charity.

CHAPTER THREE
Compensating Employees

In This Chapter

- Reasonable compensation
- Housing and the housing allowance
- Deferred compensation
- Maximizing fringe benefits
- Nondiscrimination rules
- Paying employee expenses

Compensation plans should provide tax-effective benefits. A dollar of benefit costs to the organization may be multiplied when received by the employee as tax-free or tax-deferred.

Reasonable Compensation

Employees of churches and nonprofit organizations may receive reasonable compensation for their efforts. Excessive compensation can result in private inurement and may jeopardize the tax-exempt status of the organization. Reasonable compensation is based on what would ordinarily be paid for like services by a like organization under similar circumstances.

The intermediate sanction regulations impose penalties when excessive compensation or benefits are received by certain key employees and other individuals. These penalties may be avoided if the compensation arrangement was approved by an independent board that (1) was composed entirely of individuals unrelated to and not subject to the control of the employee involved in the arrangement, (2) obtained and relied upon appropriate data as to comparability, and (3) adequately documented the basis for its determination.

A review of the changes in the Consumers Price Index from one year to the next may be helpful when projecting salary increases:

1993	2.7%	1998	1.6%	2003	1.9%
1994	2.7%	1999	2.7%	2004	3.3%
1995	2.5%	2000	3.4%	2005	3.4%
1996	3.3%	2001	1.6%	2006	2.5%
1997	1.7%	2002	2.4%	2007	2.7% (est.)

Housing and the Housing Allowance

Housing for nonministers

Housing provided to nonminister employees by a church or nonprofit organization for its convenience, as a condition of employment, and on its premises is

➤ exempt from income tax and FICA tax withholding by the church, and

➤ excluded from wages reporting by the church and employee.

If these criteria are not met, the fair rental value should be reported as compensation on Form W-2 and is subject to withholding and FICA taxation.

Qualifying for the minister's housing allowance

The 2008 edition of *The Zondervan Minister's Tax & Financial Guide* includes a thorough discussion of the availability of the housing allowance for ministers serving local churches. Ordained, commissioned, or licensed ministers *not* serving local churches may qualify as "ministers" for federal tax purposes in the situations described below.

Denominational service

This category encompasses the administration of religious denominations and their integral agencies, including teaching or administration in parochial schools, colleges, or universities that are under the authority of a church or denomination.

The IRS uses the following criteria to determine if an institution is an integral agency of a church:

➤ Did the church incorporate the institution?

➤ Does the corporate name of the institution suggest a church relationship?

➤ Does the church continuously control, manage, and maintain the institution?

➤ If it dissolved, will the assets be turned over to the church?

➤ Are the trustees or directors of the institution appointed by, or must they be approved by, the church, and may they be removed by the church?

➤ Are annual reports of finances and general operations required to be made to the church?

➤ Does the church contribute to the support of the institution?

Assignment by a church

Services performed by a minister for a parachurch organization based upon a substantive assignment or designation by a church may provide the basis for ministerial tax treatment.

Sample Housing Allowance Resolutions

Parsonage Owned by or Rented by a Church

Whereas, The Internal Revenue Code permits a minister of the gospel to exclude from gross income "the rental value of a home furnished as part of compensation" or a church-designated allowance paid as a part of compensation to the extent that actual expenses are paid from the allowance to maintain a parsonage owned or rented by the church;

Whereas, Nelson Street Church compensates the senior minister for services in the exercise of ministry; and

Whereas, Nelson Street Church provides the senior minister with the rent-free use of a parsonage owned by (rented by) the church as a portion of the compensation for services rendered to the church in the exercise of ministry;

Resolved, That the compensation of the senior minister is $2,500 per month, of which $200 per month is a designated housing allowance; and

Resolved, That the designation of $200 per month as a housing allowance shall apply until otherwise provided.

Home Owned or Rented by a Minister

Whereas, The Internal Revenue Code permits a minister of the gospel to exclude from gross income a church-designated allowance paid as part of compensation to the extent used for actual expenses in owning or renting a home; and

Whereas, Nelson Street Church compensates the senior minister for services in the exercise of ministry;

Resolved, That the compensation of the senior minister is $3,500 per month of which $1,250 per month is a designated housing allowance; and

Resolved, That the designation of $1,250 per month as a housing allowance shall apply until otherwise provided.

Evangelists

Whereas, The Internal Revenue Code permits a minister of the gospel to exclude from gross income a church-designated allowance paid as part of compensation to the extent used in owning or renting a permanent home; and

Whereas, Nelson Street Church compensates Rev. John Doe for services in the exercise of ministry as an evangelist;

Resolved, That the honorarium paid to Rev. Doe shall be $1,512, consisting of $312 travel expenses (with documentation provided to the church), $500 housing allowance, and a $700 honorarium.

The housing allowance should be designated by the employing organization, not the assigning church.

The following characteristics must be present for an effective assignment:

▶ There must be sufficient relationship between the minister and the assigning church to justify the assignment of the minister.

▶ There must be an adequate relationship between the assigning church and the parachurch organization to which the minister is assigned to justify the assignment.

To substantiate the relationship between the minister and the church, the church must determine "if there is sufficient authority, power, or legitimacy for the church to assign this particular minister." Such matters as being the ordaining church, providing ongoing supervision, having denominational affiliation, contributing significant financial support, or being the long-term "home church" would all appear to support this relationship.

In addressing the relationship between the church and the parachurch organization, the church must answer the question of "why should the church assign a minister to this particular ministry?" Essentially, the assignment of the minister must accomplish the church's ministry purposes.

Caution

Too often, a denomination lists a minister as being assigned to a parachurch ministry, for example, in an annual directory, and the minister believes he or she has been assigned for tax purposes. But effective assignments are rare because of the substantive relationship and ongoing documentation of the assignment that are needed.

In considering an assignment, it is important to distinguish between the *process* of assigning and the *documentation* of the assignment. The process of assigning expresses the church's theology, philosophy, and policy of operation: its way of doing ministry. The documentation of the assignment provides evidence that the church is doing ministry through the particular individual assigned. The keys to a proper assignment are

☐ A written policy describing the specific requirements for the relationship of the church both to the minister being assigned and to the parachurch organization to which the minister is assigned. This would include the church's theological and policy goals for the assignment.

☐ A formal review to confirm that the minister and the proposed ministry with a parachurch organization qualify.

☐ A written assignment coupled with guidelines for supervision of and reporting by the minister and the parachurch organization to the church.

☐ A periodic (at least annual) formal review of the minister's activities to confirm that the assignment continues to comply with the policy.

A sample board resolution for ministerial assignment is on page 88.

Other service

If you are not engaged in service performed in the exercise of ministry of a local church or an integral agency of a church or a church does not assign your services, the definition of a qualifying minister becomes much narrower. Tax law and regulations provide little guidance for ministers in this category. However, Tax Court cases and IRS rulings suggest that an individual will qualify for the special tax treatments of a minister only if the individual's services for the employer substantially involve conducting religious worship or performing sacerdotal functions. This definition includes conducting Bible studies and spiritual counseling.

How much time constitutes substantial involvement in conducting worship or administering the sacraments? This is difficult to say. However, in two IRS letter rulings, the IRS determined that 5% of the minister's working hours were not sufficient to qualify for tax treatment as a minister.

Caution

Many ministers are serving organizations other than local churches or integral agencies of churches and do not have an effective assignment by a church. The employer may be a rescue mission, a youth ministry, a Christian radio or TV station, or a missionary-sending organization. Qualifying for ministerial status is often based on the degree to which the individual is performing sacerdotal functions or conducting religious worship.

What if you are a minister employed by an organization that is not a church, integral agency of a church, or other religious organization? If you are an ordained, licensed, or commissioned minister conducting religious worship or performing sacerdotal functions to a substantial extent for your employer, you may qualify as a minister for tax purposes.

Based on IRS rulings, it is clear that ministers serving as chaplains in government-owned-and-operated hospitals or in state prisons fall in a special category. They are employees for social security (FICA) purposes but qualify for the housing allowance.

Individuals not qualifying for ministerial tax treatment

You do not qualify as a "minister" for federal income tax purposes if you are

- a theological student who does not otherwise qualify as a minister;
- an unordained, uncommissioned, or unlicensed church official;
- an ordained, commissioned, or licensed minister working as an administrator or on the faculty of a nonchurch-related college or seminary;
- an ordained, commissioned, or licensed minister working as an executive of a non-religious, nonchurch-related organization;
- a civilian chaplain at a VA hospital (the tax treatment of ministers who are chaplains in the armed forces is the same as that of other members of the armed forces); or
- an ordained, licensed, or commissioned minister employed by a parachurch organization but who does not meet the sacerdotal function or conducting religious worship tests.

Applying the minister's housing allowance

Qualified ministers receive preferred treatment for their housing. If a minister has a home provided as part of compensation, the minister pays no income tax on the rental value of the home. If a home is not provided but the minister receives a rental or housing allowance, the minister pays no tax on the allowance if it is used for housing expenses subject to certain limitations.

Every minister should have a portion of salary designated as a housing allowance. For a minister living in organization-owned housing, the housing allowance may be only a modest amount to cover incidental expenses such as maintenance, furnishings, and utilities. But a properly designated housing allowance may be worth thousands of dollars in tax savings for ministers living in their own homes or rented quarters.

The excludable housing allowance for ministers is the lowest of these factors:

➤ **Reasonable compensation.** While the law is clear that compensation must be "ordinary and necessary," applying these guidelines is often not easy. All forms of compensation paid by a nonprofit organization must be considered in determining whether reasonable compensation has been exceeded. This includes salary, bonuses, fringe benefits, and retirement benefits. The amount of time an individual devotes to the position is also a factor. Documentation of comparable salaries is important to justify compensation arrangements.

➤ **Amount prospectively and officially designated by the employer.** The allowance must be officially designated before payment by the organization. The designation should be evidenced in writing, preferably by resolution of the appropriate governing body, in an employment contract, or, at a minimum, in the church budget and payroll records.

If the only reference to the housing allowance is in the organization's budget, the budget should be formally approved by the top governing body. However, it is highly preferable for the governing board to use a specific resolution to authorize housing allowance designations.

➤ **Amount used from current ministerial income to provide the home.** Only actual expenses can be excluded from income.

➤ **The fair rental value of the home including utilities and furnishings.** The IRS has not provided any guidance to assist ministers in determining the fair rental value of the home.

Filing Tip

The designation of a housing allowance for a minister living in church-provided housing is often overlooked. While the largest housing allowance benefits go to ministers with mortgage payments on their own homes, a housing allowance of a few thousand dollars is often beneficial to a pastor in a church-provided home.

Deferred Compensation

In addition to 403(b) and 401(k) plans, churches and nonprofit organizations have available all the qualified retirement plan options that are available to any for-profit. These must be operated according to their terms and are generally subject to the same nondiscrimination and coverage rules as plans in for-profit organizations.

Churches and nonprofit organizations may defer the compensation of executives, but the amount of the deferral is limited in nonprofit organizations by Internal Revenue Code Section 457. For the year 2007, the annual limitation is $15,500. Salary reduction contributions to a 403(b) or 401(k) plan, however, "count" against the annual limitation. For example, if an employee contributed $15,500 to a 403(b) plan, it would use up the entire $15,500 limitation under Section 457.

Under Section 457(f) there is the ability to set aside deferred compensation without limitation if it is not "vested." The requirement is that it be subject to "significant risk of forfeiture." This is often established by requiring future years of service for it to vest. When vested, it becomes taxable income at that date.

Idea

Occasionally, churches and nonprofit organizations will set up a reserve to pay bonuses to employees at a later date. Such a reserve cannot be "designated" or "subject to an understanding" that it will be used for a specific employee. It avoids current taxation because the organization has not allocated it to specific employees nor paid it over.

Setting up the deferred compensation as a 457(f) arrangement requires a written agreement that meets the requirements. The agreement between the employee and employer to defer the income must be made before it is earned. Once it is has been earned, it is too late for the employee to request its deferral.

Amounts that are deferred are often put into a "Rabbi Trust." A Rabbi Trust is established with an independent trustee, who invests the amounts that have been deferred. The assets may still be used to pay creditors of the organization (in a bankruptcy, for instance), but cannot be reclaimed by the corporation for its operations. Essentially, a Rabbi Trust protects the executive from the board's changing its mind and using the money somewhere else.

403(b) plans

Employees of churches and other nonprofit organizations may have a Section 403(b) salary reduction arrangement based on a written plan. These plans are also called tax-sheltered annuities (TSAs).

Both nonelective and elective employer contributions for a minister to a TSA are excludable for income and social security tax (SECA) purposes. Elective contributions for non-ministers are subject to FICA. While permissible, after-tax employee contributions are the exception in TSAs.

401(k) and 403(b) Plans Compared

Provision	401(k)	403(b)
Federal taxation of employee salary reductions	Exempt from income tax Subject to FICA Exempt from SECA	Exempt from income tax Subject to FICA Exempt from SECA
State taxation of employee salary reductions	All states exempt employee salary reductions.	A few states tax employee salary reductions.
Roll-over available to 403(b) plan	Yes	Yes
Roll-over available to a pension plan or 401(k) plan, including plans of businesses	Yes	No
Roll-over available to IRA	Yes	Yes
Loans	Allowable, within certain limits	Allowable, within same limits as 401(k)
Calendar year maximum on elective deferral contributions	Lesser of percentage specified in plan document or statutory limit ($15,500 in 2007 and 2008)	Lesser of percentage specified in plan document or statutory limit ($15,500 in 2007 and 2008) NOTE: Additional catch-up contributions of $5,000 are permitted in 2007 for those 50 and older.
Per participant maximum on annual additions, including elective deferrals and employer matching contributions	Lesser of 100% of includible compensation or $45,000 (2007 limit). The 2008 limit is $46,000.	Lesser of 100% of includible compensation or $45,000 (2007 limit). The 2008 limit is $46,000. Certain modifications can be made to this limitation.
Antidiscrimination testing	Two tests are required: For the employee's 401(k) portion of the plan and for the employer's matching portion of the plan. These tests can limit 401(k) contributions and matching contributions made on behalf of highly compensated employees. Churches are not exempt.	Only the employer's matching 401(m) portion of the plan is subject to an antidiscrimination test. Therefore, if no employer contributions are made, antidiscrimination testing is not required. Churches are exempt.
Subject to ERISA with its Form 5500 filing and other requirements	Yes, for most employers. Churches are exempt.	Any employer can avoid coverage by stringent noninvolvement in plan. Churches are exempt.

See the 2008 edition of *The Zondervan Minister's Tax & Financial Guide* for additional information on TSA contribution limitations.

401(k) plans

A church or nonprofit organization may offer a 401(k) plan to its employees. Under a 401(k) plan, an employee can elect to have the employer make tax-deferred contributions to the plan (up to $15,500 for 2007), of amounts that had been withheld from employee pay.

Maximizing Fringe Benefits

Personal use of employer-provided vehicles

Vehicles provided by organizations to employees for business use are often used for personal purposes. The IRS (see IRS Publication 535) treats most types of personal use of an employer-provided vehicle as a noncash fringe benefit and generally requires the fair market value of such use to be included in the employee's gross income (to the extent that the value is not reimbursed to the employer).

If the employee reimburses the employer for the full dollar value of the personal use, it will cost the employee more than if the employer includes the personal use value in the income of the employee.

> **Example:** The personal use value of an automobile provided to a lay employee is determined to be $100; if fully reimbursed, the employee would pay $100 to the employer. If there is no reimbursement, the employer includes the $100 in the employee's income and the employee will be subject to payroll taxes on $100 of income. Assuming a federal income tax rate of 28% and an FICA rate of 7.65%, the total would be $35.65 compared with the $100 cash out-of-pocket chargeback.

Valuation of personal vehicle use

There are three special valuation rules, in addition to a set of general valuation principles, which may be used under specific circumstances for valuing the personal use of an employer-provided vehicle. This value must be included in the employee's compensation if it is not reimbursed by the employee.

Under the general valuation rule, the value is based on what the cost would be to a person leasing from a third party the same or comparable vehicle on the same or comparable terms in the same geographic area.

The special valuation rules, which are used by most employers, are

> **Cents-per-mile valuation rule.** Generally, this rule may be used if the employer reasonably expects that the vehicle will be regularly used in the employer's trade or

business, and if the vehicle is driven at least 10,000 miles a year and is primarily used by employees. This valuation rule is available only if the fair market value of the vehicle, as of the date the vehicle was first made available for personal use by employees, does not exceed a specified value set by the IRS. For 2007, this value is $15,100.

The value of the personal use of the vehicle is computed by multiplying the number of miles driven for personal purposes by the current IRS standard mileage rate (48.5 cents per mile for 2007). For this valuation rule, personal use is "any use of the vehicle other than use in the employee's trade or business of being an employee of the employer."

▶ **Commuting valuation rule.** This rule may be used to determine the value of personal use only where the following conditions are met:

- ☐ The vehicle is owned or leased by the employer and is provided to one or more employees for use in connection with the employer's trade or business and is used as such.

- ☐ The employer requires the employee to commute to and/or from work in the vehicle for bona fide noncompensatory business reasons. One example of a bona fide noncompensatory business reason is the availability of the vehicle to an employee who is on-call and must have access to the vehicle when at home.

- ☐ The employer has a written policy that prohibits employees from using the vehicle for personal purposes other than for commuting or *de minimis* personal use such as a stop for a personal errand on the way home from work.

- ☐ The employee required to use the vehicle for commuting is not a "control" employee of the employer. A control employee is generally defined as any employee who is an officer of the employer whose compensation equals or exceeds $50,000 or is a director of the employer whose compensation equals or exceeds $100,000.

> **Idea**
>
> Start with a policy that requires a contemporaneous log, with the date and personal miles recorded for all ministry vehicles. The log is the basis for determining the personal vs. business use of the vehicle. Then the employer chooses a valuation rule to determine the value of the personal use for Form W-2 reporting. Simply paying for the gas during personal use does not satisfy these rules.

The personal use of an employer-provided vehicle that meets the above conditions is valued at $1.50 per one-way commute, or $3.00 per day.

▶ **Annual lease valuation rule.** Under this rule, the fair market value of a vehicle is determined and that value is used to determine the annual lease value amount by referring to an annual lease value table published by the IRS (see below). The annual lease value corresponding to this fair market value, multiplied by the personal use percentage, is the amount to be added to the employee's gross income. If the organization provides the fuel, 5.5 cents per mile must be added to the annual lease value. Amounts reimbursed by the employee are offset.

The fair market value of a vehicle owned by an employer is generally the employer's cost of purchasing the vehicle (including taxes and fees). The fair market value of a vehicle leased by an employer generally is either the manufacturer's suggested retail price less 8%, the dealer's invoice plus 4%, or the retail value as reported in a nationally recognized publication that regularly reports automobile retail values.

If the three special valuation rules described above do not apply, the value of the personal use must be determined by using a set of general valuation principles. Under these principles, the value must be generally equal to the amount that the employee would have to pay in a normal business transaction to obtain the same or comparable vehicle in the geographic area in which that vehicle is available for use.

ANNUAL LEASE VALUE TABLE

Fair Market Value of Car	Annual Lease Value	Fair Market Value of Car	Annual Lease Value
$0 – $999	$600	22,000 – 22,999	6,100
1,000 – 1,999	850	23,000 – 23,999	6,350
2,000 – 2,999	1,100	24,000 – 24,999	6,600
3,000 – 3,999	1,350	25,000 – 25,999	6,850
4,000 – 4,999	1,600	26,000 – 27,999	7,250
5,000 – 5,999	1,850	28,000 – 29,999	7,750
6,000 – 6,999	2,100	30,000 – 31,999	8,250
7,000 – 7,999	2,350	32,000 – 33,999	8,750
8,000 – 8,999	2,600	34,000 – 35,999	9,250
9,000 – 9,999	2,850	36,000 – 37,999	9,750
10,000 – 10,999	3,100	38,000 – 39,999	10,250
11,000 – 11,999	3,350	40,000 – 41,999	10,750
12,000 – 12,999	3,600	42,000 – 43,999	11,250
13,000 – 13,999	3,850	44,000 – 45,999	11,750
14,000 – 14,999	4,100	46,000 – 47,999	12,250
15,000 – 15,999	4,350	48,000 – 49,999	12,750
16,000 – 16,999	4,600	50,000 – 51,999	13,250
17,000 – 17,999	4,850	52,000 – 53,999	13,750
18,000 – 18,999	5,100	54,000 – 55,999	14,250
19,000 – 19,999	5,350	56,000 – 57,999	14,750
20,000 – 20,999	5,600	58,000 – 59,999	15,250
21,000 – 21,999	5,850		

Employer-provided dependent care assistance plan

A church or nonprofit organization can provide employees with child care or disabled dependent care services to allow employees to work. The amount excludable from tax is limited to the smaller of the employee's earned income, the spouse's earned income, or $5,000 ($2,500 if married filing separately). The dependent care assistance must be provided under a separate written plan that does not favor highly compensated employees and that meets other qualifications.

Dependent care assistance payments are excluded from income if the payments cover expenses that would be deductible by the employee as child and dependent care expenses on Form 2441 if the expenses were not reimbursed. It may be necessary to file Form 2441, even though the dependent care assistance payments are excluded from income, to document the appropriateness of the payments.

Health insurance

Churches and other nonprofit organizations are being forced to budget for higher healthcare costs. Premiums have returned to their upward march after a brief pause. They are increasing by double digits and are projected to continue at that level for the next few years. The basic types of health coverage are

➤ **Fee-for-service coverage.** This type of insurance pays for whatever medical care an employee receives, within policy limits. Fee-for-service plans preserve the maximum choice for the individual, as there is no list of doctors or other healthcare providers that must be patronized. The use of these plans is declining due to cost factors.

➤ **Health maintenance organization (HMO).** Employees may have little choice of healthcare providers, since the HMO makes many of the decisions about how care will be rendered.

➤ **Preferred provider plans.** These plans give higher coverage if medical care is obtained from preferred provider organizations (PPOs). These providers have agreed to accept reduced fees from the insurance company as full payments.

➤ **State plans.** States generally have high-risk pools or similar arrangements if you have a health problem and can't find private coverage. Premiums may start at 50% above the normal market price for a plan with high deductibles and out-of-pocket amounts.

➤ **Denominational plans.** Ministers and other church employees who are part of a denomination may have group health coverage available through that avenue. However, there may be fewer than ten denominational plans in existence today. If a denomination allows individuals or groups to select in or out of the plan because of pricing or plan design (called "adverse selection"), the plan will eventually not succeed. The only denominations that have health plans today generally are able to do so because they can require participation.

➤ **"Newsletter" plans.** "Newsletter" approaches are modeled on the old assessment-type insurance arrangements that were popular at the turn of the twentieth century. They tend to work for a time, but eventually claims often exceed available resources, which may negatively impact the timely and full payment of claims. One would not want to be the last one in such an arrangement, as persons in that position may get to pay medical expenses for others, but then find out the plan has folded for them. Since such plans often make strong claims about not being insurance (in order to escape the scrutiny of state insurance commissioners), the payments by a church to these plans (or to reimburse a church employee's payments to these plans) are generally considered fully taxable.

- **Labor union plans.** Plans designed to serve certain labor unions have solicited church groups, but this is a questionable "insurance" solution. Some nonprofit employees have joined the unions in order to get into the plans. In several cases, these plans have failed and employees have been left without protection from significant claims. The reason some "union plans" are set up is to take advantage of the exemptions from federal and state regulation for true union plans. In some cases, they have simply been set up as elaborate Ponzi schemes with the last ones in paying premiums, but having no protection when claims are filed.

So what options exist for nonprofit employees where denominational health insurance is not available? Not many. So-called "group" coverage might be purchased with only one or two employees. But it is probably a synthetic arrangement that has a short life span. Church employees can seek outside employment that provides health coverage as a benefit. This requires working two jobs, which is not always possible. Or the spouse of a church employee may be employed and obtain group coverage.

If a person does not qualify for group health coverage but is a good health risk, purchasing an individual policy for himself or herself, and the family, may be the best answer. But the person needs to know whether the insurer is financially able to perform what is promised. Check the rating of an insurer with A.M. Best, Standard & Poor's, Moodys, and Duff & Phelps.

The largest churches and other nonprofits often self-insure. Self-funding is not an option for most churches and other nonprofits because the employee pool is too small. A fundamental element of any self-funded healthcare benefit strategy is stop-loss insurance, a risk management tool used to help control the risk of providing healthcare coverage to employees. Stop-loss insurance is designed to protect the plan sponsor from catastrophic claims for conditions such as cancer and organ transplants, or unexpected increases in overall use. Stop-loss insurance premiums have recently been increasing at double-digit annual rates, and coverage is often difficult to secure.

Specific and aggregate coverage are usually purchased in combination:

- **Specific stop-loss.** This coverage protects the plan against catastrophic claims above a specified level. Claims exceeding a specified level per individual, typically referred to as the deductible or retention, are reimbursed by the carrier. Deductibles vary depending on the level of risk that the nonprofit can retain.

- **Aggregate stop-loss.** This coverage reimburses the plan when total claims (excluding any claims reimbursable under specific stop-loss coverage) exceed a deductible. It's generally used to limit a plan's exposure to large fluctuations due to an abnormal incidence of large claims below the specific stop-loss deductible.

COBRA

The Consolidated Omnibus Budget Reconciliation Act of 1985 (COBRA) requires covered employers to offer 18 months of group health coverage beyond the time the coverage would have ended because of certain "qualifying events." Premiums are reimbursable by the former employee to the former employer.

A "qualifying event" includes any termination of the employer-employee relationship, whether voluntary or involuntary, unless the termination is caused by the employee's gross misconduct. COBRA coverage applies even if the employee retires, quits, is fired, or is laid off.

Churches are excluded from the COBRA requirements. However, churches may provide continuation benefits similar to COBRA. Other nonprofits are generally subject to COBRA if 20 or more employees are employed during a typical working day.

Reimbursing medical expenses

Securing adequate medical insurance is a high priority for church and other nonprofit employees—and their families. And following closely is the importance of having any medical expenses not covered by insurance reimbursed by the employer or covered tax-free under an employer-sponsored plan.

Medical insurance protects against catastrophic medical expenses. But even the best medical insurance policies generally do not pay all of the insured's medical expenses. These unpaid medical expenses are usually in the form of noncovered items or expenses subject to a deductible or coinsurance (or copayment) clause in a health insurance policy.

Medical expenses that are not eligible for reimbursement under a health insurance plan are deductible on Schedule A as itemized deductions. However, for many employees, receiving an itemized deduction benefit from unreimbursed medical expenses is more a dream than a reality. There are two major barriers to deducting medical expenses. First, many employees use the standard deduction instead of itemized deductions (Schedule A). This is especially true for most employees who live in church-provided housing or rent. Second, even for those employees who itemize their deductions, there is a 7.5% of adjusted gross income limitation.

> **Example:** If adjusted gross income is $30,000 and unreimbursed medical expenses are $2,000, none of these expenses are beneficial in calculating itemized deductions on Schedule A because the 7.5% adjusted gross income limitation is $2,150 ($30,000 x 7.5%).

Reimbursing medical expenses seems simple, but it is complex because employers must select from the following options:

➤ **Cafeteria plans.** The "cafeteria" (IRS Code Section 125) approach provides a flexible benefits and services program. An employee may choose from a menu of different items and "pay" for them with before-tax dollars by taking a reduced salary. Frequently, various medical insurance options and healthcare reimbursements may be items on the menu. A healthcare reimbursement option in a cafeteria plan may also be called a "healthcare flexible spending account."

➤ **Health savings account (HSA).** HSAs are individual portable, tax-free, interest-bearing accounts (typically held by a bank or insurance company) through which individuals with high-deductible health insurance save for medical expenses. The purpose of an HSA is to pay what basic coverage would ordinarily pay.

Within limits, HSA contributions made by employers are excludable from income tax and social security wages. HSA contributions may be funded through salary reduction. Earnings on amounts in an HSA are not currently taxable, and HSA distributions used to pay for medical expenses are not taxable.

➤ **Flexible spending account (FSA).** An FSA may be established without any other cafeteria plan options. The tax law is the same as for a regular cafeteria plan, but by providing only one option, the plan and administration may be simpler. It allows an employee to pre-fund medical and dental expenses in pre-tax dollars using a salary reduction election. If an FSA only covers medical expenses, it is commonly referred to as a Healthcare FSA.

➤ **Health reimbursement arrangement (HRA).** Under an HRA (Section 105), an employer may reimburse medical expenses up to a maximum dollar amount for the coverage period. HRAs do not provide a salary reduction election.

Because only larger employers typically offer full-scale cafeteria plans, the focus of this discussion is on HSAs, FSAs, and HRAs. Payments to an employee under an HSA, FSA, or HRA are not subject to federal (usually 15% to 25%) or state income tax (often 5% or so) or social security tax (15.3% for ministers and 7.65% for nonminister employees). The tax savings can easily run 40% or more of medical expenses covered under these plans.

Disability insurance

Disability insurance may be provided for nonprofit organization employees. Coverage is usually limited to 60% to 75% of the annual salary of each individual. Social security and pension benefits are often offset against disability insurance benefits. Disability insurance premiums may be paid through a flexible benefit plan (FSA) to obtain income tax and social security tax (FICA) savings.

If the organization pays the disability insurance premiums, the premiums are excluded from the employee's income. If the organization pays the premiums (and the employee is the beneficiary) as part of the compensation package, any disability policy proceeds are fully taxable to the employee. This is based on who paid the premiums for the policy covering the year when the disability started. If the premiums are shared between the employer and the employee, then the benefits are taxable in the same proportion as the payment of the premiums.

> **Idea**
>
> The probability of disability greatly exceeds the probability of death during an individual's working years. Individual or group policies may be purchased. These plans may include a probationary period, which excludes preexisting sickness from immediate coverage, and an elimination period, which specifies the time after the start of a disability when benefits are not payable.

Compensation-related loans

Some churches and nonprofit organizations make loans to employees. The loans are often restricted to the purchase of land or a residence or the construction of a residence. Before a loan is made, the organization should determine if the transaction is legal under state law. Such loans are prohibited in many states.

If an organization receives interest of $600 or more in a year relating to a loan secured by real estate, a Form 1098 must be provided to the payer (see page 109). For the interest to be deductible as an itemized deduction, an employee loan must be secured by the residence and properly recorded.

If an organization makes loans to employees at below-market rates, the organization may be required to report additional compensation to the employee. If the loan is below $10,000, there is no additional compensation to the borrower. For loans over $10,000, additional compensation is calculated equal to the forgone interest that would have been charged if the loan had been made at a market rate of interest. The market rate of interest is the "applicable federal rate" for loans of similar duration. The IRS publishes these rates monthly. The additional compensation must be reported on Form W-2, Box 1.

There are certain exceptions to the general rules on below-market loans. These exceptions relate to loans secured by a mortgage and employee relocation loans.

Social security tax reimbursement

Churches and nonprofit organizations often reimburse ministers for a portion or all of their self-employment tax (SECA) liability. Reimbursement also may be made to lay employees for all or a portion of the FICA tax that has been withheld from their pay. Any social security reimbursement must be reported as taxable income for both income and social security tax purposes. The FICA reimbursement to a lay employee is subject to income tax and FICA withholding.

Because of the deductibility of the self-employment tax in both the income tax and self-employment tax computations, a full reimbursement is effectively less than the gross 15.3% rate:

Marginal Tax Rate	Effective SECA Rate
0%	14.13%
15	13.07
27	12.22
30	12.01

For missionaries who are not eligible for the income tax deduction of one-half of the self-employment tax due to the foreign earned-income exclusion, the full reimbursement rate is effectively 14.13%.

It is usually best to reimburse an employee for self-employment tax on a monthly or quarterly basis. An annual reimbursement may leave room for misunderstanding between the organization and the employee if the employee is no longer employed at the time the reimbursement is due.

Property transfers

- **Unrestricted.** If an employer transfers property (for example, a car, residence, equipment, or other property) to an employee at no charge, this constitutes taxable income to the employee. The amount of income is generally the fair market value of the property transferred.

- **Restricted.** To recognize and reward good work, some churches or nonprofits transfer property to an employee subject to certain restrictions. The ultimate transfer may occur only if the employee lives up to the terms of the agreement. Once the terms are met, the property is transferred free and clear. Property that is subject to substantial risk of forfeiture and is nontransferable is substantially not vested. No tax liability will occur until title to the property is vested with the employee. This is a deferral of tax.

    When restricted property becomes substantially vested, the employee must report the transfer as taxable income. The amount reported must be equal to the excess of the fair market value of the property at the time it becomes substantially vested, over the amount the employee pays for the property.

    Example: A church transfers a house to the pastor subject to the completion of 20 years of service for the church. The pastor does not report any taxable income from the transfer until the 20th year. This situation will generally require advance tax planning since the pastor could have a substantial tax liability in the year of the transfer.

- **Property purchased from employer.** If the employer allows an employee to buy property at a price below its fair market value, the employer must include in income as extra wages the difference between the property's fair market value and the amount paid and liabilities assumed by the employee.

Moving expenses

Moving expenses reimbursed by an employer, based on substantiation, are excludable from an employee's gross income. To qualify for this exclusion, the expenses must be deductible as moving expenses if they are not reimbursed.

The definition of deductible moving expenses is quite restrictive. Amounts are excludable only to the extent they would be deductible as moving expenses, *i.e.*, only the cost of moving household goods and travel, other than meals, from the old residence to the new residence. Distance and timing tests must also be met.

Reimbursements to nonminister employees that do not exceed deductible moving expenses are not subject to withholding. However, excess payments are subject to FICA and federal income tax withholding. Nondeductible reimbursements to minister-employees are only subject to income tax withholding if a voluntary withholding agreement is in force.

Nondeductible payments to minister or nonminister employees must be included as taxable compensation, for income tax purposes, on Form W-2.

> **Example:** A church paid a moving company $2,200 for an employee's move. The employer also reimbursed the employee $350. All of the expenses qualify as deductible moving expenses. The employer should report $350 on Form W-2, only in Box 12, using Code P. The $2,200 of expenses paid directly to the moving company are not reportable.

Gifts

All cash gifts to employees must be included in taxable compensation. Noncash gifts of nominal value to employees are tax-free. Gifts to certain nonemployees up to $25 may be tax-free.

Workers' Compensation

Workers' Compensation insurance coverage compensates workers for losses caused by work-related injuries. It also limits the potential liability of the organization for injury to the employee related to his or her job.

Workers' Compensation insurance is required by law in all states to be carried by the employer. A few states exempt churches from Workers' Compensation coverage, and several states exempt all nonprofit employers. Most states also consider ministers to be employees regardless of the income tax filing method used by the minister, and therefore they must be covered under the Workers' Compensation policy. Contact your state department of labor to find out how your state applies Workers' Compensation rules to churches.

Workers' Compensation premiums are based on the payroll of the organization with a minimum premium charge to issue the policy. An audit is done later to determine the actual charge for the policy.

> **Key Issue**
>
> Even if a church or nonprofit organization is exempt from Workers' Compensation, the voluntary purchase of the coverage or the securing of additional general liability coverage may be prudent. This is because other types of insurance typically exclude work-related accidents: health, accident, disability, auto, and general liability insurance policies are some examples.

Most Workers' Compensation insurance is purchased through private insurance carriers. A few states provide the coverage and charge the covered organizations.

Overtime and minimum pay

The Fair Labor Standards Act (FLSA) provides protection for employees engaged in interstate commerce concerning minimum wages, equal pay, overtime pay, record keeping, and child labor (some states even have more restrictive versions of the FLSA). Any employee who makes less than $455 per week, full- or part-time, is entitled to overtime pay. Overtime pay is required regardless of whether an employee is paid on an hourly or salary basis. For employees to be exempt from the overtime and minimum wage requirements, they must be paid on a salary basis. In other words, employees paid on an hourly basis do not meet the exemption requirements.

The employees of nonprofit organizations involved in commerce or in the production of goods for commerce are generally considered covered by the provisions of the FLSA. Commerce is defined by the FLSA as "trade, commerce, transportation, transmission, or communication among the several states or between any state and any place outside thereof." Conversely, nonprofits that are not engaged in commerce or fall below the $500,000 annual gross sales volume requirement are generally exempt from the Act.

The FLSA applies to schools regardless of whether they are nonprofit entities operated by religious organizations. Church-operated day care centers and elementary and secondary schools are generally considered subject to the FLSA.

Many local churches and small nonprofits do not meet the $500,000 threshold (see above). However, individual employees are generally covered under the FLSA if they send or receive just a few emails each year across state lines. Therefore, most churches and nonprofits should follow the FLSA regulations as a precaution against possible action by the Department of Labor. Ministers are generally exempt under the professional provisions of this exemption.

> **Warning**
>
> There is significant confusion over "compensatory time," or giving time off in lieu of paying overtime. If an employee is covered under the Fair Labor Standards Act, providing compensatory time is not an option. Payment for the overtime must be made in cash.

The FLSA minimum wage was increased from $5.15 to $5.85 per hour effective July 24, 2007. It goes to $6.55 per hour effective July 24, 2008, and to $7.25 per hour effective July 24, 2009. (Caution: Thirty states have established minimum wages that exceed the federal rate.) Teenagers may be paid a training wage of any amount above $4.25 per hour for the first 90 days of employment. Minors under age 14 generally cannot be hired.

Any employee paid over $455 per week must meet the duties test in order to be classified as an exempt employee. The duties tests are divided into employee type categories. These categories are executive, administrative, and professional employees.

Executive Employees

- Primary duty is the management of the enterprise or a recognized department or subdivision.

- Customarily and regularly direct the work of two or more other employees.
- Have authority to hire or fire other employees (or make recommendations as to the hiring, firing, promotion, or other change of status of other employees).

Administrative Employees

- Primary duty is performing office or nonmanual work directly related to the management or general business operations of the employer or the employer's customers.
- Primary duty includes the exercise of discretion and independent judgment with respect to matters of significance.

Professional Employees

- **Learned Professional.** Primary duty is performing office or nonmanual work requiring knowledge of an advanced type in a field of science or learning customarily acquired by a prolonged course of specialized intellectual instruction.
- **Creative Professional.** Primary duty is the performance of work requiring invention, imagination, originality, or talent in a recognized field of artistic or creative endeavor.
- **Teacher.** Primary duty is teaching, tutoring, instructing, or lecturing in the activity of imparting knowledge as a teacher employed in an educational establishment. The $455 salary test does not apply to teacher exemption.

Nondiscrimination Rules

To qualify for exclusion from income, many fringe benefits must be nondiscriminatory. This is particularly true for many types of benefits for certain key employees. Failure to comply with the nondiscrimination rules does not disqualify a fringe benefit plan entirely. The benefit simply is fully taxable for the highly-compensated or key employees.

The nondiscrimination rules apply to the following types of fringe benefit plans:

➤ qualified tuition and fee discounts,

➤ eating facilities on or near the employer's premises,

➤ educational assistance benefits,

➤ dependent care assistance plans,

➤ tax-sheltered annuities (TSAs), 401(k) plans, and other deferred compensation plans,

➤ group-term life insurance benefits,

➤ self-insured medical plans,

- health savings accounts (including health reimbursement arrangements), and
- cafeteria plans (including a flexible spending account dependent care plan and a healthcare flexible spending account).

Fringe benefit plans that limit benefits only to officers or highly-compensated employees are clearly discriminatory. An officer is an employee who is appointed, confirmed, or elected by the board of the employer. A highly-compensated employee for 2006 and 2007 is someone who

- was paid more than $100,000, or
- if the employer elects, was in the top 20% of paid employees for compensation for the previous year.

Paying Employee Expenses

An accountable plan is a reimbursement or expense allowance arrangement that requires (1) a business purpose for the expenses, (2) employees to substantiate the expenses, and (3) the return of any excess reimbursements.

The substantiation of expenses and return of excess reimbursements must be handled within a reasonable time. The following methods meet the "reasonable time" definition:

- The fixed date method applies if
  - [ ] an advance is made within 30 days of when an expense is paid or incurred;
  - [ ] an expense is substantiated to the employer within 60 days after the expense is paid or incurred; and
  - [ ] any excess amount is returned to the employer within 120 days after the expense is paid or incurred.
- The periodic statement method applies if
  - [ ] the employer provides employees with a periodic statement that sets forth the amount paid under the arrangement in excess of substantiated expenses;
  - [ ] statements are provided at least quarterly; and
  - [ ] the employer requests that the employee provide substantiation for any additional expenses that have not yet been substantiated and/or return any amounts remaining unsubstantiated within 120 days of the statement.

If employees substantiate expenses and return any unused excess payments to the church or nonprofit organization on a timely basis, payments to the employee for business expenses have no impact on tax reporting. They are not included on Form W-2 for the employee. Although Section 179 expense deductions can be claimed by an employee on their Form 1040, Section 179 amounts are not eligible for reimbursement under an accountable expense reimbursement plan.

The timing of documenting expenses for reimbursement is of utmost importance. Under the fixed date method (see page 90), the IRS provides a safe harbor of 60 days after the expense is paid or incurred. In other words, the IRS will contest a reimbursement, based on timeliness of submitting the documentation, if the documentation is provided to the employer. Does this mean that the IRS will disallow expenses reimbursed within 61 days? Not necessarily. It simply means 60 days is a safe harbor as a "reasonable time."

> **Example:** A church approves $50,000 of compensation for the pastor and tells her to let the church know at the end of the year how much she has spent on business expenses and they will show the net amount on Form W-2. Is this valid? No. The salary must be established separately from expense reimbursements. Further, even if an accountable expense reimbursement plan is used, the annual submission of expense documentation would fail the timeliness test for expenses incurred in all but the last portion of the year.

Adopting appropriate policies

Before reimbursing expenses incurred by employees, a church or nonprofit organization should adopt adequate policies to ensure tax-exempt funds are properly expended. The following policies should be considered:

➤ Accountable expense reimbursement plan (see page 77)

➤ Travel and other expense reimbursement policy (see pages 78-81)

➤ Credit card policies and procedures (see pages 82-83)

Per diem allowance

Nonprofit employers that help their employees cover business travel expenses have two basic options: (1) The employer can pay employees the precise amount of their expenses, or (2) the employer can opt for convenience and pay a set "per diem" allowance for each day of business travel.

Per diem allowances apply to employer reimbursements and are not available for reimbursements paid to volunteers. These rates may be used to claim deductions for unreimbursed meal and incidental expenses, but the actual cost of unreimbursed travel expense must be substantiated. Higher per diem rates apply to certain locations annually identified by the IRS and are identified in IRS Publication 1542.

The per diem rates for travel within continental United States (CONUS) are (based on an October 1 to September 30 fiscal period) $60 for lodging and $39 for meals and incidentals.

Federal per diem rates for travel outside CONUS, including Alaska, Hawaii, Puerto Rico, the northern Mariana Islands, U.S. possessions, and all other foreign localities, are published at http://www.state.gov/m/a/als/prdm/.

Sample Accountable Expense Reimbursement Plan

Whereas, Income tax regulations provide that an arrangement between an employee and employer must meet the requirements of business connection, substantiation, and return of excess payments in order to be considered a reimbursement;

Whereas, Plans that meet the three requirements listed above are considered to be accountable plans, and the reimbursed expenses are generally excludable from an employee's gross compensation;

Whereas, Plans that do not meet all the requirements listed above are considered nonaccountable plans, and payments made under such plans are includible in gross employee compensation; and

Whereas, Poplar Grove Church desires to establish an accountable expense reimbursement policy in compliance with the income tax regulations;

Resolved, That Poplar Grove Church establish an expense reimbursement policy effective _____, 200__, whereby employees serving the church may receive advances for or reimbursement of expenses if

    A. There is a stated business purpose of the expense related to the ministry of the church and the expenses would qualify for deductions for federal income tax purposes if the expenses were not reimbursed,

    B. The employee provides adequate substantiation to the church for all expenses, and

    C. The employee returns all excess reimbursements within a reasonable time.

And,

Resolved, That the following methods will meet the "reasonable time" definition:

    A. An advance is made within 30 days of when an expense is paid or incurred;

    B. An expense is substantiated to the church within 60 days after the expense is paid or incurred; or

    C. An excess amount is returned to the church within 120 days after the expense is paid or incurred.

And,

Resolved, That substantiation of business expenses will include business purpose, business relationship (including names of persons present), cost (itemized accounting), time, and place of any individual nonlodging expense of $75 or more and for all lodging expenses. Auto mileage reimbursed must be substantiated by a daily mileage log separating business and personal miles. The church will retain the original copies related to the expenses substantiated.

Note: The above resolution includes the basic guidelines for an accountable expense reimbursement plan. If the employer desires to place a dollar limit on reimbursements to be made under the plan employee-by-employee, a separate resolution may be adopted for this purpose.

Travel and Other Expense Reimbursement Policy

Purpose

The Board of Directors of [name of organization] recognizes that board members, officers, and employees ("Personnel") of [name of organization] may be required to travel or incur other expenses from time to time to conduct ministry business and to further the mission of this nonprofit organization. The purpose of this Policy is to ensure that (a) adequate cost controls are in place, and that (b) travel and other expenditures are appropriate, and (c) to provide a uniform and consistent approach for the timely reimbursement of authorized expenses incurred by Personnel. It is the policy of [name of organization] to reimburse only reasonable and necessary expenses actually incurred by Personnel.

When incurring business expenses, [name of organization] expects Personnel to

- Exercise discretion and good business judgment with respect to those expenses.
- Be cost conscious and spend ministry money as carefully and judiciously as the individual would spend his or her own funds.
- Report expenses, supported by required documentation, as they were actually spent.

Expense report

Expenses will not be reimbursed unless the individual requesting reimbursement submits a written Expense Report. The Expense Report, which shall be submitted at least monthly or within two weeks of the completion of travel if travel expense reimbursement is requested, must include

- The individual's name.
- The date, origin, destination, and purpose of the trip, including a description of each organization-related activity during the trip.
- The name and affiliation of all people for whom expenses are claimed (*i.e.,* people on whom money is spent in order to conduct [name of organization]'s business).
- An itemized list of all expenses for which reimbursement is requested.

Receipts

Receipts are required for all expenditures billed directly to [name of organization], such as airfare and hotel charges. No expense in excess of $_____ will be reimbursed to Personnel unless the individual requesting reimbursement submits with the Expense Report written receipts from each vendor (not a credit card receipt or statement) showing the vendor's name, a description of the services provided (if not otherwise obvious), the date, and the total expenses, including tips (if applicable).

General travel requirements

- **Necessity of travel.** In determining the reasonableness and necessity of travel expenses, Personnel and the person authorizing the travel shall consider the ways in which [name of organization] will benefit from the travel and weigh those benefits against the anticipated costs of the travel. The same factors shall be taken into account in deciding whether the benefits to [name of organization] outweigh the costs; less expensive alternatives, such as participation by telephone or video conferencing; or the availability of local programs or training opportunities.

> **Personal and spousal travel expenses.** Individuals traveling on behalf of [name of organization] may incorporate personal travel or business with their Company-related trips; however, Personnel shall not arrange Company travel at a time that is less advantageous to [name of organization] or involving greater expenses to [name of organization] in order to accommodate personal travel plans. Any additional expenses incurred as a result of personal travel, including but not limited to extra hotel nights, additional stopovers, meals, or transportation, are the sole responsibility of the individual and will not be reimbursed by [name of organization]. Expenses associated with travel of an individual's spouse, family, or friends will not be reimbursed by [name of organization].

Air travel

Air travel reservations should be made as far in advance as possible in order to take advantage of reduced fares.

Frequent-flyer miles and compensation for denied boarding

Personnel traveling on behalf of [name of organization] may accept and retain frequent-flyer miles and compensation for denied boarding for their personal use. Individuals may not deliberately patronize a single airline to accumulate frequent-flyer miles if less expensive comparable tickets are available through another airline.

Lodging

Personnel traveling on behalf of [name of organization] may be reimbursed at the single room rate for the reasonable cost of hotel accommodations. Convenience, the cost of staying in the city in which the hotel is located, and proximity to other venues on the individual's itinerary shall be considered in determining reasonableness. Personnel shall make use of available corporate and discount rates for hotels.

Out-of-town meals

Personnel traveling on behalf of [name of organization] are reimbursed for the reasonable and actual costs of meals (including tips) subject to a maximum per diem meal allowance of $_____ per day and the terms and conditions established by [name of organization] relating to the per diem meal allowance.

Ground transportation

Employees are expected to use the most economical ground transportation appropriate under the circumstances and should generally use the following, in this order of desirability:

> **Courtesy cars.** Many hotels have courtesy cars, which will take you to and from the airport at no charge. Employees should take advantage of this free service whenever possible. Another alternative may be a shuttle or bus.

- **Airport shuttle or bus.** Airport shuttles or buses generally travel to and from all major hotels for a small fee. At major airports such services are as quick as a taxi and considerably less expensive. Airport shuttle or bus services are generally located near the airport's baggage claim area.
- **Taxis.** When courtesy cars and airport shuttles are not available, a taxi is often the next most economical and convenient form of transportation when the trip is for a limited time and minimal mileage is involved. A taxi may also be the most economical mode of transportation between an individual's home and the airport.
- **Rental cars.** Car rentals are expensive, so other forms of transportation should be considered when practical. Employees will be allowed to rent a car while out of town provided that advance approval has been given by the individual's supervisor and that the cost is less than alternative methods of transportation.

Personal cars

Personnel are compensated for use of their personal cars when used for ministry business. When individuals use their personal car for such travel, including travel to and from the airport, mileage will be allowed at the currently approved IRS rate per mile.

In the case of individuals using their personal cars to take a trip that would normally be made by air, mileage will be allowed at the currently approved rate; however, the total mileage reimbursement will not exceed the sum of the lowest available round-trip coach airfare.

Parking/tolls

Parking and toll expenses, including charges for hotel parking, incurred by Personnel traveling on organization business will be reimbursed. The costs of parking tickets, fines, car washes, valet service, etc., are the responsibility of the employee and will not be reimbursed.

On-airport parking is permitted for short business trips. For extended trips, Personnel should use off-airport facilities.

Entertainment and business meetings

Reasonable expenses incurred for business meetings or other types of business-related entertainment will be reimbursed only if the expenditures are approved in advance by [designated officer or director] of [name of organization] and qualify as tax-deductible expenses. Detailed documentation for any such expense must be provided, including

- Date and place of entertainment
- Nature of the expense
- Names, titles, and corporate affiliation of those entertained
- A complete description of the business purpose for the activity, including the specific business matter discussed
- Vendor receipts (not credit card receipts or statements) showing the vendor's name, a description of the services provided, date, and total expenses, including tips (if applicable)

Other expenses

Reasonable ministry-related telephone and fax charges due to absence of Personnel from the individual's place of business are reimbursable. In addition, reasonable and necessary gratuities that are not covered under meals may be reimbursed.

Nonreimbursable expenditures

[Name of organization] maintains a strict policy that expenses in any category that could be perceived as lavish or excessive will not be reimbursed, as such expenses are inappropriate for reimbursement by a ministry. Expenses that are not reimbursable include, but are not limited to

- Travel insurance
- First-class tickets or upgrades
- When lodging accommodations have been arranged by [name of organization] and the individual elects to stay elsewhere, reimbursement is made at the amount no higher than the rate negotiated by [name of organization]. Reimbursement shall not be made for transportation between the alternate lodging and the meeting site.
- Limousine travel
- Movie tickets, liquor or bar costs
- Membership dues at any country club, private club, athletic club, golf club, tennis club, or similar recreational organization
- Participation in or attendance at golf, tennis, or sporting events, without the advance approval of the chairman of the board or his or her designee
- Purchase of golf clubs or any other sporting equipment
- Spa or exercise charges
- Clothing purchases
- Business conferences and entertainment which are not approved by [designated officer or director] of [name of organization]
- Valet service
- Car washes
- Toiletry articles
- Expenses for spouses, friends, or relatives. If a spouse, friend, or relative accompanies staff on a trip, it is the responsibility of the staff to determine any added cost for double occupancy and related expenses and to make the appropriate adjustment in the reimbursement request.
- Overnight retreats without the prior approval of the chairman of the board or his/her designee

Sample Credit Card Policies and Procedures

Objectives

- To allow ministry personnel access to efficient and alternative means of payment for approved expenses, especially expenses related to business travel and office supplies.

- To improve managerial reporting related to credit card purchases.

- To improve efficiency and reduce costs of payables processing.

Policies

- Ministry credit cards will be issued to ministers and staff only upon approval of the Finance Committee.

- Credit cards will be used only for business purposes. Personal purchases of any type are not allowed.

- The following purchases are not allowed:
  - Capital equipment and upgrades over $5,000
  - Construction, renovation/installation
  - Items or services on term contracts
  - Maintenance agreements
  - Personal items or loans
  - Purchases involving trade-in of ministry property
  - Rentals (other than short-term autos)
  - Any items deemed inconsistent with the values of the ministry

- Cash advances on credit cards are *not* allowed without written permission from the business administrator or treasurer.

- Cardholders will be required to sign an agreement indicating their acceptance of these terms. Individuals who do not adhere to these policies and procedures will risk revocation of their credit card privileges and/or disciplinary action.

Procedures

- Credit cards may be requested for prospective cardholders by written request (Credit Card Request Form) to the business administrator or treasurer.

- Detailed receipts must be retained and attached to the credit card statements. In the case of meals and entertainment, each receipt must include the date, time, names of all persons involved in the purchase, and a brief description of the business purpose of the purchase, in accordance with Internal Revenue Service regulations.

> Monthly statements, with attached detailed receipts, must be submitted to the Accounting Department within ten days of receipt of the statement to enable timely payment of amounts due.

> All monthly statements submitted for payment must include the initials of the cardholder; the signature of the approving staff member, unless the cardholder is him/herself the staff member; and the date of approval.

> All monthly statements submitted for payment must have the appropriate account number(s) and the associated amounts clearly written on the statement.

MINISTRY CARDHOLDER AGREEMENT

I,_____, hereby acknowledge receipt of the following credit card: _____ / _____ - _____ - _____ - _____
(Type of credit card)   (Credit card number)

I understand that improper use of this card may result in disciplinary action, as outlined in the Ministry handbook, as well as personal liability for any improper purchases. As a cardholder, I agree to comply with the terms and conditions of this agreement, including the attached Ministry Credit Card Policies and Procedures agreement. I will strive to obtain the best value for the Ministry when purchasing merchandise and/or services with this card.

I acknowledge receipt of said Agreement and Policies/Procedures and confirm that I have read and understand the terms and conditions. I understand that by using the card, I will be making financial commitments on behalf of the Ministry and that the Ministry will be liable to _____ for all charges made on this card.
(Name of credit card company)

As a holder of this Ministry card, I agree to accept the responsibility and accountability for the protection and proper use of the card, as reflected above. I will return the card to the business administrator or treasurer upon demand during the period of my employment. I further agree to return the card upon termination of employment. I understand that the card is not to be used for personal purchases, and if the card is used for personal purchases or for purchases for any other entity, the Ministry will be entitled to reimbursement from me of such purchases and shall be entitled to pursue legal action, if required, to recover the cost of such purchases, together with costs of collection and reasonable attorneys' fees.

Signature _____ Date _____
(Cardholder)

Signature _____ Date _____
(Business administrator)

- **Qualifying for the housing allowance.** Determining which individuals qualify for ministerial status (and, therefore, qualify for a housing allowance designation) can be a challenging issue for the employing church or other nonprofit organization—it's always the employer's decision, not the employees. It's fairly simple to make this determination for a local church. It's easy for a denomination to figure out this issue.

  When we move beyond local churches and denominations, ministerial status is more murky. It requires an understanding of assignment of ministers, and perhaps performing significant sacerdotal functions. Then, there are ordaining, licensing, or commissioning of ministers by churches and the question whether these practices are valid. All in all, a high degree of integrity must be applied to this process.

- **Fringe benefits, stewardship, and compliance.** The decision of which fringe benefits to offer staff is often indicative of a charity's stewardship. It's isn't just how much an employee is paid; it's also how compensation is paid. Are tax-free and tax-deferred opportunities maximized? And then there is the proper reporting of taxable fringe benefits which reflects a charity's willingness to comply with tax law. For example, providing a vehicle to a key employee is an excellent fringe benefit from the employee's compensation view but there are compliance issues to be followed with respect to personal miles.

- **Fair Labor Standards Act (FLSA) issues.** The overtime and minimum wage rules included in the FLSA are often overlooked and abused by churches and other charities. Many churches and most other charities are subject to the FLSA. With the Department of Labor's generous interpretation of "interstate commerce," just a few emails sent across state lines each year by an employee will often qualify that employee for FLSA coverage even if the organization is not covered. Another common FLSA abuse is "paying" overtime by giving employees "compensatory" time off. While Congress periodically considers compensatory time off with respect to the FLSA, it has never passed.

CHAPTER FOUR: Employer Reporting

In This Chapter

- The classification of workers
- Reporting compensation
- Payroll tax withholding
- Depositing withheld payroll taxes
- Filing the quarterly payroll tax forms
- Filing the annual payroll tax forms

The withholding and reporting requirements with which employers must comply are complicated. The special tax treatment of qualified ministers simply adds another level of complexity.

Churches and nonprofit organizations are generally required to withhold federal (and state and local, as applicable) income taxes and social security taxes and to pay employer social security tax on all wages paid to all full-time or part-time employees (except qualified ministers).

The Classification of Workers

Whether an individual is classified as an employee or independent contractor has far-reaching consequences. This decision determines an organization's responsibility under the Federal Insurance Contributions Act (FICA), income tax withholding responsibilities, potential coverage under the Fair Labor Standards Act (see pages 73-74), and coverage under an employer's benefit plans. Misclassification can lead to significant penalties.

Questions frequently arise about the classification of certain nonprofit workers. Seasonal workers and those working less than full-time such as secretaries, custodians, and musicians require special attention for classification purposes. If a worker receives pay at an hourly rate, it will be difficult to justify independent contractor status. This conclusion holds true even if the workers are part-time.

Since 1935, the IRS has relied on certain common law rules (page 87) to determine whether workers are employees or independent contractors. Pressure continues to build on Congress and the IRS to provide clearer guidance on who can be an independent contractor and when.

Employees

If a worker is a nonministerial employee, the employer must withhold federal income tax (and state income tax, if applicable) and Federal Insurance Contributions Act (FICA) taxes; match the employee's share of FICA taxes; and, unless exempted, pay unemployment taxes on the employee's wages. In addition, the employer may incur obligations for employee benefit plans such as vacation, sick pay, health insurance, and pension plan contributions.

Key Issue

The employee vs. independent contractor decision is one of the most fundamental issues facing an employer making payments to workers. If a worker is truly an employee but is treated as an independent contractor, this can result in not withholding the appropriate income and FICA-type social security tax amounts.

Among other criteria, employees comply with instructions, have a continuous relationship, perform work personally, work full- or part-time, are subject to dismissal, can quit without incurring liability, are often reimbursed for expenses, and must submit reports.

Independent contractors

If the worker is classified as an independent contractor, quarterly estimated income taxes and social security taxes under the Self-Employment Contributions Act (SECA) are paid by the worker. There is no unemployment tax liability or income or social security tax withholding requirement for independent contractors.

Independent contractors normally set the order and sequence of work, set their hours of work, work for others at the same time, are paid by the job, offer their services to the

---

Independent Contractor Status Myths

- *Myth*: A written contract will characterize a person as an independent contractor.

  Fact: It is the substance of the relationship that governs.

- *Myth*: Casual labor or seasonal workers are independent contractors, or their classification is a matter of choice.

  Fact: There is never a choice. The classification is determined by the facts and circumstances.

- *Myth*: If a person qualifies as an independent contractor for federal payroll tax purposes, he or she is automatically exempt for Workers' Compensation and state unemployment tax purposes.

  Fact: State Workers' Compensation and unemployment tax laws are often broader, and an individual may actually be covered under these laws even though qualifying as an independent contractor for federal payroll tax purposes.

public, have an opportunity for profit or loss, furnish their own tools, and may do work on another's premises, and there is often substantial investment by the worker.

Common law rules

The IRS generally applies the common law rules to decide if an individual is an employee or self-employed (independent contractor) for income tax purposes. Generally, the individual is an employee if the employer has the legal right to control both what and how it is done, even if the individual has considerable discretion and freedom of action.

Workers are generally considered employees if they

- Must follow the organization's work instructions;
- Receive on-the-job training;
- Provide services that must be rendered personally;
- Provide services that are integral to the organization;
- Hire, supervise, and pay assistants for the organization;
- Have an ongoing work relationship with the organization;
- Must follow set hours of work;
- Work full-time for the organization;
- Work on the organization's premises;
- Must do their work in an organization-determined sequence;
- Receive business expense reimbursements;
- Receive routine payments of regular amounts;
- Need the organization to furnish tools and materials;
- Do not have a major investment in job facilities;
- Cannot suffer a loss from their services;
- Work for one organization at a time;
- Do not offer their services to the general public;
- Can be fired by the organization;
- May quit work at any time without penalty.

Key Issue

The amount of control and direction the employer has over a worker's services is the most important issue in deciding whether a worker is an employee or an independent contractor.

The classification of ministers

It is important that the organization decide whether the services of ministers employed by the organization qualify for special tax treatment as ministerial services.

Most ordained, commissioned, or licensed ministers serving local churches are eligible for these six special tax provisions with respect to services performed in the exercise of ministry. The IRS and courts apply certain tests to ministers serving local churches, including whether the minister administers the sacraments, conducts worship services, is considered a spiritual leader by the church, and performs management services in the "control, conduct, or maintenance of a religious organization." It may not be necessary for a minister to meet all of these tests to qualify for the special tax treatment. For a complete discussion of this topic, see the 2008 edition of *The Zondervan Minister's Tax & Financial Guide*.

Ordained, commissioned, or licensed ministers not serving local churches may qualify as ministers for federal tax purposes without meeting additional tests if their duties include the following (also see pages 56, 58-59):

➤ Administration of church denominations and their integral agencies, including teaching or administration in parochial schools, colleges, or universities that are under the authority of a church or denomination.

➤ Performing services for an institution that is not an integral agency of a church pursuant to an assignment or designation by ecclesiastical superiors, but only if the services relate to church purposes.

If a church does not assign the minister's services, they will be qualified services only if they substantively involve performing sacerdotal functions or conducting religious worship (including preaching, leading Bible studies, spiritual counseling, etc.).

Sample Board Resolution for Ministerial Assignment

Whereas, _____Name of assigning church_____ recognizes the calling of _____Name of minister assigned_____ as a minister and is (ordained, licensed, or commissioned), and

Whereas, We believe that the assignment of _____Name of minister assigned_____ will further the efforts and mission of our church and we desire to provide support and encouragement;

Resolved, That _____Name of minister assigned_____ is hereby assigned to _____Name of ministry to which assigned_____ effective_____, 200__ to serve as _____Position title_____, and

Resolved, That this assignment is made for a period of one year upon which time it will be reviewed and may be renewed, and

Resolved, That this assignment is contingent upon the quarterly submission of activity and financial reports by _____Name of minister assigned_____ to our church.

Special Tax Provisions for Ministers

- Exclusion for income tax purposes of the housing allowance and the fair rental value of a ministry-owned housing provided rent-free to clergy.

- Exemption of clergy from self-employment tax under very limited circumstances.

- Treatment of clergy (who do not elect social security exemption) as self-employed for social security tax purposes for income from ministerial services.

- Exemption of clergy compensation from mandatory income tax withholding.

- Eligibility for a voluntary income tax withholding arrangement between the minister-employee and the employer.

- Potential double deduction of mortgage interest and real estate taxes as itemized deductions and as housing expenses for housing allowance purposes.

Reporting Compensation

Minister-employees

Forms W-2 are annually provided to minister-employees. There is no requirement to withhold income taxes, but they may be withheld under a voluntary agreement. Social security taxes are not withheld.

Nonminister-employees

If an employee does not qualify for tax treatment as a minister, the organization is liable to withhold and pay FICA and income taxes. Certain FICA tax exceptions are discussed on page 90.

Nonemployees

Self-employed recipients of compensation should receive Form 1099-MISC instead of Form W-2 (if the person has received compensation of at least $600 for the year).

Payroll Tax Withholding

FICA social security

Most churches and nonprofit organizations must withhold FICA taxes from their employees' wages and pay them to the IRS along with the employer's share of the tax. Minister-employees are an exception to this rule.

In 2007 both the employer and the employee pay a 6.2% tax rate on the social security wage base of up to $97,500 (up from $94,200 for 2006). Similarly, both the employer and the employee pay a 1.45% Medicare tax rate on all pay above $97,500. The 2008 social security wage base is $102,000.

There are a few exceptions to the imposition of FICA. Generally, wages of less than $100 paid to an employee in a calendar year are not subject to FICA. Services excluded from FICA include

Warning

FICA-type social security taxes should never be withheld from the compensation of a qualified minister. Ministers are self-employed for social security purposes, even when working for a parachurch organization. They must file Schedule SE to compute self-employment social security tax, unless they have opted out of social security.

➤ services performed by a minister of a church in the exercise of ministry or by a member of a religious order in the exercise of duties required by such order;

➤ services performed in the employ of a church or church-controlled organization that opposes for religious reasons the payment of social security taxes (see later discussion of filing Form 8274); and

➤ services performed by a student in the employ of a school, college, or university.

Churches and church-controlled organizations opposed to social security taxes

In 1984 the law was changed to allow qualifying churches and church-controlled organizations to claim exemption from payment of FICA taxes. An organization must certify opposition "for religious reasons to the payment of employer social security taxes." Very few organizations qualify to file Form 8274.

Organizations in existence on September 30, 1984, were required to file Form 8274 by October 30, 1984. Any organization created after September 30, 1984, must file before the first date on which a quarterly employment tax return is due from the organization.

Organizations desiring to revoke their exemption made earlier by filing Form 8274 should file Form 941 with full payment of social security taxes for that quarter.

Federal income tax

Most nonprofit organizations are exempt from the payment of federal income tax on the organization's income (see pages 32-39 for the tax on unrelated business income). But they must withhold and pay federal, state, and local income taxes on the wages paid to each employee. Minister-employees are an exception to this rule.

An employee-minister may have a voluntary withholding agreement with a church or nonprofit employer relating to the minister's income taxes (or he or she may file Form 1040-ES, or both). An agreement to withhold income taxes from wages must be in writing. There is no required form for the agreement. A minister may request voluntary withholding by submitting Form W-4 (Employee Withholding Allowance Certificate) to the employer, indicating the additional amount to be withheld in excess of the tax table, or the written request may be in another format.

Federal income taxes for all employees (except ministers) are calculated based on the chart and tables shown in IRS Publication 15. State and local income taxes are usually required to be withheld according to state withholding tables.

> **Form W-4.** All employees, part- or full-time, must complete a W-4 form. (Ministers are an exception to this requirement unless a voluntary withholding arrangement is used.) The withholding allowance information completed on this form gives the basis to determine the amount of income tax to be withheld.
>
> Charities must file all Forms W-4 with the IRS on which employees claim exempt status from withholding (and the employees' wages would normally exceed $200 weekly) or claim more than 10 withholding allowances.

> **Caution**
>
> Social security taxes (FICA) should never be withheld from the salary of an employee. But under the voluntary withholding agreement for ministers' federal income taxes, additional federal income tax may be withheld sufficient to cover the minister's self-employment tax liability. This withholding must be identified as "federal income tax withheld" (and not social security taxes withheld).

> **Form W-5.** An eligible employee uses Form W-5 to elect to receive advance payments of the earned income tax credit (EITC). Employees may be eligible for the EITC if their 2007 taxable and nontaxable earned income was less than $14,590 if there is no qualifying child; less than $35,241 if there is one qualifying child; or less than $39,783 if there are two or more qualifying children.

> **Form W-7.** Certain individuals who are not eligible for a social security number (SSN) may obtain an individual taxpayer identification number. The following individuals may file Form W-7: (1) nonresident aliens who are required to file a U.S. tax return, (2) nonresident aliens who are filing a U.S. tax return only to claim a refund, (3) individuals being claimed as dependents on U.S. tax returns and who are not eligible to obtain a social security number, (4) individuals being claimed as husbands or wives for exemptions on U.S. tax returns and who are not eligible to obtain an SSN, and (5) U.S. residents who must file a U.S. tax return but are not eligible for an SSN.

Personal liability for payroll taxes

Church and nonprofit officers and employees may be personally liable if payroll taxes are not withheld and paid to the IRS. If the organization has willfully failed to withhold and pay the taxes, the IRS has the authority to assess a 100% penalty of withheld income and social security taxes.

2008 CHURCH AND NONPROFIT TAX & FINANCIAL GUIDE

---------- Cut here and give Form W-4 to your employer. Keep the top part for your records. ----------

Form **W-4**	**Employee's Withholding Allowance Certificate**	OMB No. 1545-0074
Department of the Treasury Internal Revenue Service	▶ Whether you are entitled to claim a certain number of allowances or exemption from withholding is subject to review by the IRS. Your employer may be required to send a copy of this form to the IRS.	20**07**

1 Type or print your first name and middle initial.   Walter R.
Last name   Knight
2 Your social security number   511 02 7943

Home address (number and street or rural route)
601 Oakridge Boulevard

3 ☐ Single ☒ Married ☐ Married, but withhold at higher Single rate.
Note. If married, but legally separated, or spouse is a nonresident alien, check the "Single" box.

City or town, state, and ZIP code
Vinton, VA 24179

4 If your last name differs from that shown on your social security card, check here. You must call 1-800-772-1213 for a replacement card. ▶ ☐

5 Total number of allowances you are claiming (from line H above **or** from the applicable worksheet on page 2) 5 **4**
6 Additional amount, if any, you want withheld from each paycheck . . . . 6 $
7 I claim exemption from withholding for 2007, and I certify that I meet **both** of the following conditions for exemption.
 • Last year I had a right to a refund of **all** federal income tax withheld because I had **no** tax liability **and**
 • This year I expect a refund of **all** federal income tax withheld because I expect to have **no** tax liability.
 If you meet both conditions, write "Exempt" here . . . . ▶ 7

Under penalties of perjury, I declare that I have examined this certificate and to the best of my knowledge and belief, it is true, correct, and complete.

Employee's signature
(Form is not valid unless you sign it.) ▶ *Walter R. Knight*   Date ▶ 1-1-07

8 Employer's name and address (Employer: Complete lines 8 and 10 only if sending to the IRS.)   9 Office code (optional)   10 Employer identification number (EIN)

For Privacy Act and Paperwork Reduction Act Notice, see page 2.   Cat. No. 10220Q   Form **W-4** (2007)

This form must be completed by all lay employees, full- or part-time. Your exemption for 2007 expires February 16, 2008. If a minister completes this form, it can be the basis to determine income tax withholding under a voluntary agreement.

Form **W-5**	**Earned Income Credit Advance Payment Certificate**	OMB No. 1545-0074
Department of the Treasury Internal Revenue Service	▶ Use the current year's certificate only. ▶ Give this certificate to your employer. ▶ This certificate expires on December 31, 2008.	20**08**

Print or type your full name
Daniel L. Wheeler

Your social security number   511 20 7843

Note. If you get advance payments of the earned income credit for 2008, you **must** file a 2008 federal income tax return. To get advance payments, you **must** have a qualifying child and your filing status must be any status **except** married filing a separate return.

1 I expect to have a qualifying child and be able to claim the earned income credit for 2008 using that child. I do not have another Form W-5 in effect with any other current employer, and I choose to get advance EIC payments . . . . ☒ Yes ☐ No
2 Check the box that shows your expected filing status for 2008:
  ☐ Single, head of household, or qualifying widow(er) ☒ Married filing jointly
3 If you are married, does your spouse have a Form W-5 in effect for 2008 with any employer? . . . . . ☐ Yes ☒ No

Under penalties of perjury, I declare that the information I have furnished above is, to the best of my knowledge, true, correct, and complete.

Signature ▶ *Daniel L. Wheeler*   Date ▶ 1-1-07
Cat. No. 10227P

This form should be completed if an employee elects to receive advance payments of the earned income credit.

This penalty may be assessed against the individual responsible for withholding and paying the taxes, even if the person is an unpaid volunteer such as a church treasurer.

Depositing Withheld Payroll Taxes

The basic rules for depositing payroll taxes are as follows:

➤ If your total accumulated and unpaid employment tax (income tax withheld, social security tax withheld and matched by the organization) is less than $2,500 in a calendar quarter, taxes can be paid directly to the IRS when the organization files Form 941. These forms are due one month after the end of each calendar quarter.

➤ If payroll taxes are over $2,500 for a quarter, payroll tax deposits must be made monthly or before the 15th day of each month for the payroll paid during the preceding month. Large organizations with total employment taxes of over $50,000 per year are subject to more frequent deposits.

To determine if an organization is a monthly depositor, you must determine if the accumulated liabilities in the "look-back period" reached a threshold of $50,000. Those with an accumulated liability of less than $50,000 in the look-back period are generally monthly depositors (except those qualifying for quarterly deposits with liabilities of $1,000 or less).

The cost of missing deposit deadlines can be very high. Besides interest, the organization can be hit with penalties at progressively stiffer rates. These range from 2% if you deposit the money within 5 days of the due date to 15% if it is not deposited within 10 days of the first delinquency notice or on the day that the IRS demands immediate payment, whichever is earlier.

> **Remember**
>
> A new organization (or one filing payroll tax returns for the first time) will be required to file monthly until a "look-back period" is established. A look-back period begins on July 1 and ends on June 30 of the preceding calendar year.

Deposit coupons

➤ **Form 8109.** Use Form 8109 deposit coupons to make deposits of the taxes covered by the following forms: Form 941, Form 990-T, and Schedule A.

The preprinted name and address of the organization and the employer identification number (EIN) appear on the coupons. Deliver or mail the completed coupon with the appropriate payment to a qualified depository for federal taxes.

➤ **Form 8109-B.** Use Form 8109-B deposit coupons to make tax deposits only in the following two situations:

☐ You have reordered preprinted deposit coupons (Form 8109) but have not yet received them.

☐ You are a new entity and have already been assigned an EIN, but have not yet received your initial supply of preprinted deposit coupons (Form 8109).

Form 8109-B may be obtained only from the IRS.

Filing the Quarterly Payroll Tax Forms

Employers must report covered wages paid to their employees by filing Form 941 with the IRS.

Form 941

Church and other nonprofit employers who withhold income tax and both social security and medicare taxes must file Form 941 quarterly. There is no requirement to file Form 941 if your organization has not been required to withhold payroll taxes even if you have one or more employee-ministers. However, if the only employee is a minister and voluntary federal income tax has been withheld, Form 941 must be filed.

Most common errors made on Form 941

The IRS has outlined the most common errors discovered during the processing of Form 941, Employer's Quarterly Federal Tax Return, and the best way to avoid making these mistakes. A checklist for avoiding errors follows:

> **Idea**
> Do not file more than one Form 941 per quarter even if you deposit payroll taxes monthly. If you have multiple locations or divisions, you must file only one Form 941 per quarter. Filing more than one return may result in processing delays and require correspondence with the IRS.

- ▶ Do not include titles or abbreviations, such as Dr., Mr., or Mrs.

- ▶ On line 2, do not include amounts designated as housing allowance for qualified ministers.

- ▶ Make sure that taxable social security wages and the social security tax on line 5a and the taxable Medicare wages and the Medicare tax on line 5c are reported separately. Most employers will need to complete both lines 5a and 5c.

- ▶ The preprinted form sent by the IRS should be used. If the return is prepared by a third-party preparer, make certain that the preparer uses exactly the name that appears on the preprinted form that was sent.

- ▶ Check the math for lines 5d, 10, and 11.
  Line 11 should always be the sum of lines 3, 5d, and 9.

- ▶ Make sure the social security tax on line 5a is calculated correctly (social security wages x 12.4%).

- ▶ Make sure the Medicare tax on line 5c is calculated correctly (Medicare wages x 2.9%).

CHAPTER 4 > EMPLOYER REPORTING

File this form to report social security (FICA) and Medicare taxes and federal income tax withheld.

95

Form **941c** (Rev. October 2006) Department of the Treasury Internal Revenue Service	**Supporting Statement To Correct Information** **Do Not File Separately** ▶ File with Forms 941, 941-M, 941-SS, 943, 944, 944(SP), 944-SS, 945, or Form 843.	OMB No. 1545-0256 Page No.

Name: Little Valley Church
Employer identification number (EIN): 35 : 6309294

Telephone number (optional):

A This form supports adjustments to Form: Check only one box. (see instructions)
- [X] 941
- [ ] 941-M
- [ ] 941-SS
- [ ] 943
- [ ] 944
- [ ] 944(SP)
- [ ] 944-SS
- [ ] 945

B This form is **attached to** and filed with the return for the period ending (month, year) ▶

C Enter the date that you discovered the error(s) reported on this form. (If you are making more than one correction and the errors were not discovered at the same time, explain in Part V.)   ▶ **2-01-08**

Part I — Signature and Certification
(You **must** complete this part for the IRS to process your adjustments for overpayments.) Skip Part I if all of your adjustments are underpayments. **(Part I applies to wages only.)**

I certify that Forms W-2c, Corrected Wage and Tax Statement, have been filed (as necessary) with the Social Security Administration, and that (check appropriate boxes):

- [ ] All overcollected federal income taxes for the current calendar year and all social security and Medicare taxes for the current and prior calendar years have been **repaid** to employees. For claims of overcollected employee social security and Medicare taxes in earlier years, a written statement has been obtained from each employee stating that the employee has not claimed and will not claim refund or credit for the amount of the overcollection.

- [ ] All affected employees have given their **written consent** to the allowance of this credit or refund. For claims of overcollected employee social security and Medicare taxes in earlier years, a written statement has been obtained from each employee stating that the employee has not claimed and will not claim refund or credit for the amount of the overcollection.

- [ ] The social security tax and Medicare tax adjustments represent the **employer's share only.** An attempt was made to locate the employee(s) affected, but the affected employee(s) could not be located or will not comply with the certification requirements.

- [ ] None of this refund or credit was withheld from employee wages.

Sign Here   Signature *Curtis R. Lee*   Title ▶ Treasurer   Date ▶ 4/30/08

Part II — Federal Income Tax Withholding (Including Backup Withholding) Adjustment

	(a) Period Corrected (For quarterly returns, enter date quarter ended. For annual returns, enter year.)	(b) Withheld Income Tax Previously Reported for Period	(c) Correct Withheld Income Tax for Period	(d) Withheld Income Tax Adjustment
1	12/31/07	400	600	200
2				
3				
4				

5 Net withheld income tax adjustment. If more than one page, enter total of **all** columns (d) on first page only. Enter here and on the **appropriate** line of the return with which you file this form. ▶ **5**

Part III — Social Security Tax Adjustment
(Use the tax rate in effect during the period(s) corrected. You must also complete Part IV.)

	(a) Period Corrected (For quarterly returns, enter date quarter ended. For annual returns, enter year.)	(b) Wages Previously Reported for Period	(c) Correct Wages for Period	(d) Tips Previously Reported for Period	(e) Correct Tips for Period	(f) Social Security Tax Adjustment
1	12/31/07	2000	4500			155
2						
3						
4						
5	**Totals.** If more than one page, enter totals on first page only. ▶					155

6 Net social security tax adjustment. If more than one page, enter total of **all** columns (f) on first page only. Enter here and on the appropriate line of the return with which you file this form. ▶ **6**

7 Net wage adjustment. If more than one page, enter total of **all** lines 7 on first page only. If line 5(c) is smaller than line 5(b), enter difference in parentheses. ▶ **7** 2500

8 Net tip adjustment. If more than one page, enter total of **all** lines 8 on first page only. If line 5(e) is smaller than line 5(d), enter difference in parentheses. ▶ **8**

For Paperwork Reduction Act Notice, see page 4.   Cat. No. 11242O   Form **941c** (Rev. 10-2006)

Use this form to correct income, social security (FICA), and Medicare tax information reported on Form 941. It may be necessary to issue Form W-2c to employees relating to prior year data.

- Be sure to use the most recent Form 941 that the IRS sends. The IRS enters the date the quarter ended after the employer identification number. If the form is used for a later quarter, the IRS will have to contact the employer.

- Make sure there is never an entry on both lines 12 and 13. There cannot be a balance due and a refund.

Filing the Annual Payroll Tax Forms

Form W-2

By January 31 each employee must be given a Form W-2. Be sure to reconcile the data reflected on Forms W-2, W-3, and 941 before distributing Forms W-2 to employees. If these forms do not reconcile, the IRS generally sends a letter to the employer requesting additional information. For additional help, call 304-263-8700.

Make all entries without a dollar sign or comma but with a decimal point and cents (do not use whole dollars).

Void – Put an X in this box when an error has been made on this W-2.

Box 1 – Wages, tips, other compensation. Items to include in Box 1 (before any payroll deductions) are

- total wages paid during the year (including love offerings paid by the church or nonprofit organization to a minister or other employee);

- the value of noncash payments, including taxable fringe benefits;

- business expense payments under a nonaccountable plan;

- payments of per diem or mileage allowance paid for business expense purposes that exceed the IRS-specified rates;

- payments made by a church or nonprofit organization to an employee's Individual Retirement Account;

- payments for nonexcludable moving expenses;

- all other compensation, including taxable fringe benefits;
  ("Other compensation" represents amounts an organization pays to an employee from which federal income tax is not withheld. If you prefer, you may show other compensation on a separate Form W-2.)

- the cash housing allowance or the fair market rental value of housing and utilities, which must be reported as taxable income for lay employees unless lodging is furnished on the employer's premises and the employee is required to accept the lodging as a condition of employment.

Exclude the following:

➤ the fair rental value of a church-provided parsonage or a properly designated housing allowance for ministers;

➤ auto, business, or qualified moving expense reimbursements paid through an accountable expense plan; and

➤ contributions to 403(b) tax-sheltered annuities or 401(k) plans.

Box 2 – Federal income tax withheld. Enter the total federal income tax withheld according to the chart and tables in IRS Publication 15.

A minister-employee may enter into a voluntary withholding arrangement with the employing organization. Based on Form W-4 or other written withholding request, federal income tax withholding may be calculated from the chart and tables in Publication 15, excluding any housing allowance amount.

The minister may request that an additional amount of income tax be withheld to cover self-employment tax. However, the additional amount withheld is reported as income tax withheld on the quarterly Form 941 and in Box 2 of Form W-2.

An organization that provides additional compensation to the employee-minister to cover part or all of the self-employment tax liability may

➤ pay the additional compensation directly to the IRS by entering that amount on the organization's Form 941 and in Boxes 1 and 2 of Form W-2, or

➤ pay the additional compensation to the minister with the minister being responsible for remitting the amounts to the IRS with a Form 1040-ES. If this procedure is followed, the organization reports this amount only as additional compensation on Form 941 and only in Box 1 of Form W-2.

> **Remember**
>
> One of an employer's primary challenges is to determine if all of an employee's compensation is reported on Form W-2. Taxable compensation that is often erroneously omitted includes life insurance premiums paid for the employee (only group-term-life up to $50,000 is tax-free) and expense allowances (only expenses reimbursed under an accountable plan are tax-free).

Box 3 – Social security wages. Show the total wages paid (before payroll deductions) subject to employee social security tax (FICA). This amount must not exceed $97,500 in 2007 (the maximum social security tax wage base). Include nonaccountable employee business expenses reported in Box 1. Generally, all cash and noncash payments reported in Box 1 must also be shown in Box 3. Voluntary salary reduction tax-sheltered annuity contributions for nonminister employees are included in Box 3.

Box 3 should be blank for a qualified minister (an individual who meets the ministerial tests of the IRS).

CHAPTER 4 > EMPLOYER REPORTING

Checklist for Completing Box 1 of Form W-2

Data Included for			
Minister Only	Both	Nonminister Only	
	yes		Salary
no		yes	Housing/furnishings allowance (designated in advance)
no		yes	Parsonage rental value
no		yes	Utilities paid by church or nonprofit
	yes		Social security/Medicare "allowance" or reimbursement
	no		Transportation/travel and other business and professional expense reimbursements *only if* paid under a board-adopted accountable reimbursement plan
	yes		"Reimbursements" if not paid under an accountable reimbursement plan
	yes		Love offerings or cash gifts in excess of $25
	no		Contributions to a tax-sheltered annuity plan
	no		Health/dental/long-term care insurance premiums paid directly or reimbursed by the employer
	no		Group-term life insurance premiums (for up to $50,000 coverage) paid directly by the employer
	no		Excludable moving expense paid for or reimbursed to an employee
	yes		Nonexcludable moving expenses paid for or reimbursed to an employee
	yes		Value of personal and nonbusiness use of organization's vehicle

Box 4 – Social security tax withheld. Show the total FICA social security tax (not including the organization's share) withheld or paid by the organization for the employee. The amount shown must equal 6.2% of the amount in Box 3 and must not exceed $6,045 for 2007. Do not include the matching employer FICA tax.

Some organizations pay the employee's share of FICA tax for some or all nonminister employees instead of deducting it from the employee's wages. These amounts paid by the organization must be included in Boxes 1, 3, and 5 as wages and proportionately in Boxes 4 and 6 as social security and Medicare tax withheld. In these instances, the effective cost to the employer is 8.28% instead of 7.45% for wages up to $97,500 and 1.47% rather than 1.45% for wages above $97,500.

Box 4 should be blank for qualified ministers. Any amount of withholding to meet the minister's SECA tax liability must be reported in Box 2, not in Box 4 or Box 6.

Box 5 – Medicare wages. The wages subject to Medicare tax are the same as those subject to social security tax (Box 3), except there is no wage limit for the Medicare tax.

Example: A nonminister employee is paid wages of $98,000. The amount shown in Box 3 (social security wages) should be $97,500, but the amount

99

```
22222  Void [ ]   a Employee's social security number   For Official Use Only ▶
                                                       OMB No. 1545-0008
```

b Employer identification number (EIN)		1 Wages, tips, other compensation	2 Federal income tax withheld
35-2948039		93800.00	7000.00
c Employer's name, address, and ZIP code		3 Social security wages	4 Social security tax withheld
ABC Charity		94200.00	5840.40
2870 North Hull Road		5 Medicare wages and tips	6 Medicare tax withheld
Traverse City, MI 49615		95000.00	1377.50
		7 Social security tips	8 Allocated tips
d Control number		9 Advance EIC payment	10 Dependent care benefits
517-38-6451			
e Employee's first name and initial Last name Suff.		11 Nonqualified plans	12a See instructions for box 12 E $1200.00
Michael A. Black		13 Statutory employee [ ] Retirement plan [X] Third-party sick pay [ ]	12b P $984.73
15550 Cleveland Avenue		14 Other	12c
Traverse City, MI 49615			12d
f Employee's address and ZIP code			

15 State	Employer's state ID number	16 State wages, tips, etc.	17 State income tax	18 Local wages, tips, etc.	19 Local income tax	20 Locality name
MI	6309294	93800.00	700.00			

Form **W-2** Wage and Tax Statement **2007** Department of the Treasury—Internal Revenue Service

Copy A For Social Security Administration — Send this entire page with Form W-3 to the Social Security Administration; photocopies are **not** acceptable.

For Privacy Act and Paperwork Reduction Act Notice, see back of Copy D.
Cat. No. 10134D

Do Not Cut, Fold, or Staple Forms on This Page — Do Not Cut, Fold, or Staple Forms on This Page

Form W-2 must be filed for each employee who received taxable compensation or for whom income tax or FICA-type social security tax was withheld.

shown in Box 5 (Medicare wages) should be $98,000. If the wages are less than $97,500, the amounts entered in Boxes 3 and 5 will be the same.

Box 5 should be blank for qualified ministers. Nonqualified moving expense reimbursements and payments for lay employees are included in Box 5.

Box 6 – Medicare tax withheld. Enter the total employee Medicare tax (not your share) withheld or paid by you for your employee. The amount shown must equal 1.45% of the amount in Box 5. Box 6 should be blank for qualified ministers.

Box 9 – Advance EIC payment. Show the total paid to the employee as advance earned income credit payments.

Box 10 – Dependent care benefits. Show the total amount of dependent care benefits under Section 129 paid or incurred by you for your employee, including any amount over the $5,000 exclusion. Also include in Box 1, Box 3, and Box 5 any amount over the $5,000 exclusion.

Box 11 – Nonqualified plans. Enter the total amount of distributions to the employee from a nonqualified deferred compensation plan. Nonqualified plans do not include a tax-sheltered annuity or a "Rabbi Trust." Include an amount in Box 11 only if it is also includible in Box 1 or Boxes 3 and 5.

Box 12 – Additional entries. The following items are most frequently inserted in Box 12 by churches and other nonprofit organizations:

- C – Group-term life insurance. If you provided your employee more than $50,000 of group-term life insurance, show the cost of the coverage over $50,000. Also include the amount in Box 1 (also in Boxes 3 and 5 if a lay employee).

- D – Section 401(k) cash or deferred arrangement.

- E – Section 403(b) voluntary salary reduction agreement to purchase an annuity contract. This amount would not be included in Box 1 for either ministerial or lay employees. This amount would be included in Boxes 3 and 5 for a lay employee.

- F – Section 408(k)(6) salary reduction simplified employee pension (SEP).

- L – Generally, payments made under an accountable plan are excluded from the employee's gross income and are not required to be reported on Form W-2. But if the organization pays a per diem or mileage allowance, and the amount paid exceeds the amount substantiated under IRS rules, you must report as wages on Form W-2 the amount in excess of the amount substantiated. Report the amount substantiated (the nontaxable portion) in Box 12. In Box 1, show the portion of the reimbursement that is more than the amount treated as substantiated. For lay employees the excess amount is subject to income tax withholding, social security tax, Medicare tax, and possibly federal unemployment tax.

    Example 1: An employee receives mileage reimbursement at the rate of 48.5 cents per mile during 2007 and substantiates the business miles driven to the organization. The mileage reimbursement is not reported on Form W-2.

    Example 2: An employee receives a mileage allowance of $2,000 per year and does not substantiate the business miles driven. The $2,000 allowance is includible in Box 1 as compensation for a minister and Boxes 1, 3, and 5 for a lay employee. The business mileage is deductible as a miscellaneous deduction on the employee's Schedule A, subject to limitations.

    Payments made to nonminister employees under a nonaccountable plan are reportable as wages on Form W-2 and are subject to income tax withholding, social security tax, Medicare tax, and possibly federal unemployment tax.

    Payments made to minister-employees under a nonaccountable plan are reportable as wages on Form W-2 and may be subject to income tax withholding under a voluntary agreement, but are not subject to mandatory withholding or social security (FICA) or Medicare tax.

- P – Qualified moving expenses paid directly to an employee. Report nonqualified moving expense reimbursements and payments in Box 1 for either ministerial or lay employees. This amount is included in Boxes 3 and 5 for lay employees.

- R – Employer contributions to a medical savings account.

S – Salary reductions to a savings incentive match plan for employees with a SIMPLE retirement account.

T – Employer payments under an adoption assistance plan.

Y – Deferrals under a section 409A nonqualified deferred compensation plan.

Z – Income under a section 409A nonqualified deferred compensation plan.

Box 13 – Check the appropriate boxes. The box that may apply to employees of churches and nonprofit organizations is the retirement plan box:

Retirement plan. Mark this checkbox if the employee was an active participant (for any part of the year) in any of the following:

1. A qualified pension plan described in section 401(a), including a 401(k) plan.

2. An annuity plan described in section 403(a).

3. An annuity contract or custodial account described in section 403(b).

4. A simplified employee pension (SEP) plan described in section 408(k).

Box 14 – Other. You may use this box for any other information the employer wishes to provide to an employee. Label each item and include information such as health insurance premiums deducted or educational assistance payments.

If the organization owns or leases a vehicle for an employee's use, the value of the personal use of the vehicle is taxable income. The value of the use of the vehicle is established by using one of the methods described on pages 63-65. The amount of the personal use must be included in Box 1 (and in Boxes 3 and 5 if a lay employee) or on a separate statement to the employee. The employee is required to maintain a mileage log or similar records to substantiate business and personal use of the vehicle and submit this to the employer. If its use is not substantiated, the employer must report 100% of the use of the vehicle as taxable income.

If the employee fully reimburses the employer for the value of the personal use of the vehicle, then no value would be reported in either Box 1 or in Box 14. Reimbursement of the amount spent for gas on personal trips does not constitute a reimbursement of the full value of the personal use of the vehicle.

> **Filing Tip**
>
> The minister's housing allowance could be included in this box with the words "Housing Allowance." However, some employers prefer to provide the minister with a separate statement reflecting the housing allowance amount.

> **Caution**
>
> Do not include any per diem or mileage allowance or other reimbursements for employee business expenses under an accountable plan in Boxes 1 or 14 if the total reimbursement is less than or equal to the amount substantiated.

Form W-3

A Form W-3 is submitted to the IRS as a transmittal form with Forms W-2. Form W-3 and all attached W-2s must be submitted to the Social Security Administration Center by February 28. No money is sent with Form W-3.

Form W-2c and W-3c

Use Form W-2c to correct errors on a previously filed Form W-2. Use Form W-3c to transmit corrected W-2c forms to the Social Security Administration. If you are correcting only an employee's name or social security number, you do not have to file Form W-3c with Form W-2c. File Forms W-2c and W-3c as soon as possible after you discover an error. Also provide Form W-2c to employees as soon as possible.

If you are correcting only an employee's name and/or social security number, complete Form W-2c through Box g, as appropriate. Do not complete Boxes 1 through 20.

Wages paid in error in a prior year remain taxable to the employee for that year. This is because the employee received and had use of those funds during that year. The employee is not entitled to file an amended return (Form 1040X) to recover the income tax on these wages. Instead, the employee is entitled to a deduction for the repaid wages on his or her Form 1040 for the year of repayment.

Unemployment taxes

The federal and state unemployment systems provide temporary unemployment compensation to workers who have lost their jobs. Employers provide the revenue for this program by paying federal unemployment taxes, under the Federal Unemployment Tax Act (FUTA), and state unemployment taxes. These are strictly employer taxes, and no deductions are taken from employees' wages.

The current federal unemployment tax law exempts from coverage

- services performed in the employment of a church, a convention, or an association of churches or an organization that is operated primarily for religious purposes (to qualify for exemption, employees must be performing strictly religious duties);

- services performed by an ordained, commissioned, or licensed minister of a church in the exercise of ministry or by a member of a religious order in the exercise of duties required by such order;

- services performed in the employment of an unincorporated church-controlled elementary or secondary school;

- services performed in the employment of an incorporated religious elementary or secondary school if it is operated primarily for religious purposes and is operated, supervised, controlled, or principally supported by a church or a convention or association of churches;

Form W-3 is the "cover sheet" or transmittal form for all Forms W-2.

Form W-2c is used to submit changes to data previously filed on Form W-2.

> services performed in the employment of an elementary or secondary school that is operated primarily for religious purposes and is not operated, supervised, controlled, or principally supported by a church or a convention or association of churches.

States may expand their coverage of unemployment taxes beyond the federal minimum. In many states, exemption is also provided for

> services performed in the employ of a separately incorporated church school if the school is operated primarily for religious purposes and is operated, supervised, controlled, or principally supported by a church or convention or association of churches.

Unemployment reporting requirements

Nonprofit organizations that are liable for FUTA taxes are required to file Form 940, or 940-EZ Employer's Annual Federal Unemployment Tax Return, due on January 31, if one of the following tests apply:

> You paid wages of $1,500 or more in any calendar quarter in the current or prior year, or

> You had one or more employees for at least some part of a day in any 20 or more different weeks in the current or prior year.

Filing Tip

Recent court cases reflect attempts by states to subject religious organizations, including churches, to state unemployment taxes. Except for an Oregon case and a New York case, most courts have held that churches are not subject to state unemployment tax.

Although Form 940 covers a calendar year, you may have to make deposits of the tax before filing the return. Generally, deposit FUTA tax quarterly if your FUTA tax exceeds $100. You must use Form 8109, Federal Tax Deposit Coupon, when making each federal unemployment tax deposit.

The taxable wage base under FUTA is $7,000 for 2007. (The state wage base may be different.) The tax applies to the first $7,000 you pay each employee as wages during the year. For example, if you had only one employee for the year and the salary was $20,000, only $7,000 is subject to FUTA. The gross FUTA tax rate is 6.2% for 2007.

Generally, you can take a credit against your FUTA tax for amounts you paid into the state unemployment funds. This credit cannot be more than 5.4% of taxable wages. If you are entitled to the maximum 5.4% credit, the FUTA tax rate after the credit is 0.8%.

Use Form 940 or 940-EZ, Employer's Annual Federal Unemployment (FUTA) Tax Return, to report this tax. You may be able to use Form 940-EZ instead of Form 940 if (1) you paid unemployment taxes ("contributions") to only one state, (2) you paid state unemployment taxes by the due date of Form 940 or 940-EZ, and (3) all wages that were taxable for FUTA tax purposes were also taxable for your state's unemployment tax.

Integrity*Points*

- **Worker classification issues.** Classifying workers correctly is a big deal in the minds of two important federal government agencies: the Department of Labor (DOL) and the IRS. The DOL's interest relates to being sure workers who are employees are classified as such so the Fair Labor Standards Act (minimum wage and overtime), workers' compensation and other fringe benefit purposes. The IRS wants to see Federal income tax and FICA-type social security tax (for lay employees) withheld for all workers who qualify as employees.

    Too often churches and other charities make a decision on employee vs. independent contractor based on how much the FICA social security cost (and perhaps other paperwork costs) will be for the charity. Actually, the social security cost factor has no relationship to an appropriate employee vs. independent contractor decision. Integrity requires proper evaluation of worker classification to insure workers receive the benefits to which they are entitled.

- **Ministers and social security.** One of the most common mistakes made by churches and other charities is to withhold FICA-type social security tax from a qualified minister. But what if the employing charity wants to give a minister a choice (of FICA withholding or paying their own social security) or the minister requests FICA tax withheld because it was done this way by his or her previous employer. Unfortunately, there is no choice on this issue.

    Qualified ministers must pay their own social security by completing Schedule SE, filed with their Form 1040. If a charity withholds and matches FICA-type social security tax from the pay of a minister, it has not correctly reported the minister's taxable compensation because the matched portion (7.65%) of the FICA tax escapes income tax when it is fully taxable for a minister. A charity must apply these rules with integrity, sometimes in spite of pressure to do otherwise.

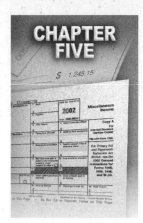

CHAPTER FIVE

Information Reporting

In This Chapter

- General filing requirements
- Reporting on the receipt of funds
- Reporting on the payment of funds
- Summary of payment reporting requirements

Information reporting may be required for many noncontribution funds received by your organization. Payments to nonemployees will often require filings with the IRS also.

General Filing Requirements

Information forms (1098 and 1099) must be provided to the payers/recipients on or before January 31 following the calendar year that the funds were paid or received. Copies of the forms (or electronic media) must be filed with the IRS by February 28 following the year that the funds were paid or received.

An extension of time to file may be requested by filing Form 8809, Request for Extension of Time to File Information Returns, by the due date of the returns.

Magnetic media reporting may be required for filing information returns with the IRS. If an organization is required to file 250 or more information returns, magnetic media filing must be used. The 250-or-more requirement applies separately to each type of form. Form 4419, Application for Filing Information Returns on Magnetic Media, must be filed to apply to use magnetic media.

Payers filing returns on paper forms must use a separate transmittal Form 1096, Annual Summary and Transmittal of U.S. Information Returns, for each different type of information form. For example, when filing Forms 1098, 1099-MISC, and 1099-S, complete one Form 1096 to transmit Forms 1098, another Form 1096 to transmit Forms 1099-MISC, and a third Form 1096 to transmit Forms 1099-S.

2008 CHURCH AND NONPROFIT TAX & FINANCIAL GUIDE

Form W-9 (Rev. August 2007)
Department of the Treasury
Internal Revenue Service

Request for Taxpayer Identification Number and Certification

Give form to the requester. Do not send to the IRS.

Name (as shown on your income tax return): Richard Bennett

Business name, if different from above:

Check appropriate box: [X] Individual/Sole proprietor [ ] Corporation [ ] Partnership
[ ] Limited liability company. Enter the tax classification (D=disregarded entity, C=corporation, P=partnership) ▶ ....
[ ] Other (see instructions) ▶

[ ] Exempt from backup withholding

Address (number, street, and apt. or suite no.): 829 Garner Street
City, state, and ZIP code: Thomasville, SC 27360

Requester's name and address (optional):

List account number(s) here (optional):

Part I — Taxpayer Identification Number (TIN)

Enter your TIN in the appropriate box. The TIN provided must match the name given on Line 1 to avoid backup withholding. For individuals, this is your social security number (SSN). However, for a resident alien, sole proprietor, or disregarded entity, see the Part I instructions on page 3. For other entities, it is your employer identification number (EIN). If you do not have a number, see *How to get a TIN* on page 3.

Note. If the account is in more than one name, see the chart on page 4 for guidelines on whose number to enter.

Social security number: 403 99 1297

or

Employer identification number:

Part II — Certification

Under penalties of perjury, I certify that:

1. The number shown on this form is my correct taxpayer identification number (or I am waiting for a number to be issued to me), and
2. I am not subject to backup withholding because: (a) I am exempt from backup withholding, or (b) I have not been notified by the Internal Revenue Service (IRS) that I am subject to backup withholding as a result of a failure to report all interest or dividends, or (c) the IRS has notified me that I am no longer subject to backup withholding, and
3. I am a U.S. citizen or other U.S. person (defined below).

Certification instructions. You must cross out item 2 above if you have been notified by the IRS that you are currently subject to backup withholding because you have failed to report all interest and dividends on your tax return. For real estate transactions, item 2 does not apply. For mortgage interest paid, acquisition or abandonment of secured property, cancellation of debt, contributions to an individual retirement arrangement (IRA), and generally, payments other than interest and dividends, you are not required to sign the Certification, but you must provide your correct TIN. See the instructions on page 4.

Sign Here — Signature of U.S. person ▶ *Richard K. Bennett*   Date ▶ 1-2-08

Use this form to obtain the taxpayer identification number in non-employee situations.

Do Not Staple   6969

Form 1096
Department of the Treasury
Internal Revenue Service

Annual Summary and Transmittal of U.S. Information Returns

OMB No. 1545-0108
2007

FILER'S name: ABC Charity
Street address (including room or suite number): 2670 North Hull Road
City, state, and ZIP code: Traverse City, MI 49615

Name of person to contact: Marianne Smith
Telephone number: (616) 435-2201
Email address: marsmith@msn.com
Fax number: (616) 435-2205

For Official Use Only

1 Employer identification number: 35-7431062
2 Social security number:
3 Total number of forms: 10
4 Federal income tax withheld: $
5 Total amount reported with this Form 1096: $ 5842.00

Enter an "X" in only one box below to indicate the type of form being filed. If this is your **final return**, enter an "X" here ▶ [ ]

W-2G 32	1098 81	1098-C 78	1098-E 84	1098-T 83	1099-A 80	1099-B 79	1099-C 85	1099-CAP 73	1099-DIV 91	1099-G 86	1099-H 71	1099-INT 92	1099-LTC 93
[ ]	[ ]	[ ]	[ ]	[ ]	[ ]	[ ]	[ ]	[ ]	[ ]	[ ]	[ ]	[ ]	[ ]

1099-MISC 95	1099-OID 96	1099-PATR 97	1099-Q 31	1099-R 98	1099-S 75	1099-SA 94	5498 28	5498-ESA 72	5498-SA 27
[X]	[ ]	[ ]	[ ]	[ ]	[ ]	[ ]	[ ]	[ ]	[ ]

Return this entire page to the Internal Revenue Service. Photocopies are not acceptable.

Under penalties of perjury, I declare that I have examined this return and accompanying documents, and, to the best of my knowledge and belief, they are true, correct, and complete.

Signature ▶ *Daniel L. Lewis*   Title ▶ Treasurer   Date ▶ 1-31-08

This form is the "cover sheet" or transmittal form that must accompany all your Forms 1099-MISC and other information forms.

CHAPTER 5 ➢ INFORMATION REPORTING

Obtaining correct identification numbers

Organizations required to file information returns with the IRS must obtain the correct taxpayer identification number (TIN) to report real estate transactions, mortgage interest paid to or by the organization, and certain other transactions.

Form W-9, Request for Taxpayer Identification Number and Certification, is used to furnish the correct TIN to the organization and in certain other situations to

> ➤ certify that the TIN furnished is correct,
>
> ➤ certify that the recipient of the income is not subject to backup withholding, or
>
> ➤ certify exemption from backup withholding.

Remember

If the recipient does not furnish a completed Form W-9, the church or nonprofit organization is required to withhold 28% of the payment for amounts paid, deposit the withholding with Form 8109 or 8109-B, and report amounts withheld on Form 1099-INT, 1099-MISC, or 1099-R, as applicable.

Reporting on the Receipt of Funds

Receipt of interest on mortgages

Use Form 1098, Mortgage Interest Statement, to report mortgage interest of $600 or more received by an organization during the year from an individual, including a sole proprietor. There is no requirement to file Form 1098 for interest received from a corporation, partnership, trust, estate, or association. A transmittal Form 1096 must accompany one or more Forms 1098.

Reporting on the Payment of Funds

Payments of interest

File Form 1099-INT, Statement for Recipients of Interest Income, for each person to whom an organization paid interest reportable in Box 1 of at least $10 in any calendar year. This form is also required if any federal income tax was withheld under the backup withholding rules (28% rate), regardless of the amount of the payment. In certain instances, the $10 limit increases to $600. There is no requirement to file Form 1099-INT for payments made to a corporation or another tax-exempt organization.

The $10 limit applies if the interest is on "evidences of indebtedness" (bonds and promissory notes) issued by a corporation in "registered form." A note or bond is in "registered form" if its transfer must be effected by the surrender of the old instrument and either the corporation's reissuance of the old instrument to the new holder or its reissuance of a new instrument to the new holder.

```
9292          ☐ VOID    ☐ CORRECTED
PAYER'S name, street address, city, state, ZIP code, and telephone no.   Payer's RTN (optional)   OMB No. 1545-0112
                                              1 Interest income        2007      Interest Income
  Lanaster Community Church                   $
  1425 Spencer Avenue                         2 Early withdrawal penalty
  Logansport, IN 46957                        $                        Form 1099-INT
PAYER'S federal identification number  RECIPIENT'S identification number  3 Interest on U.S. Savings Bonds and Treas. obligations   Copy A
  35-7921873                                  $ 913.00                                              For
RECIPIENT'S name                              4 Federal income tax withheld   5 Investment expenses   Internal Revenue
  James R. Moore                                                                                   Service Center
                                              $                        $                           File with Form 1096.
Street address (including apt. no.)           6 Foreign tax paid       7 Foreign country or U.S.   For Privacy Act
  804 Linden Avenue                           $                        possession                  and Paperwork
                                                                                                   Reduction Act
City, state, and ZIP code                     8 Tax-exempt interest    9 Specified private activity   Notice, see the
  Wabash, IN 46992                                                     bond interest               2007 General
Account number (see instructions)   2nd TIN not.                                                   Instructions for
                                    ☐        $                         $                           Forms 1099, 1098,
                                                                                                   5498, and W-2G.
Form 1099-INT                       Cat. No. 14410K                    Department of the Treasury - Internal Revenue Service
Do Not Cut or Separate Forms on This Page  —  Do Not Cut or Separate Forms on This Page
```

Use this form to report certain interest payments to the recipients.

Example 1: Sleepy Hollow Church financed a new church by issuing registered bonds. A 1099-INT form must be provided to each bond investor receiving $10 or more in interest during any calendar year.

If Sleepy Hollow engaged a bond broker to handle the issuance of the bonds, the broker would issue 1099-INT forms. If Sleepy Hollow issued the bonds without using a bond broker, the church would issue the 1099-INT forms.

Example 2: Sleepy Hollow Church borrows funds from church members. The notes are transferable. There is no requirement to return the bonds to the church for reissuance. The $600 limit applies for the issuance of 1099-INT forms for the payment of interest on these notes.

Payments to annuitants

File Form 1099-R for each person to whom an organization made a designated distribution that is a total distribution from a retirement plan or a payment to an annuitant of $1 or more. If part of the distribution is taxable and part is nontaxable, Form 1099-R should reflect the entire distribution.

Example: ABC Charity makes payments of $1,000 during the year to one of its annuitants, Mary Hughes. (Several years earlier, Mary entered into the charitable gift annuity agreement by giving a check to ABC.)

A portion of each annuity payment is a tax-free return of principal, and the remainder is annuity income for Mary. ABC will generally report the

CHAPTER 5 ➤ INFORMATION REPORTING

```
9898    ☐ VOID    ☐ CORRECTED
```

PAYER'S name, street address, city, state, and ZIP code	1 Gross distribution	OMB No. 1545-0119	Distributions From Pensions, Annuities, Retirement or Profit-Sharing Plans, IRAs, Insurance Contracts, etc.
ABC Charity 8049 Riverside Blvd. Sacramento, CA 95831	$ 1000.00	2007	
	2a Taxable amount $	Form **1099-R**	
	2b Taxable amount not determined [X]	Total distribution ☐	Copy A For Internal Revenue Service Center File with Form 1096.
PAYER'S federal identification number 35-0179214	RECIPIENT'S identification number 703-41-3669	3 Capital gain (included in box 2a) $	4 Federal income tax withheld $
RECIPIENT'S name Mary Hughes	5 Employee contributions /Designated Roth contributions or insurance premiums $	6 Net unrealized appreciation in employer's securities $	For Privacy Act and Paperwork Reduction Act Notice, see the 2007 General Instructions for Forms 1099, 1098, 5498, and W-2G.
Street address (including apt. no.) PO Box 9042	7 Distribution code(s)	IRA/ SEP/ SIMPLE ☐	8 Other $ %
City, state, and ZIP code El Toro, CA 92630	9a Your percentage of total distribution %	9b Total employee contributions $	
	1st year of desig. Roth contrib.	10 State tax withheld $ $	11 State/Payer's state no.	12 State distribution $ $
Account number (see instructions)	13 Local tax withheld $ $	14 Name of locality	15 Local distribution $ $

Form **1099-R**   Cat. No. 14436Q   Department of the Treasury — Internal Revenue Service

Do Not Cut or Separate Forms on This Page — Do Not Cut or Separate Forms on This Page

Use this form for retirement or annuity payments.

entire $1,000 in Box 1 on Form 1099-R and check Box 2b unless ABC determines the taxable amount for the year.

Form W-4P, Withholding Certificate for Pension or Annuity Payments, should be completed by recipients of income from annuity, pension, and certain other deferred compensation plans to inform payers whether income tax is to be withheld and on what basis.

Payments to nonresident aliens

Payments for personal services made to noncitizens who are temporarily in this country (nonresident aliens) are often subject to federal income tax withholding at a 30% rate. Some payments may be exempt from income tax withholding if the person is from a country with which the United States maintains a tax treaty. A nonresident alien is a person who is neither a U.S. citizen nor a resident of the United States. Salary payments to nonresident aliens employed in the United States are subject to income tax withholding based on the regular withholding tables.

Caution

Generally, you must withhold 30% from the gross amount paid to a foreign payee unless you can reliably associate the payment with valid documentation that establishes the payee is a U.S. person. If you do not have documentation or if you believe the documentation is unreliable or incorrect, you must follow the presumption rules outlined in IRS Publication 515.

Single, nonrecurring, fixed or determinable payments to nonresident aliens are generally not subject to withholding. Honoraria paid to visiting speakers usually fit this definition. It is not clear if love offerings are subject to withholding.

All payments to nonresident aliens, other than expense reimbursements and amounts reported on Form W-2, must be reported on Forms 1042 and 1042-S. These forms are filed with the IRS Service Center in Philadelphia by March 15 for the previous calendar year, and a copy of Form 1042-S must be sent to the nonresident alien.

Payments of royalties and for other services

An organization must file Form 1099-MISC for each recipient (other than corporations) to whom it has paid

- at least $10 in royalties, or
- at least $600 in rents (for example, office rent or equipment rent), payments for services (nonemployee compensation), or medical healthcare payments.

Payments of attorneys' fees to a lawyer or law firm must be included, generally in Box 7, even if the firm providing the legal services is incorporated.

Caution

There is more misunderstanding about the use of the Form 1099-MISC than about most IRS forms. Payments of $600 or more per calendar year to noncorporate providers of services trigger the filing of this form. This form should not be used for employee compensation payments. So a church should not report the pastor's compensation (or the housing allowance) on this form.

Example: A charity has established a written, nondiscriminatory employee health reimbursement arrangement under which the charity pays the medical expenses of the employee, spouse, and dependents.

If $600 or more is paid in the calendar year to a doctor or other provider of healthcare services, a Form 1099-MISC must be filed. Amounts paid to an employee under a health reimbursement arrangement (or healthcare flexible spending account) are not reportable on Form W-2 or 1099-MISC.

Benevolence payments to nonemployees are not reportable on Form 1099-MISC (or any other information form). Benevolence payments to employees are reportable on Form W-2.

Do not include the payment of a housing allowance to a minister on Form 1099-MISC. Advances, reimbursements, or expenses for traveling and other business expenses of an employee are not reportable on Form 1099-MISC. These payments may be reportable on Form W-2 if they do not comply with the accountable expense plan rules.

Advances, reimbursements, or expenses for traveling and other business expenses of a self-employed person are not reportable on Form 1099-MISC if made under an accountable expense reimbursement plan. Under this type of plan, expenses are reimbursed only if they are substantiated as to amount, date, and business nature, and any excess reimbursements must be returned to the organization.

CHAPTER 5 ➤ INFORMATION REPORTING

On Form 1099-MISC, report all advances, reimbursements, or expenses for traveling and other business expenses of a self-employed person for income tax purposes that are not substantiated to the paying organization.

Example 1: ABC Ministry organizes a seminar and engages a speaker. The speaker is paid a $750 honorarium, and ABC reimburses the travel expenses of $200 upon presentation of proper substantiation by the speaker. Form 1099-MISC should be issued to the speaker for $750.

Example 2: Same facts as Example 1, except of the $750 payment, $250 is designated for travel expenses and the speaker substantiates to ABC for the travel. Since the honorarium is $500, after excluding the substantiated payments, and therefore is less than the $600 limit, there is no requirement to issue a Form 1099-MISC to the speaker.

If ABC paid an honorarium to the same speaker during the same calendar year of $100 or more, bringing the total for the year to the $600 level, a Form 1099-MISC should be issued.

Example 3: ABC Ministry contracts for janitorial services with an unincorporated janitorial service and pays $2,000 during the year for this service. ABC should issue a Form 1099-MISC for these payments.

9595	☐ VOID	☐ CORRECTED		
PAYER'S name, street address, city, state, ZIP code, and telephone no. ABC Charity 110 Harding Avenue Cincinnati, OH 45963	1 Rents $ 2 Royalties $	OMB No. 1545-0115 **2007** Form **1099-MISC**	**Miscellaneous Income**	
	3 Other income $	4 Federal income tax withheld $	Copy A For Internal Revenue Service Center	
PAYER'S federal identification number 35-1148942	RECIPIENT'S identification number 389-11-8067	5 Fishing boat proceeds $	6 Medical and health care payments $	File with Form 1096.
RECIPIENT'S name Mark A. Mitchell		7 Nonemployee compensation $ 2400.00	8 Substitute payments in lieu of dividends or interest $	For Privacy Act and Paperwork Reduction Act Notice, see the 2007 General Instructions for Forms 1099, 1098, 5498, and W-2G.
Street address (including apt. no.) 1512 Warren Avenue		9 Payer made direct sales of $5,000 or more of consumer products to a buyer (recipient) for resale ▶ ☐	10 Crop insurance proceeds $	
City, state, and ZIP code Norwood, OH 45212		11	12	
Account number (see instructions)	2nd TIN not. ☐	13 Excess golden parachute payments $	14 Gross proceeds paid to an attorney $	
15a Section 409A deferrals $	15b Section 409A income $	16 State tax withheld $ $	17 State/Payer's state no.	18 State income $ $

Form **1099-MISC**   Cat. No. 14425J   Department of the Treasury - Internal Revenue Service
Do Not Cut or Separate Forms on This Page   —   Do Not Cut or Separate Forms on This Page

Use this form to report royalty and nonemployee services payments.

Payments to volunteers

Payments to volunteers that represent a reimbursement under an accountable business expense reimbursement plan for expenses directly connected with the volunteer services are not reportable by the charity.

Payments for auto mileage up to the maximum IRS rate for business miles are generally considered to be tax-free for volunteers. When an organization provides liability insurance for its volunteers, the value of the coverage can be excluded from the volunteer's income as a working condition fringe benefit.

Payments to or on behalf of volunteers that are not business expenses are reported on Form W-2 or Form 1099-MISC, depending on whether or not a common law employee relationship exists. When the relationship takes the form of an employer-employee relationship, payments other than expense reimbursement are reported on Form W-2. Payments to nonemployee volunteers for medical, education, or personal living expenses must be reported as nonemployee compensation on Form 1099-MISC. Payments to volunteers for lodging, meals, and incidental expenses may be made under the per diem rules if the duration of the travel is under one year.

> **Remember**
>
> Tax law does not specifically address what deductions are allowable for volunteers. However, if the volunteer renders services under the direction and supervision of the ministry, then the tax provisions for expense reimbursement of employees appear to apply to such volunteers, including mileage reimbursement payments at the business mileage rate.

Moving expenses

Qualified moving expenses an employer pays to a third party on behalf of the employee (for example, to a moving company) and services that an employer furnishes in kind to an employee are not reported on Form W-2.

A taxpayer must move at least 50 miles to qualify to deduct moving expenses or receive a tax-free reimbursement. Many ministers move less than 50 miles, which makes the expenses nondeductible and reimbursements by the church fully taxable for both income and social security tax purposes.

> **Filing Tip**
>
> Employer reimbursements of moving expenses are excludable from Form W-2 reporting only to the extent that the expenses would qualify for a moving expense deduction if they had been paid by the employee and not reimbursed. For example, many employees move less than 50 miles. This makes the expenses nondeductible and reimbursements by the employer fully taxable both for income and social security tax purposes.

Racial discrimination

Form 5578, Annual Certification of Racial Nondiscrimination for a Private School Exempt from Federal Income Tax, must be filed by churches that operate, supervise, or control a private school. The form must be filed by the 15th day of the fifth month following the end

CHAPTER 5 › INFORMATION REPORTING

> **Form 5578** (Rev. June 1998)
> Department of the Treasury
> Internal Revenue Service
>
> **Annual Certification of Racial Nondiscrimination for a Private School Exempt From Federal Income Tax**
> (For use by organizations that do not file Form 990 or Form 990-EZ)
>
> OMB No. 1545-0213
> For IRS use ONLY
>
> For the period beginning _____, and ending _____
>
> **1a** Name of organization that operates, supervises, and/or controls school(s).
> Fellowship Church
> Address (number and street or P.O. box no., if mail is not delivered to street address) Room/suite
> East Main Street
> City or town, state, and ZIP + 4 (If foreign address, list city or town, state or province, and country. Include postal code.)
> Lamont, KS 66855
> **1b** Employer identification number
> 73 : 0896893
>
> **2a** Name of central organization holding group exemption letter covering the school(s). (If same as 1a above, write "Same" and complete 2c.) If the organization in 1a above holds an individual exemption letter, write "Not Applicable."
> N/A
> Address (number and street or P.O. box no., if mail is not delivered to street address) Room/suite
> City or town, state, and ZIP + 4 (If foreign address list city or town, state or province, and country. Include postal code.)
> **2b** Employer identification number
> **2c** Group exemption number (see instructions under **Definitions**)
>
> **3a** Name of school. (If more than one school, write "See Attached," and attach a list of the names, complete addresses, including postal codes, and employer identification numbers of the schools.) If same as 1a above, write "Same."
> Fellowship Christian School
> Address (number and street or P.O. box no., if mail is not delivered to street address) Room/suite
> Same
> City or town, state, and ZIP + 4 (If foreign address, list city or town, state or province, and country. Include postal code.)
> Same
> **3b** Employer identification number, if any
> Same
>
> Under penalties of perjury, I hereby certify that I am authorized to take official action on behalf of the above school(s) and that to the best of my knowledge and belief the school(s) has (have) satisfied the applicable requirements of sections 4.01 through 4.05 of Rev. Proc. 75-50, 1975-2 C.B. 587, for the period covered by this certification.
>
> *Ralph Winzeler* (Signature)   Ralph Winzeler, Superintendent (Type or print name and title.)   5-16-08 (Date)

of the organization's fiscal year. For organizations that must file Form 990, there is no requirement to file Form 5578 since the information is included in Part V of Schedule A.

The "private school" definition includes preschools; primary, secondary, preparatory, and high schools; and colleges and universities, whether operated as a separate legal entity or an activity of a church.

Immigration control

The Immigration Reform and Control Act (IRCA) prohibits all employers from hiring unauthorized aliens, imposes documentation verification requirements on all employers, and provides an "amnesty" program for certain illegal aliens. The law also prohibits employers with three or more employees from discriminating because of national origin. An I-9 Form (see page 116) must be completed and retained on file by all employers for each employee. The form must be available for inspection at any time. Form I-9 may be obtained by calling 800-375-5283 or at http://uscis.gov/graphics/formsfee/forms/i-9.htm.

The Form I-551 Alien Registration Receipt Card issued after August 1, 1989, is the exclusive registration card issued to lawful permanent residents as definitive evidence of identity and U.S. residence status.

Department of Homeland Security
U.S. Citizenship and Immigration Services

OMB No. 1615-0047; Expires 03/31/07

Employment Eligibility Verification

Please read instructions carefully before completing this form. The instructions must be available during completion of this form. ANTI-DISCRIMINATION NOTICE: It is illegal to discriminate against work eligible individuals. Employers CANNOT specify which document(s) they will accept from an employee. The refusal to hire an individual because of a future expiration date may also constitute illegal discrimination.

Section 1. Employee Information and Verification. To be completed and signed by employee at the time employment begins.

Print Name: Last	First	Middle Initial	Maiden Name
Hendricks	Fred	W.	

Address (Street Name and Number)	Apt. #	Date of Birth (month/day/year)
406 Forest Avenue		06/12/1949

City	State	Zip Code	Social Security #
Cincinnati	OH	45960	514-42-9087

I am aware that federal law provides for imprisonment and/or fines for false statements or use of false documents in connection with the completion of this form.

I attest, under penalty of perjury, that I am (check one of the following):
[X] A citizen or national of the United States
[ ] A Lawful Permanent Resident (Alien #) A _____
[ ] An alien authorized to work until _____
(Alien # or Admission #)

Employee's Signature: *Fred W. Hendricks*
Date (month/day/year): 1-3-08

Preparer and/or Translator Certification. (To be completed and signed if Section 1 is prepared by a person other than the employee.) I attest, under penalty of perjury, that I have assisted in the completion of this form and that to the best of my knowledge the information is true and correct.

Preparer's/Translator's Signature	Print Name

Address (Street Name and Number, City, State, Zip Code)	Date (month/day/year)

Section 2. Employer Review and Verification. To be completed and signed by employer. Examine one document from List A OR examine one document from List B and one from List C, as listed on the reverse of this form, and record the title, number and expiration date, if any, of the document(s).

	List A	OR	List B	AND	List C
Document title:			Driver's License		Birth Certificate
Issuing authority:			Ohio		Ohio
Document #:			514-42-9087		
Expiration Date (if any):			6-30-08		
Document #:					
Expiration Date (if any):					

CERTIFICATION - I attest, under penalty of perjury, that I have examined the document(s) presented by the above-named employee, that the above-listed document(s) appear to be genuine and to relate to the employee named, that the employee began employment on (month/day/year) _____ and that to the best of my knowledge the employee is eligible to work in the United States. (State employment agencies may omit the date the employee began employment.)

Signature of Employer or Authorized Representative	Print Name	Title
David L. Brown	David L. Brown	Business Manager

Business or Organization Name Address (Street Name and Number, City, State, Zip Code)	Date (month/day/year)
Fairfield Church, 110 Harding Avenue, Cincinnati, OH 45960	1-31-08

Section 3. Updating and Reverification. To be completed and signed by employer.

A. New Name (if applicable)	B. Date of Rehire (month/day/year) (if applicable)

C. If employee's previous grant of work authorization has expired, provide the information below for the document that establishes current employment eligibility.

Document Title:	Document #:	Expiration Date (if any):

I attest, under penalty of perjury, that to the best of my knowledge, this employee is eligible to work in the United States, and if the employee presented document(s), the document(s) I have examined appear to be genuine and to relate to the individual.

Signature of Employer or Authorized Representative	Date (month/day/year)

NOTE: This is the 1991 edition of the Form I-9 that has been rebranded with a current printing date to reflect the recent transition from the INS to DHS and its components.

Form I-9 (Rev. 05/31/05)Y Page 2

This form must be completed and retained on file by all employers for employees hired after November 6, 1986. (For more information on completing this form, go to www.uscis.gov.)

Summary of Payment Reporting Requirements

Below is an alphabetical list of some payments and the forms necessary to report them. It is not a complete list of payments, and the absence of a payment from the list does not suggest that the payment is exempt from reporting.

Types of Payment	Report on Form
Advance earned income credit	W-2
Annuities, periodic payments	1099-R
* Attorneys' fees	1099-MISC
** Auto, personal use of employer-owned vehicle	W-2
Auto reimbursements (nonaccountable plan):	
Employee	W-2
Nonemployee	1099-MISC
Awards:	
Employee	W-2
Nonemployee	1099-MISC
Bonuses:	
Employee	W-2
Nonemployee	1099-MISC
Cafeteria/flexible benefit plan	5500, 5500-C, or 5500-R
Car expense (nonaccountable plan):	
Employee	W-2
Nonemployee	1099-MISC
Christmas bonuses:	
Employee	W-2
Nonemployee	1099-MISC
Commissions:	
Employee	W-2
Nonemployee	1099-MISC
Compensation:	
Employee	W-2
Nonemployee	1099-MISC
Dependent care payments	W-2
Director's fees	1099-MISC
Education expense reimbursement (nonaccountable plan):	
Employee	W-2
Nonemployee	1099-MISC

Types of Payment	Report on Form
Employee business expense reimbursement (nonaccountable plan)	W-2
Fees:	
Employee	W-2
Nonemployee	1099-MISC
Group-term life insurance (PS 58 costs)	W-2 or 1099-R
Interest, mortgage	1098
Interest, other than mortgage	1099-INT
Long-term care benefits	1099-LTC
Medical expense reimbursement plan (employee-funded)	5500, 5500-C, or 5500-R
Mileage (nonaccountable plan):	
Employee	W-2
Nonemployee	1099-MISC
Mortgage interest	1098
Moving expense:	
*** Employee	W-2
Nonemployee	1099-MISC
Prizes:	
Employee	W-2
Nonemployee	1099-MISC
Real estate proceeds	1099-S
Rents	1099-MISC
Royalties	1099-MISC
Severance pay	W-2
Sick pay	W-2
Supplemental unemployment	W-2
Vacation allowance:	
Employee	W-2
Nonemployee	1099-MISC

* The exemption from reporting payments made to corporations does not apply to payments to a lawyer or a law firm for legal services, even if the provider of the legal services is incorporated.

** Or, the value may be reported on a separate statement to the employee.

*** Qualified moving expenses paid directly to an employee must be reported on Form W-2, only in Box 13, using Code P.

# IntegrityPoints

- **Obtaining a completed Form W-9.** The proper completion of forms in the 1099 series all starts with obtaining a completed Form W-9 before the applicable payments are made by the church or other charity. Unless the Form W-9 is obtained before payments are made, it may be very difficult to obtain the form at a later date and could complicate the filing of the appropriate 1099 form. Integrity requires having procedures to obtain a Form W-9 at the beginning of the relationship with a recipient of certain charity payments.

- **Reporting of payments to independent contractors.** Because there is generally no tax to withhold, it is easy for a church or other charity to overlook the filing of Form 1099-MISC. When a charity fails to file a required Form 1099-MISC, the charity may be inadvertently giving an independent contractor a license to not report taxable income. Integrity requires the proper filing of Form 1099-MISC and all other forms in the 1099 series, if applicable.

- **Reporting of payments to noncitizens.** Churches and other charities often make payments to individuals who are not U.S. citizens and are temporarily in the U.S. The proper reporting to the IRS is often overlooked. For example, payments might be made by a church to a national worker (noncitizen) visiting the church to report on the effectiveness of gifts made by a church to an international mission field.

    While reimbursements made under an accountable expense reimbursement plan are not reportable, other payments must be reported on Form 1042-S and some payments are even subject to federal income tax withholding. Integrity requires a charity to understand the rules relating to payment to noncitizens before the payments are made.

Financial Records

CHAPTER SIX

In This Chapter

- Handling incoming funds
- Handling outgoing funds
- Accounting records
- Financial reports
- Budgeting
- Audits, reviews, and compilations

It takes a practical set of accounting records and financial reports to communicate the financial condition of your organization. Sound written procedures should be developed, installed, and maintained. These procedures will be different for every organization, depending on its size and the capability and availability of personnel.

Handling Incoming Funds

Donations are one of the most fundamental elements of income for most nonprofit organizations. And church offerings are the financial lifeblood of churches. The proper handling of donations, including adequate internal controls, must be one of the first priorities for every church and other nonprofit organization.

Church offerings come in various forms. Most commonly, the offering plates are passed during the service. In other churches, offerings are placed in containers located outside the sanctuary.

Most offerings received by churches are unrestricted. But nearly every church receives some donor-restricted funds. These donor-restricted funds require special treatment in the process of counting and recording offerings.

Why do money-handling problems arise in churches? It's primarily because cash is so easily misappropriated. It is small, lacks owner identification, and has immediate transferability. If offerings are not counted before they go from two-person control to one-person control, some or all of the cash can easily disappear.

Guidelines for Handling Church Offerings

- **Adopt policies to prevent problems.** Written policies are the ounce of prevention that could avoid serious problems at your church. Adopt a series of detailed policies that outline the procedures to be followed from the time the money goes into the offering plate—in worship services, Sunday school classes, other services, received in the mail, or delivered to the church—until the money is deposited in the bank.

- **Make accountability and confidentiality dual goals.** Too many churches focus so much on confidentiality that accountability takes too low a priority. True, some confidentiality is sacrificed when good accountability exists. But the church that does not balance confidentiality and accountability is treading on dangerous ground.

- **Use confidentiality statements.** Counters should sign a written statement of confidentiality before participating in the counting process. If the commitment of confidentiality is broken, the individual(s) should be removed from the team of counters.

- **Always follow the principle of two.** When a church leaves the offering in control of a single person—even for a short time period—before the count has been recorded or the uncounted offering has been dropped at the bank, it is a blatant invitation for problems. When sole access to the offering is allowed, most people will not take any money. However, for some, the temptation may be too great.

  Even when the principle of joint control is carefully followed, collusion between the two people is still possible—leading to a loss of funds. The risk of collusion can be reduced by rotating ushers and offering-counters so they don't serve on consecutive weeks. Church treasurers, financial secretaries, and other church-elected individuals should serve for limited terms, such as two or three years. A pastor or the church treasurer should not be involved in the counting process. A husband and wife could serve on the same counting team only if a third party is always present.

  > **Example:** The Sunday offerings go from the ushers to the head usher and then to the financial secretary, who takes the money, makes the initial count, records the donations by donor, and then makes the bank deposit. Problem: This violates the principle of having offerings in the control of two individuals until they are counted. The head usher and financial secretary both have the opportunity to remove cash. Or they could be accused of mishandling the funds and have no system of controls to support their innocence.

- **Keep the offering plates in plain view.** When the offering is being received, it is important that each offering plate always be kept in plain view of two ushers. When a solo usher takes an offering plate down a hall, upstairs to the balcony, behind a curtain, or out a door, there is a possibility of losing cash from the plate.

- **Be sure the guidelines cover Sunday school offerings.** Too often churches are very careful with offerings from the worship services but not so careful with offerings received in church school classes. These offerings should be counted in the class and turned over to an usher or counting team comprised of at least two individuals.

- ❑ **Encourage the use of offering envelopes.** Members should be encouraged to use offering envelopes. The envelopes provide a basis for recording contributions in the church's donor records.

  Some churches emphasize this concept by providing each individual or church family with a series of prenumbered offering envelopes to be used throughout the calendar year. The numbering system identifies the donor. This can ease the process of posting donations and is an excellent approach.

- ❑ **Count the offerings as soon as possible.** A frequent reason given by churches for not counting offerings immediately is that church members don't want to miss the service. This is very understandable. In some churches, the Sunday offerings are counted on Monday. Adequate control over the money is maintained by providing a secure place to store the funds, usually a safe, and carefully limiting access to the storage location.

  However, the greater the length of time between receiving and counting the offering, the greater the potential for mishandling of funds. When offerings are immediately counted, secure storing of the funds is important but not as critical because an audit trail has been established.

- ❑ **Have counters complete offering tally sheets.** Tally sheets should be completed that separately account for loose checks and cash that were placed in offering envelopes. Checks or cash placed in blank, unidentified offering envelopes should be recorded with the loose funds. This separation of money serves as a control amount for the later posting to donor records.

- ❑ **Use a secure area for counting.** For safety of the counting team, confidentiality, and avoidance of interruptions, provide a secure area in which the offering can be counted. (When offerings are significant, consider providing armed security when offerings are transported to the bank.) The counters should have an adding machine, coin wrappers, offering tally sheets, and other supplies. The adding machine should have a tape (instead of a paperless calculator) so the counting team can run two matching adding machine tapes of the offering.

- ❑ **Deposit all offerings intact.** Offerings should always be counted and deposited intact. Depositing intact means not allowing cash in the offering to be used for the payment of church expenses or to be exchanged for other cash or a check.

  If offerings are not deposited intact, an unidentified variance between the count and the deposit could occur. Additionally, if an individual is permitted to cash a check from offering funds, the church may inadvertently provide the person with a cancelled check that could be used in claiming a charitable tax deduction.

- ❑ **Verify amounts on offering envelopes with the contents.** As the counting team removes the contents from offering envelopes, any amounts written on the envelope by the donors should be compared with the contents. Any variances should be noted on the envelope.

- ❑ **Properly identify donor-restricted funds.** All donor restrictions should be carefully preserved during the counting process. These restrictions are usually noted on an offering envelope, but they can take the form of an instruction attached to a check or simply a notation on the check.

- ❏ **Use a restrictive endorsement for checks.** During the counting process, it is important to add a restrictive endorsement, with a "For Deposit Only" stamp, to the back of all checks.

- ❏ **Place offerings in a secure location when they are stored in the church.** If offerings are stored in the church, even for short periods of time, the use of a secure location is important. A safe implies security, while an unlocked desk drawer connotes lack of security. But defining security is often not that easy.

  Again, the principle is that no one person should have access to the funds at any time. This can be accomplished by

  ✓ obtaining a safe with two locks,

  ✓ changing the combination and distributing portions of the new combination to different people, or

  ✓ placing the safe in a locked room or building and placing the offerings in locked bags before locking them in the safe.

  Ideally, offerings are counted during or after the service and a deposit is made immediately. Alternately, the cash portion of the offering is recorded and the uncounted offerings are immediately transported to the bank drop box by two people. When these two preferable options are not used, the offerings are generally stored at the church for a period of time on Sunday or perhaps until Monday morning. This process requires a secure storage location, preferably a safe, and highly structured controls over access to locked bank bags and the safe.

- ❏ **Use proper controls when dropping uncounted funds at the bank.** If your church drops uncounted offerings at the bank, several key principles should be followed:

  ✓ The funds should be placed in locked bank bags with careful control of the number of persons who have keys to the bags.

  ✓ Two individuals should transport the funds to the bank.

  ✓ Two people should pick up the funds from the bank on the next business day, count the funds, and make the deposit.

- ❏ **Control deposit variances.** Provide written instructions to the bank concerning procedures to be followed if the bank discovers a discrepancy in the deposit. The notification should go to someone other than the individual(s) who participated in preparation of the deposit.

- ❏ **Segregate duties when recording individual contributions.** Someone other than a member of the counting team should record individual gifts in donor records. This segregation of duties reduces the possibility of misappropriation of gifts.

Cash Count Summary

March 9, 2008

	Sunday School	Sunday A.M.	Sunday P.M.	Received During Week	TOTAL
Coins	83.12	21.82	10.42		115.36
Currency	320.00	431.00	108.00		859.00
Checks	25.00	1,855.00	360.00	185.00	2,425.00
TOTALS	428.12	2,307.82	478.42	185.00	3,399.36

Breakdown by Type of Gift

	Sunday School	Sunday A.M.	Sunday P.M.	Received During Week	TOTAL
Regular Tithes and Offerings		1,942.82	368.42	140.00	2,451.24
Sunday School	428.12				428.12
Building Fund		85.00	50.00	15.00	150.00
Missions		100.00	30.00	20.00	150.00
Other Designated Funds:					
Benevolence Fund		40.00			40.00
School Project		30.00	10.00		40.00
Choir Robes		50.00			50.00
Youth Trip		40.00	20.00	10.00	70.00
Parking Lot		20.00			20.00
TOTALS	428.12	2,307.82	478.42	185.00	3,399.36

Counted by: Mike Anderson / Helen David / Bob Wells

Deposited on: March 13, 2008

Contributions by Donor

March 9, 2008   (X) A.M. ( ) P.M. (_____)

Name of Contributor	Regular Tithes & Offerings	Sunday School	Building Fund	Missions	Other Description	Amount
Wilson, M/M Mark	50.00		10.00	20.00		
Young, Frank	35.00					
Jackson, Ellen	60.00		15.00			
Avery, Lori	40.00					
Floyd, M/M Mike	100.00	10.00			Benevolence	40.00
Long, M/M Harold	45.00		5.00	10.00		
Martin, Mary	75.00					
Ross, M/M Steve	80.00			20.00		
Harris, M/M Joe	65.00		5.00		School Project	30.00
York, Kelly	50.00					
Walker, Peggy	30.00					
Franklin, M/M Bob	75.00	5.00		15.00		
Gilles, Don	40.00		10.00			
Shields, Lou	200.00					
White, M/M Ron	80.00		20.00			
Howe, Art	100.00	10.00	20.00		Choir Robes	50.00
Plunkett, M/M Stan	60.00				Youth Trip	40.00
Robbins, Nancy	75.00			5.00		
Lyon, M/M Bill	50.00					
Clark, M/M David	80.00		20.00		Parking Lot	20.00
Bowers, James	40.00			10.00		
Burr, Cindy	60.00					
TOTALS	1,490.00	25.00	85.00	100.00		180.00

Handling offerings with care will generate credibility. Few happenings can cause more consternation in a church than just the possibility that the offerings have been mishandled. And yet many churches leave the door wide open or at least ajar for problems with the handling of offerings. Often overlooked is the fact that sound controls over the offering protect church leaders in the event of false accusations regarding mishandling of funds.

All funds received should be recorded to reflect the date, the nature of the offering, and the name of the donor, if this information has been provided, and the donation amount by donor. The bulk of the income for a church is received in Sunday offerings. Counting sheets are used by offering tellers to record the offerings in detail. Non-offering income for churches and other organizations should be receipted in detail. Funds received in the church office between Sundays may be held over for inclusion in the next deposit, but they must be held in a secure place.

> **Idea**
>
> So, how does a church avoid having problems with the handling of offerings? Procedures vary from church to church. It is impossible to totally eliminate all problems. But handling church funds with integrity will always start with written procedures which incorporate the guidelines on pages 120-22.

Use of offering envelopes

Donors should be encouraged to donate by check and use offering envelopes for designated gifts (without an adequate paper trail, the mishandling of designated gifts may occur) and cash. Checks, payable to the church, are more difficult to steal than cash. Loose cash could more easily be removed without detection during the cash collection and counting process. The money counters should verify that the contents of the offering envelopes are identical to any amounts written on the outside of the envelopes.

Checks still provide proof of contributions for IRS purposes for single gifts of less than $250. The use of offering envelopes is essential when cash is given since loose cash in the offering plate does not qualify the donor for a tax deduction.

Offering envelopes should be retained in the church office. Their retention is important if individual contributions need to be verified.

Handling Outgoing Funds

Payment of expenses

One of the most important principles of handling funds is to pay virtually all expenses by check. The use of the petty cash fund should be the only exception to payment by check. Cash from a deposit should never be used to pay expenses.

If checks are prepared manually, a large desk-type checkbook is often helpful. Such a checkbook usually has three checks to a page and large stubs on which to write a full description of each expenditure. But most churches and other nonprofit organizations should be using computer-prepared checks that provide a stub with adequate space to identify the type of expense and account number(s) charged.

Use preprinted, consecutively numbered checks. All spoiled checks should be marked "void" and kept on file with the cancelled checks.

In some instances, it may be wise to require two signatures on every check or on checks over a certain amount. In other situations, one signature may be appropriate. The level of controls over the funds will help determine if more than one signature is necessary. Access to a checking account should generally be limited to no more than two or three individuals. A church pastor should not have access to the checking account. Checks should never be signed and delivered to anyone without completing the payee and the amount.

Caution

Checks should not be written until near the time there are funds available to cover them. Some organizations write checks when bills are due without regard to available cash. Checks are held for days, weeks, or sometimes months until they are released for payment. This is an extremely confusing practice that makes it very difficult to determine the actual checkbook balance.

The use of check request forms, including the approval by the appropriate church office or committee, is often a good expense-control procedure. Large churches may use a formal purchase order system. In either case, oral requests for funds should not be permitted.

Every check should have some type of written document to support it—an invoice, petty cash receipt, payroll summary, and so on. If such support is not available for some good reason, a memo should be written to support the expenditure. For example, an honorarium paid to a visiting speaker would not be supported by an invoice but should be documented by indicating the date of the speaking engagement and the event.

Occasionally it may be necessary to advance funds before supporting documentation is available (for example, a travel advance for future travel). In these instances, the treasurer must devise a system to ensure documentation is provided on a timely basis and any excess funds are returned.

Payments to vendors should be based on *original* copies of invoices. Payments should not be based on month-end statements that do not show the detail of the service or products provided. After payment has been made, all supporting material should be filed in a paid-bills file in alphabetical order by payee.

Expense approval and recording

If funds are approved in a church or other organization budget, this may be sufficient authority for the treasurer to pay the bills. In other instances, the approval of department heads or supervising personnel may be appropriate. Expenses that exceed the budget may need specific approval.

2008 CHURCH AND NONPROFIT TAX & FINANCIAL GUIDE

CASH EXPENSE REPORT

Name: Pastor Frank Morris
Address: 3801 North Florida Avenue
Miami, FL 33168
Period Covered: From: 6-01-07 To: 6-14-07

DATE	TRAVEL								OTHER *		ACCOUNT to be Charged
	City	Purpose of Travel	Brkfast	Lunch	Dinner	Snack	Lodging	Trans.	Description	Amount	
6-02-07									Lunch w/Bob Cox	18.21	644-002
6-06-07	Atlanta, GA	Continuing Ed. Sem.		10.80	13.40	2.10	90.50	265.08	Tips	8.00	644-010
6-06-07	" "	" " " "	6.40								644-010
6-06-07									Lunch w/Al Lane	12.80	641-002
6-14-07									Lunch w/Sam Lee	11.12	641-002
	TOTAL CASH EXPENSES		6.40	10.80	13.40	2.10	90.50	265.08		50.13	

*If this is entertainment, please use the entertainment worksheet on the back of this form.

Frank Morris   6-16-07
Signature (person requesting reimbursement) Date

Bob Davis   6-16-07
Approved by   Date

Total cash expenses 438.41
Personal auto business mileage 96.52
(Complete worksheet on the back of this form.)
199 miles X 48.5 ¢ per mile
Less travel advance .... (300.00)
Balance due 234.93
Refund due organization ....

PERSONAL AUTO BUSINESS MILEAGE

Date	Purpose/Destination	Miles	Account to be charged
6-01-07	Calls/Valley View Rest Home	23	638-000
6-02-07	Brown Funeral Home/Harold Boone	18	"
6-03-07	Calls/Various Homes	20	"
6-06-07	Calls/Memorial Hospital	15	"
6-05-07	Kiwanis Speaker/Pat's Cafeteria	25	"
6-07-07	Calls/Various Homes	10	"
6-08-07	Calls/St. Luke's Hospital	17	"
6-09-07	Calls/Cannon Nursing Home	12	"
6-10-07	Calls/Various Homes	8	"
6-12-07	Calls/Memorial Hospital	15	"
6-15-07	Ministerial Convention/Webb City	36	"
	TOTAL MILES TRAVELED	199	

To mileage summary on page one

ENTERTAINMENT WORKSHEET
(Expenses paid in behalf of individuals(s) other than the person filing this expense report.)

Date	Persons Entertained	Purpose of Entertainment	Place	Amount
6-02-07	M/M Bob Cox	Prospective Members	Olive Garden	18.21
6-06-07	Al Lane	Discuss Ch. Bldg Plans	Chi-Chi's	12.80
6-14-07	Sam Lee	Church Goals w/Bd. Chair	Damon's	11.12
			TOTAL AMOUNT SPENT	42.13

To "other" expense column on page one

Although every organization should have a budget, many do not. Even without a budget, routine expenses for utilities, salaries, and mortgage payments normally do not need specific approval before payment by the treasurer.

All checks should be recorded in a cash disbursements journal. The type of expense is reflected in the proper column in a manually prepared journal. Expense account numbers are used to identify the type of expense in a computerized journal. Expenses should be categorized in sufficient detail to provide an adequate breakdown of expenses on the periodic financial statements.

Petty cash system

To avoid writing numerous checks for small amounts, it is wise to have a petty cash fund (with a fixed base amount) from which to make small payments. For example, if the church office needs a roll of stamps, the use of the petty cash fund for the expense is more efficient than writing a check for the minor amount.

A petty cash fund of $50 or $100 is often adequate for small organizations. Large organizations may have multiple petty cash funds in various departments. The amount of the fund may vary based on need, such as the average per month petty cash expenditures.

As funds are disbursed from the petty cash fund, a slip detailing the expense is completed and placed in the petty cash box. If an invoice or receipt is available, it should be attached to the petty cash slip for filing. The petty cash slips are kept with the petty cash. At all times, the total of the unspent petty cash and the petty cash slips should equal the fixed amount of the petty cash fund.

> **Idea**
>
> Virtually every organization should have a petty cash fund—large organizations may have petty cash funds in every department. Adequate physical and accounting controls must be established over each fund to ensure proper use and reimbursement of the fund.

When the cash in the fund is getting low, a check is written payable to "Petty Cash Fund" for an amount equal to the expense slips plus or minus any amounts the fund is out of balance. The check is cashed and the cash returns the fund to the fixed balance. Expenses are allocated and recorded based on the purposes reflected on the slips.

Accounting Records

Accounting systems differ in shape, size, complexity, and efficiency. The objectives of the system should be to measure and control financial activities and to provide financial information to an organization's governing body, a congregation, and donors. In choosing the accounting records for your organization, the most important consideration is the ability of the individual(s) keeping the records.

Cash and accrual methods

Most small-to-medium-size churches and nonprofit organizations use the cash or modified cash basis of accounting. These methods do not conform to generally accepted accounting standards (GAAP). When the accrual basis of accounting is required for audit purposes, the cash basis is often used throughout the year with the conversion to accrual at year-end.

Advantages of cash method

Under this method, revenue is recorded only when cash is received, and expenses are recorded when they are paid. For example, office supplies expense is shown in the month when the bill is paid, even though the supplies were received and used in the previous month. Pledges are not recorded as receivables, and the revenue from pledges is recorded as the cash is received.

The primary advantage of the cash method is its simplicity. It is easier for nonaccountants to understand and keep records on this basis. When financial statements are required, the treasurer just summarizes the transactions from the checkbook stubs or runs the computer-prepared financial statements with fewer adjusting entries required. For smaller organizations, the difference between financial results on the cash and on the accrual basis are often not significantly different.

Advantages of accrual method

Many organizations use the accrual method of accounting when the cash basis does not accurately portray the financial picture. Under the accrual method, revenue is recorded when earned. For example, a church charges a fee for the use of the fellowship hall for a wedding. Under accrual accounting, the revenue is recorded in the month earned even though the cash might not be received until a later month.

Under accrual accounting, expenses are recorded when incurred. For example, telephone expense is recorded in the month when the service occurs although the bill may not be paid until the next month.

> **Idea**
>
> Even when obtaining an accrual basis audit, you can keep your books on the cash basis during the year and record journal entries on the last day of the year to convert to accrual. Too many organizations struggle to keep their books on the accrual basis (recording accounts receivable, accounts payable, etc.) when their financial life would be much simpler if the cash basis were used.

Generally accepted accounting principles for nonprofit organizations require the use of accrual basis accounting. Organizations that have their books audited by Certified Public Accountants and want the CPAs to report that the financial statements appear according to "generally accepted accounting principles" (GAAP) must either keep their records on the accrual basis or make the appropriate adjustments at the end of the year to convert to this basis. Financial statements prepared on a cash or other comprehensive basis may qualify under GAAP if the financial statements are not materially different from those prepared on an accrual basis.

Modified cash method

The modified cash method of accounting is a combination of certain features of the cash and accrual methods. For example, accounts payable may be recorded when a bill is received although other payables or receivables are not recorded. The modified cash method portrays the financial picture more accurately than the cash method but not as well as the full accrual method.

Fund accounting

Fund accounting (or accounting by classes of net assets) provides an excellent basis for stewardship reporting. It is a system of accounting in which separate records are kept for resources donated to an organization that are restricted by donors or outside parties to certain specified purposes or uses.

GAAP requires that net assets be broken down into the following three classes, based on the presence or absence of donor-imposed restrictions and their nature:

> **Remember**
>
> Fund accounting does not necessarily require multiple bank accounts. One bank account is all that is usually necessary. However, it may be appropriate to place restricted funds into a separate bank account to ensure that the funds are not inadvertently spent for other purposes.

- ▶ **Permanently restricted.** These assets are not available for program expenses, payments to creditors, or other organizational needs. An example is an endowment gift with a stipulation that the principal is permanently not available for spending but the investment income from the principal may be used in current operations.

- ▶ **Temporarily restricted.** These assets may be restricted by purpose or time, but the restrictions are not permanent. An example of the purpose-restricted gift is a gift for a certain project or for the purchase of some equipment. An example of a time-restricted gift is a contribution in the form of a trust, annuity, or term endowment (the principal of the gift is restricted for a certain term of time).

- ▶ **Unrestricted.** These net assets may be used for any of the organization's purposes. According to accounting standards, "the only limits on unrestricted net assets are broad limits resulting from the nature of the organization and the purposes specified in its articles of incorporation or bylaws."

Donor-imposed restrictions normally apply to the use of net assets and not to the use of specific assets. Only donors or outside parties may "restrict" funds given to a nonprofit organization. The organization's board may not "restrict" monies—they may only "designate" funds. For example, if a donor gives money for a new church organ, the funds should be placed in a restricted fund. If the church board sets funds aside in a debt retirement fund, this is a designated fund, a subdesignation of unrestricted net assets.

Records Retention

Proper maintenance of corporate documents and records is critical from both management and legal aspects. An organization's preparedness for a financial or IRS audit, legal action and/or response, public inquiry, and loss by theft or natural catastrophe, among other things, depends largely on keeping accurate records for as long as necessary.

The following is a partial listing of recommended retention times for several types of corporate records. Progressive churches and nonprofit organizations will retain many of these documents on their computer network.

Permanent Records:

Accounting

Audit reports of independent accountants or internal auditors

Checks used for important payments; *i.e.,* taxes, property, etc.

Fixed asset records, including depreciation schedules

End-of-year financial statements

Tax and information returns (state and federal)

Legal

Articles of incorporation and bylaws

Corporate charter, constitution

IRS examinations, rulings comments

Litigation-related documents

Board and executive committee minutes

Tax-exemption application and approval letter

Contracts and leases (active)

Insurance matters (policies, claims, accident and fire inspection reports)

Leases

Three Years:

Accounting

Accounts payable and receivable documents

Bank reconciliations

Invoices (after payment)

Monthly financial reports and statements

Working papers (accounting, budgets, cash flow, audits)

Legal

Service contracts (after termination)

Seven Years:

Accounting

Bank statements and canceled checks

Brokerage statements

Credit card statements

Donor contributions (numbered receipts)

General ledger and journals

Sales invoices

Credit card statements

Legal

Contracts and leases (expired)

Accident reports (after settlement)

Employment tax records

Depreciation

Some organizations charge off or record land, buildings, and equipment as expense at the time of purchase. Other organizations capitalize land, buildings, and equipment at cost and do not record depreciation. Other organizations record land, buildings, and equipment at cost and depreciate them over their estimated useful life. GAAP requires this last method. This provides the most consistent and reasonable presentation of these transactions for financial reporting purposes.

Organizations may set dollar limits for the recording of buildings and equipment as assets. For example, one organization might properly expense all equipment purchases of less than $2,000 per item and record items as assets above that amount.

Nonprofit software

When many churches and other charities are formed, their accounting needs are very basic and may be served by accounting packages such as QuickBooks plus a nonintegrated donor or fund-raising accounting package. As a nonprofit grows, it is generally more effective to begin integrating donor software with a nonprofit's accounting system. Many packages feature links to donor packages.

Software with additional features generally causes the cost to jump significantly. The total for several key packages (general ledger, accounts payable, payroll, etc.) can easily run to $10,000 or more per organization. The more sophisticated software often requires the assistance of consultants in the installation and training process. Consider the total costs, software and installation consulting, before making a software decision.

Entry-level accounting systems often provide only basic financial statement customizations. Moving to higher-level packages adds the ability to customize the look of financial statements to the specifications of the board, auditors, and management.

> **Remember**
>
> Software providers that have large numbers of users are more likely to continue to update the software regularly. Widely used products also tend to have fewer bugs, more enhancement releases, and better training and consultant availability.

It is not unusual for a nonprofit to grow so that larger account numbers are needed. These additional characters are often used to represent different funds or projects/grants that are being tracked for reporting purposes.

New accounting options are available through application service providers (ASP). Under the ASP model, organizations log on to a website and enter their data into a central computer that is far removed from the users' operations. Only those with the proper security access can see the data. Over the Internet, it's available anytime. Software upgrades can be implemented more easily under the ASP approach.

Before purchasing an accounting software package, here are a few questions to help you evaluate key product features:

- Does the software allow you to adequately track donor-restricted funds? This includes revenue, expense, and beginning- and end-of-year balances for each donor-restricted fund.

- Does it allow an account number consistent with the account numbers of your organization? Examine your account code needs carefully in comparison with software packages.

- Does the software offer security? Application access should be limited by program and user.

- Do the reports generated by the system meet the needs of your organization? Do the reports adequately reflect comparisons between actual revenues and expenses versus budgets?

An excellent summary of nonprofit software prepared by Nick B. Nicholaou, President, Ministry Business Services, Inc., P.O. Box 1567, Huntington Beach, CA 92647 (714-840-5900, www.mbsinc.com) is reprinted with permission on pages 133-36. Included are the number of active users, how long the vendor has been in business, technical support hours, and how often the vendor updates its software.

The symbol ■ is used on those options currently available and that they provide directly. The symbol ▰ is used on those options the provider offers through an outside (third-party) source. Some providers rely on QuickBooks for their accounting modules.

Financial Reports

In preparing financial reports, there is one basic rule: Prepare different reports for different audiences. For example, a church board would normally receive a more detailed financial report than the church membership. Department heads in a nonprofit organization might receive reports that only relate to their department.

Financial statements should

- ▶ be easily comprehensible so that any person taking the time to study them will understand the financial picture;

- ▶ be concise so that the person studying them will not get lost in detail;

- ▶ be all-inclusive in scope and embrace all activities of the organization;

Key Issue

"Dashboard" financial reporting is increasingly used by nonprofits. It gets its name because it's like a financial dashboard—with gauges, redlines, and warning lights. It cuts through the barrage of uninterrupted data and delivers a clear view of the organization's performance. It often includes a visualization of historical information and personalized reports for key staff members.

Church and Ministry Management Systems
2008 Survey

(Feature comparison chart across the following products: ACS Technologies, Acts Group, Blackbaud, By The Book, C.A.A. Ministries, CCIS Church Software, CDM+, Church Community Builder, Church Windows, Concordia Technology Solutions, ConnectionPower.com, Diakonia, Excellerate, Fellowship Technologies, Group Publishing, Helpmate Technology Solutions, Logos Management Software, Membership Plus, MyFlock.com, Nuverb Systems, People Driven Software, PowerChurch Software, QuickBooks Nonprofit Edition, Shelby Systems, Specialty Software, Vian.)

Features surveyed:

- Software is Focused for Church Management
- Software is Focused for Parachurch Donor Management
- Congregation / Donor Database
- Can Separately Track Multiple Congregations
- Can Move a Family Member w/Their Data Intact
- Individual **and** Family Photos
- Prints Color Photo Directories
- Tracks Individual's Communication Preferences (Mail, Email, Fax, etc)
- Prints U.S. Postal Bar Codes
- Certified Postal CASS/PAVE
- National Change of Address (NCOA) Updates
- Tracks Contribution of Gifts in Kind
- Gifts in Kind Can Satisfy Pledge without Setting GIK Value
- Can Post Gifts Received via Website
- Can Store Check & Envelope Images
- Can Reassign Envelope Numbers
- Statements Can Be Automatically Sent via Email
- Tracks Attendance
- Has Security / Check-In Capability
- Manages Small Groups
- Facility / Equipment Calendar Scheduler
- Calendar Scheduler Can Feed Ministry's Website
- Retreat / Event Registrations with A/R Tracking
- Can Post Event Registrations Received via Website
- Bookstore (Inventory / POS) Module
- General Ledger
- Automatically Tracks Multiple Fund Balances
- Automatically Balances Funds when Transferring Between Funds
- Has a Secure, Unalterable Audit Trail (not just password protected)
- Can Select Either Fixed (Straight Line) or Variable (Seasonal) Budgeting
- Graphic Analysis
- Fixed Assets Tracking (Inventory, Depreciation, Maintenance, etc)
- Accounts Payable
- Can Set Up as Either Accrual or Cash Basis
- Invoices Can Be Automatically Distributed to Expense Accts
- Annual 1099's
- Purchase Order Tracking (Authorization Process, Budget & GL Interface)
- Payroll with Minister's Salary Capabilities (Housing, SECA, etc)
- Time Clock Interface
- Payroll ACH Direct Deposit
- Accrues Vacation & Sick Time Available
- Vacation Scheduler w/ Ability to Show Composite Schedule
- All Federal & State Payroll Tax Forms
- Workers' Comp Audit
- Can Send Individually-Addressed Bulk Email
- Email Can Have Attachments
- Bulk Email is Mail Merge Capable
- Data Accessible in Real-Time via PDA (Palm, PocketPC, etc)
- Can be Network Based w/ Multiple Concurrent User Access
- Intranet / Internet Web Browser Interface
- Congregants Can Update Contact Info Online
- Users Can Add / Modify Fields to Database
- Data is Accessible & Fully Exportable in Multiple Formats
- Includes Dashboard
- Field-Level Access / Entry Security
- Denomination "Editions" Available
- Runs on Ministry's Local / Internal Server
- Runs Hosted on Off-Site Hosted Server
- If Hosted, Server(s) is Geographically Mirrored
- If Hosted, Server(s) is Multi-Homed to Different Internet Backbones

Church Management Software Providers — 2008 Survey
Compiled by Ministry Business Services, Inc.

ACS Technologies
Phone: (800) 736-7425
Email: solutions@acstechnologies.com
Web: www.acstechnologies.com
Company Founded in 1978
Years Marketing CMS: 30
Ministries Currently Using: 23000
Number on Team: 320
Tech Support: 9a-8p (-6p F) Eastern
Last Major Release: 8/2007
Updates per Year: Ongoing Via Web

By The Book
Phone: (800) 554-9116
Email: info@bythebook.com
Web: www.bythebook.com
Company Founded in 1991
Years Marketing CMS: 16
Ministries Currently Using: 1125
Number on Team: 5
Tech Support: 8a-5p (-12p F) Central
Last Major Release: 6/2006
Updates per Year: Ongoing Via Web

CDM+
Phone: (877) 891-4236
Email: sales@cdmplus.com
Web: www.cdmplus.com
Company Founded in 1986
Years Marketing CMS: 21
Ministries Currently Using: 3600
Number on Team: 20
Tech Support: 8:30a-7p (-5p F) Eastern
Last Major Release: 7/2007
Updates per Year: Ongoing Via Web

Acts Group
Phone: (877) 564-8300
Email: drmiller@actsgroup.net
Web: www.actsgroup.net
Company Founded in 2003
Years Marketing CMS: 1
Ministries Currently Using: 15
Number on Team: 8
Tech Support: Online 24•7
Last Major Release: 9/2007
Updates per Year: Ongoing Via Web

C.A.A. Ministries
Phone: (706) 864-4055
Email: mike@caaministries.org
Web: www.caaministries.org
Company Founded in 2005
Years Marketing CMS: 2
Ministries Currently Using: 250
Number on Team: 4
Tech Support: 8a-7p Eastern
Last Major Release: 2/2007
Updates per Year: 1

Church Community Builder
Phone: (866) 242-1199
Email: solutions@churchcommunity-builder.com
Web: www.churchcommunitybuilder.com
Company Founded in 2001
Years Marketing CMS: 7
Ministries Currently Using: 750
Number on Team: 15
Tech Support: 7a-5p Mountain
Last Major Release: 8/2007
Updates per Year: 6

Blackbaud
Phone: (800) 443-9441
Email: solutions@blackbaud.com
Web: www.blackbaud.com
Company Founded in 1981
Years Marketing CMS: 15
Ministries Currently Using: 1000
Number on Team: 900
Tech Support: Online 24•7
Last Major Release: 8/20007
Updates per Year: 2

CCIS Church Software
Phone: (800) 295-7551
Email: sales@ccissoftware.com
Web: www.ccissoftware.com
Company Founded in 1981
Years Marketing CMS: 27
Ministries Currently Using: 6487
Number on Team: 60
Tech Support: 8a-5p Eastern
Last Major Release: 1/2007
Updates per Year: 2

Church Windows
Phone: (800) 533-5227
Email: info@churchwindows.com
Web: www.churchwindows.com
Company Founded in 1986
Years Marketing CMS: 22
Ministries Currently Using: 10000
Number on Team: 28
Tech Support: 9a-6p Eastern
Last Major Release: 4/2007
Updates per Year: 2

Church Management Software Providers — 2008 Survey *(continued)*
Compiled by Ministry Business Services, Inc.

Concordia Technology Solutions
Phone: (800) 325-2399
Email:
  softwaresales@shepherdsstaff.org
Web: www.cts.cph.org
Company Founded in 1869
Years Marketing CMS: 25
Ministries Currently Using: 7500
Number on Team: 14
Tech Support: 7:30a-5p Central
Last Major Release: 4/2007
Updates per Year: 1

ConnectionPower.com
Phone: (800) 801-9297
Email: allen@connectionpower.com
Web: www.connectionpower.com
Company Founded in 2002
Years Marketing CMS: 4
Ministries Currently Using: 3000
Number on Team: 20
Tech Support: 7a-5p Pacific
Last Major Release: 8/2007
Updates per Year: Ongoing Via Web

Diakonia
Phone: (800) 325-6642
Email: info@faithfulsteward.com
Web: www.faithfulsteward.com
Company Founded in 1992
Years Marketing CMS: 13
Ministries Currently Using: 1051
Number on Team: 4
Tech Support: 9a-5p Central
Last Major Release: 1/2007
Updates per Year: Varies

Excellerate
Phone: (888) 371-6878
Email: info@msdweb.com
Web: www.excellerate.com
Company Founded in 1989
Years Marketing CMS: 10
Ministries Currently Using: 1175
Number on Team: 4
Tech Support: 9a-5p Central
Last Major Release: 1/2007
Updates per Year: 3

Fellowship Technologies
Phone: (866) 690-1104
Email: sales@fellowshiptech.com
Web: www.fellowshiptech.com
Company Founded in 2004
Years Marketing CMS: 4
Ministries Currently Using: 620
Number on Team: 59
Tech Support: 6a-10p, 7 Days Central
Last Major Release: 5/2007
Updates per Year: Ongoing Via Web

Group Publishing
Phone: (800) 747-1565
Email: buzzinfo@group.com
Web: www.group.com/buzz
Company Founded in 1974
Years Marketing CMS: 1
Ministries Currently Using: 70
Number on Team: 4
Tech Support: 8a-5p Mountain
Last Major Release: 2/2007
Updates per Year: Ongoing Via Web

Helpmate Technology Solutions
Phone: (888) 858-3247
Email: sales@helpmate.net
Web: www.helpmate.net
Company Founded in 1996
Years Marketing CMS: 11
Ministries Currently Using: 1750
Number on Team: 6
Tech Support: 9:30a-5p Eastern
Last Major Release: 4/2006
Updates per Year: 1

Logos Management Software
Phone: (800) 266-3311
Email: dsmith@logoscms.com
Web: www.logoslbe.com
Company Founded in 1980
Years Marketing CMS: 27
Ministries Currently Using: 8400
Number on Team: 54
Tech Support: 6a-5p Pacific
Last Major Release: 7/2007
Updates per Year: 4

Membership Plus
Phone: (888) 459-0078
Email: sales@quickverse.com
Web: www.memplushome.com
Company Founded in 1988
Years Marketing CMS: 16
Ministries Currently Using: 40000
Number on Team: 25
Tech Support: 8a-5:30p Central
Last Major Release: 12/2006
Updates per Year: 2

Church Management Software Providers — 2008 Survey *(continued)*
Compiled by Ministry Business Services, Inc.

MyFlock.com
Phone: (866) 852-6648
Email: info@myflock.com
Web: www.myflock.com
Company Founded in 2001
Years Marketing CMS: 6
Ministries Currently Using: 400
Number on Team: 4
Tech Support: 8a-5p Eastern
Last Major Release: 8/2007
Updates per Year: 20

PowerChurch Software
Phone: (800) 486-1800
Email: info@powerchurch.com
Web: www.powerchurch.com
Company Founded in 1984
Years Marketing CMS: 23
Ministries Currently Using: 27000
Number on Team: 12
Tech Support: 9a-6p Eastern
Last Major Release: 11/2006
Updates per Year: 1

Specialty Software
Phone: (800) 568-6350
Email: sales@specialtysoftware.com
Web: www.specialtysoftware.com
Company Founded in 1983
Years Marketing CMS: 24
Ministries Currently Using: 5000
Number on Team: 10
Tech Support: 9a-5p Eastern
Last Major Release: 9/2007
Updates per Year: 4

Nuverb Systems
Phone: (888) 479-4636
Email: info@nuverb.com
Web: www.donarius.com
Company Founded in 1993
Years Marketing CMS: 9
Ministries Currently Using: 850
Number on Team: 1
Tech Support: 9a-5p Eastern
Last Major Release: 3/2007
Updates per Year: 20

QuickBooks Nonprofit Edition
Phone: (888) 729-1996
Email: www.quickbooks.com/callme
Web: www.quickbooks.com
Company Founded in 1983
Years Marketing CMS: 5
Ministries Currently Using: 28000
Number on Team: 130
Tech Support: 6a-6p Pacific
Last Major Release: 9/2006
Updates per Year: 1

Vian
Phone: (908) 537-4642
Email: vian@vian.com
Web: www.vian.com
Company Founded in 1982
Years Marketing CMS: 23
Ministries Currently Using: 3650
Number on Team: 2
Tech Support: 4:30p-6p Eastern
Last Major Release: 3/2007
Updates per Year: Ongoing Via Web

People Driven Software
Phone: (866) 737-9273
Email: info@peopledrivensoftware.com
Web: www.peopledrivensoftware.com
Company Founded in 2002
Years Marketing CMS: 5
Ministries Currently Using: 650
Number on Team: 10
Tech Support: 9a-5p Eastern
Last Major Release: 8/2007
Updates per Year: 12

Shelby Systems
Phone: (800) 877-0222
Email: mktg@shelbyinc.com
Web: www.shelbyinc.com
Company Founded in 1976
Years Marketing CMS: 31
Ministries Currently Using: 8700
Number on Team: 116
Tech Support: 7a-6p Central
Last Major Release: 5/2007
Updates per Year: Ongoing Via Web

➤ have a focal point for comparison so that the person reading them will have some basis for making a judgment (usually this will be a comparison with a budget or data from the corresponding period of the previous year); and

➤ be prepared on a timely basis (the longer the delay after the end of the period, the longer the time before corrective action can be taken).

For additional reading, see the *Accounting and Financial Reporting Guide for Christian Ministries* (Evangelical Joint Accounting Committee, 800-323-9473) and *Financial and Accounting Guide for Not-for-Profit Organizations* by Melvin J. Gross Jr., John H. McCarthy, and Nancy E. Shelmon (John Wiley & Sons).

Statement of activity

The statement of activity (also referred to as a statement of revenues and expenses) reflects an organization's support and revenue, expenses, and changes in net assets for a certain period of time. It shows the sources of an organization's income and how the resources were used. The form of the statement will depend on the type of organization and accounting method used. But the statement must present the change in unrestricted, temporarily restricted, permanently restricted, and total net assets.

Many smaller organizations will have several lines for support and revenue such as contributions, sales of products, investment income, and so on. Expenses are often listed by natural classification such as salaries, fringe benefits, supplies, and so on.

Organizations desiring to meet GAAP accounting standards must reflect functional expenses (for example, by program, management and general, fund-raising, and membership development) in the statement of activity or footnotes. Some organizations will also show expenses by natural classification in the statement of activity or in the footnotes. While the reporting of expenses by natural classification is not generally required under GAAP, readers of the financial statements will often find the additional reporting very helpful.

Statement of financial position

A statement of financial position shows assets, liabilities, and net assets as of the end-of-period date. This statement is also called a balance sheet because it shows how the two sides of the accounting equation (assets minus liabilities equal net assets) "balance" in your organization.

Anything an organization owns that has a money value is an asset. Cash, land, buildings, furniture, and fixtures are examples of assets. Anything the organization owes is a liability. Liabilities might include amounts owed to suppliers (accounts payable) or to the bank (notes payable and other amounts due).

SAMPLE CHART OF ACCOUNTS FOR A CHURCH

Assets (101)
- 101 Cash and cash equivalents
- 110 Prepaid expenses
- 120 Short-term investments
- Land, buildings, and equipment
  - 160 Church buildings
  - 161 Parsonage
  - 162 Furnishings
- 180 Long-term investments

Liabilities (200)
- 201 Accounts payable
- 210 Notes payable
- 220 Long-term debt

Revenues and Support (300)
- Contributions
  - 301 Regular offerings
  - 302 Sunday school offerings
  - 303 Missions offerings
  - 304 Building fund offerings
  - 319 Other offerings
- Investment income
  - 321 Interest income
  - 322 Rental income
- Other income
  - 331 Tape sales
  - 335 Other sales
  - 339 Other income

Expenses (400-500)
- Salaries and wages
  - 401 Salary including cash housing allowance
  - 402 Tax-deferred payments (TSA/IRA)
- Benefits
  - 411 Pension
  - 412 Social security (SECA) reimbursement
  - 413 Social security (FICA)
  - 414 Medical expense reimbursement
  - 415 Insurance premiums
- Supplies
  - 421 Postage
  - 422 Literature and printing
  - 423 Office supplies
  - 424 Maintenance supplies
  - 425 Food
  - 426 Kitchen supplies
  - 427 Flowers
  - 439 Other supplies
- Travel and entertainment
  - 441 Auto expense reimbursements
  - 442 Vehicle rental
  - 449 Other travel expense
- 450 Continuing education
- Insurance
  - 461 Workers' Compensation
  - 462 Health insurance
  - 463 Property insurance
  - 469 Other insurance
- Benevolences
  - 471 Denominational budgets
  - 479 Other benevolences
- Services and professional fees
  - 481 Speaking honoraria
  - 482 Custodial services
  - 483 Legal and audit fees
  - 489 Other fees
- Office and occupancy
  - 491 Rent
  - 492 Telephone
  - 493 Utilities
  - 494 Property taxes
  - 499 Other office and occupancy
- 500 Depreciation
- 510 Interest expense
- Other
  - 591 Banquets
  - 592 Advertising

Suffix digits may be used to indicate the functional expense category, such as

- -10 Program expenses
- -11 Pastoral
- -12 Education
  - -121 Sunday school
  - -122 Vacation Bible school
  - -123 Camps and retreats
- -13 Music and worship
- -14 Missions
- -15 Membership and evangelism
- -16 Youth
- -17 Singles
- -18 Seniors
- -20 Management and general
  - -21 Church plant
  - -22 Parsonages
  - -23 Office
- -30 Fund-raising

Shenandoah Valley Church
Statement of Activity
Year Ended June 30, 2008

	Unrestricted	Temporarily Restricted	Permanently Restricted	Total
Support and revenues				
Contributions				
Regular offerings	$260,000			$260,000
Sunday school offerings	45,000			45,000
Missions offerings	50,000			50,000
Other offerings	25,000	$10,000		35,000
Investment income				
Interest income	1,000		$2,000	3,000
Rental income	3,000			3,000
Total revenues	384,000	10,000	2,000	396,000
Expenses				
Program expenses				
Worship	25,000	9,000		34,000
Sunday school	35,000			35,000
Youth	30,000			30,000
	90,000	9,000		99,000
Management and general	296,000			296,000
Fund-raising	5,000			5,000
Total expenses	391,000	9,000		400,000
Change in net assets	(7,000)	1,000	2,000	(4,000)
Net assets at beginning of year	645,000	4,000	18,000	667,000
Net assets at end of year	$ 638,000	$ 5,000	$ 20,000	$ 663,000

Expenses incurred were for:

	Worship	Sunday School	Youth	Mgt. & Gen.	Fund Raising	Total
Salaries, wages, and benefits	$5,000	$6,000		$131,000		$142,000
Supplies	25,000	24,000	$24,000			73,000
Travel			1,000	10,000	$5,000	16,000
Insurance	20,000			20,000		40,000
Benevolences						
Denominational budgets				20,000		20,000
Other benevolences				50,000		50,000
Services and professional fees	4,000	5,000	5,000			14,000
Office and occupancy				30,000		30,000
Depreciation	10,000			10,000		
Interest	25,000			25,000		
	$ 34,000	$ 35,000	$ 30,000	$296,000	$ 5,000	$400,000

This is a multicolumn presentation of a statement of activity. Reporting of expenses by natural classification (at bottom of page), though often useful, is not required.

Castle Creek Church
Statement of Activity
Year Ended June 30, 2008

Changes in unrestricted net assets:
Revenues

Contributions	$ 141,000
Fees	6,250
Income on long-term investments	5,400
Other	20,100
Total unrestricted revenues	172,750

Expenses (Note A)

Salaries, wages, and benefits	90,500
Supplies	3,000
Travel	5,000
Insurance	7,500
Benevolences	
Denominational budgets	10,000
Other benevolences	20,000
Services and professional fees	8,000
Office and occupancy	7,000
Depreciation	5,000
Interest	20,000
Total expenses	176,000

Net assets released from restrictions:

Satisfaction of program restrictions	2,000
Expiration of time restrictions	3,000
Total net assets released from restrictions	5,000
Increase in unrestricted net assets	1,750

Changes in temporarily restricted net assets:

Contributions	23,000
Net assets released from restrictions	(5,000)
Increase in temporarily restricted net assets	18,000

Changes in permanently restricted net assets:

Contributions	7,000
Increase in permanently restricted net assets	7,000
Increase in net assets	26,750
Net assets at beginning of year	910,000
Net assets at end of year	$936,750

Note A:
Functional expense breakdown:

Program expenses:	
Worship	$16,000
Sunday school	7,000
Youth	5,000
Management and general	145,500
Fund-raising	2,500
Total expenses	$176,000

This is an alternate, single-column presentation of a statement of activity. If the natural classification of expenses is shown in the body of the statement, as in this example, the functional expenses must be reflected in a footnote to meet accounting standards.

Hayward First Church
Statement of Financial Position
June 30, 2008 and 2007

	2008	2007
Assets		
Cash and cash equivalents	$20,000	$15,000
Prepaid expenses	5,000	4,000
Short-term investments	10,000	8,000
Land, buildings, and equipment:		
Church buildings	525,000	525,000
Parsonage	110,000	110,000
Furnishings	175,000	160,000
Long-term investments	30,000	25,000
Total assets	875,000	847,000
Liabilities and net assets		
Accounts payable	$8,000	$7,000
Notes payable	9,000	10,000
Long-term debt	195,000	205,000
Total liabilities	212,000	222,000
Net assets		
Unrestricted	638,000	601,000
Temporarily restricted (Note 1)	5,000	4,000
Permanently restricted (Note 2)	20,000	20,000
Total net assets	663,000	625,000
Total liabilities and net assets	$875,000	$847,000

Note 1: Restricted net assets result when a donor has imposed a stipulation to use the funds or assets contributed in a manner which is more limited than the broad purpose for which tax-exempt status is granted to an organization. For example, a church may receive a contribution to establish a scholarship fund with the principal and earnings available for scholarship payments. This gift is a temporarily restricted contribution. If the scholarship funds were all expended in the church's fiscal year when the gift was received, the contribution would be unrestricted.

Note 2: Permanently restricted contributions are those which contain a stipulation that will always be present. For example, if a scholarship gift is made with the stipulation that only the earnings from the fund may be spent for scholarships, this is a permanently restricted net asset.

The financial statements illustrated on pages 139-41 are presented based on Statement No. 117 issued by the Financial Accounting Standards Board (FASB) of the American Institute of Certified Public Accountants.

Common Nonprofit Financial Statement Errors

Statement of Financial Position

- **Omitting net assets by class.** Net assets must be categorized by unrestricted, temporarily restricted, and permanently restricted. When unrestricted net assets are subdivided into components such as net investment in plant, board-designated, and other, a total for all these components must be shown.

- **Reflecting negative balances in the temporarily restricted net asset class.** It is improper to show either a negative total of temporarily restricted net assets or a component of this net asset class, perhaps in a footnote to the financial statements. When the balance in a temporarily restricted account has been totally released, additional expenditures must be charged to the unrestricted class.

Statement of Activities

- **Reporting exchange transactions as temporarily restricted revenue.** All earned income should be reported as unrestricted revenue. Contributions with specific donor restrictions as to time or purpose and investment return relating to the investment of temporarily restricted contributions are the only types of temporarily restricted revenue.

- **Reporting fund-raising events, conferences, thrift shops, etc. as a net amount.** It is appropriate to show the two gross numbers (gross proceeds of an activity, less expenses of activity—net revenue from activity) for each activity in the statement of activities. The display of the gross data is typically shown in the revenue section of the statement unless expenses exceed revenue for this activity. In this case, the display is generally shown in the expense section.

- **Failure to recognize all gifts-in-kind revenue.** Examples of revenue that should be reflected include free rent and services provided by another organization.

- **Failure to report qualifying contributed services of volunteers.** All contributed services must be recorded unless the services do not meet the recognition criteria in Statement of Financial Account Standards 116 or there is no reasonable way to assign a value to the services.

- **Failure to disclose fund-raising expense.** Fund-raising expenses must be disclosed except in the very rare circumstances where these expenses are immaterial.

- **Failure to properly allocate expenses functionally.** Expenses must be allocated and reported functionally; *e.g.*, program, general and administration, fund-raising. Depreciation, interest, and occupancy expenses must be functionally allocated unless the amounts are immaterial.

- **Reporting expenses in either of the restricted classes of net assets.** Although losses may be reported in any class, all expenses should be reported as decreases in unrestricted net assets.

Statement of cash flows

The statement of cash flows provides information about the cash receipts and disbursements of your organization and the extent to which resources were obtained from, or used in, operating, investing, or financing activities. The direct method of presenting a cash flow statement starts by listing all sources of cash from operations during the period and deducts all operating outflows of cash to arrive at the net cash flow. The indirect method begins with the change in net assets and adjusts backwards to reconcile the change in net assets to net cash flows. The Financial Accounting Standards Board encourages the use of the direct presentation method.

Budgeting

A budget is an effective tool for allocating financial resources and planning and controlling spending even for smaller organizations. A budget matches anticipated inflows of resources with outflows of resources. Preparing a budget requires considerable effort. It includes looking back at revenue and expense trends. Projected plans and programs must be converted into estimated dollar amounts. Too many organizations budget expenses with some degree of precision and then set the income budget at whatever it takes to cover the total expenses. This is often a disastrous approach.

Separate budgets should be prepared for all funds of an organization. Even capital and debt-retirement funds should be budgeted. The separate budgets are then combined into a unified budget.

Line-item budgets within each fund reflect the projected cost of salaries, fringe benefits, utilities, maintenance, debt retirement, and other expenses. The line-item approach is generally used by a treasurer in reporting to department heads or other responsible individuals.

Program budgets are often presented to the board of a nonprofit organization or a church's membership. In this approach, the cost of a program is reflected rather than the cost of specific line-items such as salaries or fringe benefits.

Audits, Reviews, and Compilations

An annual audit, review, or compilation of the financial statements and the disclosure of the financial statements are key components of transparency, both within a church or other charity and to donors and the public. This flows directly from biblical principles: "This is the verdict: Light has come into the world, but men loved darkness instead of light because their deeds were evil. Everyone who does evil hates the light, and will not come into the light for fear that his deeds will be exposed" (John 3:19-20 NIV).

External audits, reviews, and compilations should be performed by an independent auditor who has no impairing relationship to the organization and has maximum objectivity. Internal audits are generally performed by members or those closely associated with the organization.

External audits, reviews, and compilations

An **audit** is a formal examination of financial statements intended to assess the accuracy and thoroughness of financial records. An independent CPA performs this procedure on a set of financial statements in order to render an opinion based on the accounting records provided. An unqualified audit opinion states that the financial statements are in conformity with accounting principles generally accepted in the United States (GAAP). Audits are performed according to auditing standards generally accepted in the United States (GAAS). An audit is more expensive than a review or compilation because an opinion on the accuracy of financial statements requires significantly more work than that involved in either a review or a compilation.

A **review** is the performance of limited procedures as a basis for expressing limited assurance on financial statements. Although not as comprehensive as an audit, a review provides more assurance than a compilation. A review report states that: 1) the accountants do not express an opinion on the financial statements and, 2) based on their review, they are not *aware* of any material modifications that should be made to the financial statements.

A review is less expensive than an audit but more expensive than a compilation. In performing this accounting service, the accountant must conform to the AICPA *Statements on Standards for Accounting and Review Services* (SSARS). ECFA requires that the compiled financial statements include disclosures and be prepared either in conformity with U.S. GAAP or the modified cash basis of accounting.

A **compilation** is the gathering of financial information and the creation of financial statements for an organization. A compilation involves no assurance on the financial statements, as the accountant simply assembles the financial statements for the organization. In performing this accounting service, the accountant must conform to SSARS. ECFA requires that the compiled financial statements include disclosures and be prepared either in conformity with U.S. GAAP or the modified cash basis of accounting.

> **Filing Tip**
>
> Independence is the cornerstone of the auditing profession. It means the auditor is not related to the entity and is therefore objective. The independent auditor should have no ties to management and no responsibility for governance of finance. The public can place faith in the audit function because an auditor is impartial and recognizes an obligation of fairness.

Internal audits

Members of the organization may form an audit committee to perform an internal audit to determine the validity of the financial statements. (Sample internal audit guidelines for churches are shown on page 145-49.) If the committee takes its task seriously, the result may be significant improvements in internal control and accounting procedures.

Church Internal Audit Guidelines

Financial statements

- Are monthly financial statements prepared on a timely basis and submitted to the organization's board?
- Do the financial statements include all funds (unrestricted, temporarily restricted, and permanently restricted)?
- Do the financial statements include a statement of financial condition and statement of activity?
- Are account balances in the financial records reconciled with amounts presented in financial reports?

Cash receipts

- **General**
  - Are cash handling procedures in writing?
  - Has the bank been notified to never cash checks payable to the church?
  - Are Sunday school offerings properly recorded and delivered to the money counters?
  - Are procedures established to care for offerings and monies delivered or mailed to the church office between Sundays?

- **Offering counting**
  - Are at least two members of the counting committee present when offerings are counted? (The persons counting the money should not include a pastor of the church or the church treasurer.)
  - Do money counters verify that the contents of the offering envelopes are identical to the amounts written on the outside of the envelopes?
  - Are all checks stamped with a restrictive endorsement stamp immediately after the offering envelope contents are verified?
  - Are money counters rotated so the same people are not handling the funds each week?
  - Are donor-restricted funds properly identified during the process of counting offerings?

➢ **Depositing of funds**
- Are two members of the offering counting team in custody of the offering until it is deposited in the bank, or placed in a night depository or the church's safe?
- Are all funds promptly deposited? Compare offering and other receipt records with bank deposits.
- Are all receipts deposited intact? Receipts should not be used to pay cash expenses.

➢ **Restricted funds**
- Are donations for restricted purposes properly recorded in the accounting records?
- Are restricted funds held for the intended purpose(s) and not spent on operating needs?

Donation records/receipting

➢ Are individual donor records kept as a basis to provide donor acknowledgments for all single contributions of $250 or more?

➢ If no goods or services (other than intangible religious benefits) were provided in exchange for a gift, does the receipt include a statement to this effect?

➢ If goods or services (other than intangible religious benefits) were provided in exchange for a gift, does the receipt
- inform the donor that the amount of the contribution that is deductible for federal income tax purposes is limited to the excess of the amount of any money and the value of any property contributed by the donor over the value of the goods and services provided by the organization, and
- provide the donor with a good faith estimate of the value of such goods and services?

➢ Are the donations traced from the weekly counting sheets to the donor records for a selected time period by the audit committee?

Cash disbursements

➢ Are all disbursements paid by check except for minor expenditures paid through the petty cash fund?

➢ Is written documentation available to support all disbursements?

➢ Has the church established an accountable reimbursement plan for expenses?

➢ Do employees report and substantiate expenses within 60 days of incurring the expense?

➢ Does the substantiation include original receipts and documentation of the time, place, amount, and purpose of expenditure?

➢ If a petty cash fund is used, are vouchers prepared for each disbursement from the fund?

- Are prenumbered checks used? Account for all the check numbers including voided checks.
- Are blank checks ever signed in advance? This should never be done.

Information reporting

- Has the church filed Form 990-T for gross unrelated business income over $1,000 per fiscal year, if required?
- Did the church make payments to recipients (other than corporations) of at least $10 in royalties or at least $600 in rents, payments for services, prizes and awards, or medical and healthcare payments?
- Did the church obtain W-9 for all applicable recipients and file Form 1099-MISC?
- Did the church provide Form 1099-INT to all recipients of interest totaling $600 or more during the calendar year?
- If the church operates a preschool or private school which is not separately incorporated, did the church file Form 5578 concerning a statement of racial nondiscrimination with the IRS?

Payroll tax reporting

- Does the church withhold and pay the employee's share of FICA taxes for all nonministerial employees?
- Does the church pay the employer's share of FICA taxes for all nonministerial employees?
- Did the church make timely deposits of employment taxes?
- Did the church file Form 941 for each quarter of the previous calendar year?
- Did the church verify that the totals from the four quarterly Forms 941 agree with the totals on Form W-3 prepared at year-end?
- Did the church provide Form W-2 to all persons classified as employees (including ministers) by January 31?
- Was Form W-2 and Transmittal Form W-3 provided to the IRS for all persons classified as employees (including ministers) by February 28?

Petty cash funds

- Is a petty cash fund used for disbursements of a small amount? If so, is the fund periodically reconciled and replenished based on proper documentation of the cash expenditures?

Bank statement reconciliation

➤ Are written bank reconciliations prepared on a timely basis? Test the reconciliation for the last month in the fiscal year. Trace transactions between the bank and the books for completeness and timeliness.

➤ Are there any checks that have been outstanding over three months?

➤ Are there any unusual transactions in the bank statement immediately following year-end? Obtain the bank statement for the first month after year-end directly from the bank for review by the audit committee. Otherwise, obtain the last bank statement (unopened) from the church treasurer.

Savings and investment accounts

➤ Are all savings and investment accounts recorded in the financial records? Compare monthly statements to the books.

➤ Are earnings or losses from savings and investment accounts recorded in the books?

Land, buildings, and equipment records

➤ Are there detailed records of land, buildings, and equipment including date acquired, description, and cost or fair market value at date of acquisition?

➤ Was a physical inventory of equipment taken at year-end?

➤ Have the property records been reconciled to the insurance coverages?

Accounts payable

➤ Is there a schedule of unpaid invoices including vendor name, invoice date, and due date?

➤ Are any of the accounts payable items significantly past due?

➤ Are there any disputes with vendors over amounts owed?

Insurance policies

➤ Has a schedule been prepared of insurance coverage in force? Does it reflect effective and expiration dates, kind and classification of coverages, maximum amounts of each coverage, premiums, and terms of payment?

➤ Is Workers' Compensation insurance being carried as provided by law in most states? Are all employees (and perhaps some independent contractors) covered under the Workers' Compensation policy?

Amortization of debt

- Is there a schedule of debt such as mortgages and notes?
- Have the balances owed to all lenders been confirmed directly in writing?
- Have the balances owed to all lenders been compared to the obligations recorded on the balance sheet?

Securities and other negotiable documents

- Does the church own any marketable securities or bonds? If so, are they kept in a safe-deposit box, and are two signatures (excluding a pastor's) required for access?
- Have the contents of the safe-deposit box been examined and recorded?

Copyright and licensing issues

- Does the church have a policy of prohibiting the unlawful duplication or use of copyrighted works?
- Does the church pay an annual fee to Christian Copyright Licensing, Inc., of Portland, Oregon, for the right to reproduce copyrighted music?
- Does the church have a policy which prohibits the showing of rented or purchased videos without authorization of the copyright owner?
- Does the church post a copyright notice at each photocopy machine?
- Does the church comply with all computer software licensing agreements?

General

- If the church operates a preschool, day care, or school, does the church comply with federal (and state) minimum wage and overtime requirements?
- If overtime payments are required, has the church taken steps to avoid paying overtime through compensatory time off?
- Does the church have a record retention policy specifying how long records should be kept?
- Are record retention and storage requirements formally considered at year-end?
- Do you know the location of the original deed of church property?
- Is the church in full compliance with restrictions imposed by the deed?
- Did the church refrain from participating in or directly opposing a particular candidate's political campaign?

- **Handling incoming funds.** The handling of incoming funds by a church or other charity is one of the most critical elements of the financial management process. The potential of embezzlement is often high at the point funds are received.

    Sound policies and procedures should be adopted and followed to ensure no funds are lost at the point of entry. Sound internal controls also protect the staff members or volunteers handling the funds. Pastors and ministry leaders should stay far away from handling funds.

- **Choosing an accounting method.** The choice of an accounting method has many implications for a church or other charity. Large charities generally use the accrual basis of accounting throughout the year and use the same approach for budgeting. The basis of accounting used for interim financial statements can be changed at year end by posting a few journal entries. Reverse the entries on the first day of the subsequent accounting year and the books are back to the previous accounting method. The following are a few of the accounting methods used:

    o   Cash basis through the year/accrual basis at year end.

    o   Modified cash through the year/accrual basis at year end.

    o   Cash basis through the year/cash basis at year end.

    To ensure comparative financial data, it is important that the same approach (accrual, modified cash, or cash) be used on the accounting records through the year as is used for budgeting purposes.

- **Audits.** Churches and other charities with significant financial activities (perhaps annual revenue of $1 million or more) should generally obtain a formal examination by an independent CPA of financial statements intended to assess the accuracy and thoroughness of the financial records—called an audit. Smaller organizations may opt for a review (limited procedures performed by a CPA as a basis for expressing limited assurance on financial statement) or a compilation which involves no assurance on the financial statements.

CHAPTER SEVEN

Charitable Gifts

In This Chapter

- Charitable gift options
- Percentage limitations
- Gifts that may not qualify as contributions
- Charitable gift timing
- Acknowledging and reporting charitable gifts
- Quid pro quo disclosure requirements
- Deputized fund-raising
- Short-term missions trips
- Other special charitable contribution issues

While most donors care more about the reason for giving than they do about the tax implications, the spirit of giving should never be reduced by unexpected tax results.

A gift is an unconditional transfer of cash or property with no personal benefit to the donor. The mere transfer of funds to a church or charitable nonprofit is not necessarily a gift. Thus, when a parent pays the college tuition for a child, there is no gift or charitable deduction.

If payments are made to a charity to receive something in exchange, the transaction is more in the nature of a purchase. The tax law states that a transfer to a nonprofit is not a contribution when made "with a reasonable expectation of financial return commensurate with the amount of the transfer." When one transfer comprises both a gift and a purchase, only the gift portion is deductible.

The two broad categories of charitable gifts are *outright* gifts and *deferred* gifts. Outright gifts require that the donor immediately transfer possession and use of the gift property to the donee. In deferred giving, the donor also makes a current gift, but the gift is of a future interest. Accordingly, actual possession and use of the gift property by the donee is deferred until the future.

Charitable contributions are deductible if given "to and for the use" of a "qualified" tax-exempt organization to be used under its control to accomplish its exempt purposes. ("Qualified" organizations are churches and other domestic 501[c][3] organizations.)

Three types of gifts commonly given to a church or other nonprofit organization are

➤ **Gifts without donor stipulations.** Contributions received without donor restriction (*e.g.,* "use where needed most") are generally tax-deductible.

➤ **Personal gifts.** Gifts made through an organization to an individual, where the donor has specified, by name, the identity of the person who is to receive the gift, generally are not tax-deductible. Processing of personal gifts through a church or nonprofit organization should be discouraged by the organization unless it is done as a convenience to donors and the ultimate recipients where communication between the two parties might otherwise be difficult (*e.g.,* a missionary supported by the organization who is serving in a foreign country).

> **Remember**
>
> The practice of raising funds by ministries with the gifts preferenced for the support of certain employees of the charity is often called deputized or staff-support fund-raising. The IRS acknowledges that deputized fund-raising is a widespread and legitimate practice, and contributions properly raised by this method are tax-deductible (see pages 181-84).

➤ **Donor restricted gifts.** Contributions may be restricted (also referred to as *designated*) by the donor for a specific exempt purpose of the organization rather than being given without donor stipulation. If the gifts are in support of the organization's exempt program activities and not restricted for an individual, they are generally tax-deductible.

If gifts are earmarked for a specific individual, no tax deduction is generally allowed unless the church or nonprofit organization exercises adequate discretion and control over the funds and they are spent for program activities of the organization (see pages 153-55 for preferenced gifts).

Tax-deduction receipts should not be issued to a donor for personal gifts, and the organization should affirmatively advise donors that the gifts are not tax-deductible.

Two fundamental concepts relating to donor-restricted gifts are charity control and donor preferences:

➤ **Charity control over donor-restricted gifts.** A common misconception is that the control a charity board must exercise over any donor-restricted gift is in conflict with, or contradictory to, stipulations by donors. *This is not true.* Some believe that organizations should not follow donor restrictions, from time to time, to demonstrate their control. *This is inappropriate.*

Board control and donor restrictions are really a "hand in glove" concept. It is not *either/or* but *both/and*! Restricted gifts must be used for a specific exempt purpose, whereas unrestricted gifts may be used for any exempt purpose.

The board must control all contributions to an exempt organization, unrestricted and restricted, to be used exclusively for its exempt purposes. In addition, the board must provide reasonable measures to assure that donor-restricted gifts are used for the intended exempt purpose(s).

Notifying the donor on the gift response vehicle that the charity will exercise control and discretion over the gift does not remove the donor's restriction placed on a gift. Charities must exercise control and discretion over all charitable gifts, whether unrestricted (may be used for any exempt purpose) or restricted (must be used for a specific purpose) by the donor.

Donor restrictions arise when a charity accepts contributions that are solicited for or restricted by a donor for a specific area of ministry, such as a program, project, or a type of missionary work (vs. missionary work anywhere in the world); *e.g.*, missionary work in Sri Lanka preferenced for a particular missionary. Unrestricted contributions have no implicit or explicit donor restrictions and are available to be used in any exempt operations of the charity.

Donors often like to retain some control over their gifts. However, if too much control is retained, the donor's income tax deduction may be endangered.

➤ **Donor preferences vs. restrictions.** In charitable giving, there is a distinction between a donor's restriction and a donor's preference. This distinction can make a difference between the donor's eligibility for a charitable tax deduction and no tax deduction.

The preferencing of gift does not dictate whether the gift is unrestricted or restricted. When a gift is preferenced to support a particular worker, the preferencing may qualify the gift for a charitable tax deduction, but other factors must be reviewed to determine whether the gift is unrestricted or restricted for accounting purposes.

> **Example 1:** Accompanying a gift, a donor communicates: "My preference is that the gift be used for scholarships. However, I give the charity permission to use the gift for any exempt purpose consistent with the charity's mission statement." This gift is an unrestricted gift because the charity has full discretion as to the use of the gift.
>
> **Example 2:** A prayer letter or appeal letter from a charity that conducts works in several countries describes the need for religious workers in India. The request is for funds preferenced to enable a particular worker employed by the charity to carry out certain work in India. A gift in response to this appeal is temporarily restricted for the ministry's program in India and the gift is preferenced to support a particular worker.

A donor's *restriction* on a gift limits the charity's use of the funds to the purposes specified by the donor, *e.g.*, "This gift is made on the condition that," or "This gift is restricted for XYZ project." This type of gift is generally tax-deductible as a charitable contribution.

It may be inappropriate for a charity to accept a gift if the restrictions accompanying a gift:

- prevent the charity from using the donation in the furtherance of its charitable purposes. For example, if a donor restricts a gift for the benefit of a specific individual in a way that prevents the charity from exercising discretion and control over the gift (such as a gift restricted for a particular benevolent recipient, an employee of the charity, etc.), the gift is generally not deductible as a charitable contribution.

- are incompatible with the mission of the charity. Even though a restricted gift is exclusively charitable, it would be inappropriate for a charity to accept a gift requiring the expenditure of funds outside the mission of the charity. For example, if a ministry whose sole purpose is international child sponsorship is offered a gift restricted for inner-city evangelism in the U.S., the gift should not be accepted by the charity because it is inconsistent with the mission of the charity (the overall mission of the charity is generally described in the organization's governing documents).

- are at odds with the best interests of the charity. A restricted gift could be exclusively charitable and compatible with the mission of the charity and still not be in the best interests of the charity. A charity might not have the capacity to comply with gift restrictions. For example, the amount of funds raised for a particular disaster may exceed the charity's capacity to effectively spend the funds in a reasonable period of time.

Alternatively, the administrative requirements of a restricted gift could consume an inordinate amount of the charity's resources. For example, the gift of a time share property could be offered to a ministry. However, the charity may decide the time share is not in the best interest of the charity because (1) time shares are often unmarketable properties laden with annual costs, and (2) even when sales are made, the low resale market prices can minimize or erase profits.

A donor's *preference* communicates a desire or suggestion which is advisory in nature. A desire or suggestion does not restrict the use of the gift and allows the charity full discretion to use the gift in relation to the desire or suggestion or use the funds for any other purpose. Factors that imply a charity has received a donor preferenced gift and not a restricted gift include:

- The donor intends to only express a desire or make a suggestion with respect to a gift.

- Both the solicitation letter and response form (and perhaps the gift acknowledgment) from the charity clearly communicate to the donor that preferenced gifts are sought. Materials include statements such as: "We appreciate your desire or suggestion as the use of the funds. While we will endeavor to use the funds as you desire or suggest, we may use the gift for another purpose." This is very different from the statement: "Gifts made to our charity are under the discretion and control of the charity." All gifts must be under the discretion and control of the charity so making that statement does not turn an otherwise donor-restricted gift into an unrestricted gift.

☐ The donor communicated in writing or verbally a desire or suggestion as to the use of the funds, but the donor did not restrict the funds for a certain purpose.

If the donor preferences a gift, even when the preference is for the funds to go to a particular individual, the gift may often qualify for a charitable tax deduction if the charity exercises adequate due diligence with respect to the gift. For example, a gift restricted for missions and preferenced for the missionary endeavors involving a certain identified individual or a gift for benevolence preferenced for a particular benevolent recipient may qualify for a charitable tax deduction if the charity exercises adequate due diligence related to the gift.

Some charities inform donors not to place the name of a preferred worker on the memo line of the donor's check. This practice may send an inappropriate message to donors—*e.g.*, improperly implying that hiding information from the IRS is an acceptable and/or desirable practice. If a donor wants to use the memo line on the check to indicate a preference to support the work of a particular individual (preferenced for the ministry of Jill Smith), this should be no more problematic for IRS purposes than checking a box on the response form which contains similar wording.

Charitable Gift Options

Irrevocable nontrust gifts

▶ **Cash.** A gift of cash is the simplest method of giving. The value of the gift is easily known. A cash gift is deductible within the 50% or 30% of adjusted gross income limitations, depending on the type of the recipient organization. Generally the 50% limit applies.

▶ **Securities.** The contribution deduction for stocks and bonds held long-term (12 months or more) is the mean between the highest and lowest selling prices on the date of the gift where there is a market for listed securities. The contribution deduction is limited to cost for securities held short-term.

> **Example:** An individual taxpayer plans to make a gift of $50,000 to a college. To provide the capital, the taxpayer planned to sell stock that had cost $20,000 some years earlier yielding a long-term capital gain of $30,000. The taxpayer decides to donate the stock itself instead of the proceeds of its sale. The taxpayer receives a contribution deduction of $50,000 and the unrealized gain on the stock is not taxable. By contributing the stock, the taxpayer's taxable income is $30,000 less than if the stock were sold.

▶ **Real estate.** The contribution deduction for a gift of real estate is based on the fair market value on the date of the gift. If there is a mortgage on the property, the value must be reduced by the amount of the debt.

▶ **Life insurance.** The owner of a life insurance policy may choose to give it to a charitable organization. The deduction may equal the cash surrender value of the policy, its replacement value, its tax basis, or its "interpolated terminal reserve" value (a value slightly more than cash surrender value). The deduction cannot exceed the donor's tax basis in the policy.

▶ **Bargain sale.** A bargain sale is part donation and part sale. It is a sale of property in which the amount of the sale proceeds is less than the property's fair market value. The excess of the fair market value of the property over the sales price represents a charitable contribution to the organization. Generally, each part of a bargain sale is a reportable event, so the donor reports both a sale and a contribution.

▶ **Remainder interest in a personal residence or life estate.** A charitable contribution of the remainder interest in a personal residence (including a vacation home) or farm creates an income tax deduction equal to the present value of that future interest.

▶ **Charitable gift annuity.** With a charitable gift annuity, the donor purchases an annuity contract from a charitable organization for more than its fair value. This difference in values between what the donor could have obtained and what the donor actually obtained represents a charitable contribution. The contribution is tax-deductible in the year the donor purchases the annuity.

> **Idea**
>
> The American Council on Gift Annuities suggests charitable gift annuity rates for use by charities and their donors. The latest are available at www.acga-web.org.

▶ **Donor-advised funds.** Donor advised gifts may be made to a donor-advised fund (DAF). Although DAFs have been used for many years, the concept was only codified in 2006. A DAF is defined as a fund or account that is separately identified by reference to contributions of a donor or donors, is owned and controlled by a charitable sponsoring organization, and to which a donor (or any person appointed or designated by the donor) has advisory privileges with respect to the distribution or investment of amounts in the fund.

A donor makes an irrevocable contribution of cash and/or securities to the separate fund or account. The donor is eligible for a tax deduction at the time of the contribution to the DAF even though the DAF may distribute the funds to one or more charities in a subsequent tax year. The donor makes recommendations to the trustees for grants to be made out of his or her separate fund with the DAF. The representatives of the DAF then review these recommended grants to verify whether the target organization is a qualified charity.

The right of a donor to make recommendations to the trustees of a DAF generally does not constitute a restricted gift. However, if a gift to a DAF is restricted by the donor as to purpose or time, with the right to make recommendations as to the eventual charitable recipient(s) of the funds, this gift is temporarily or permanently restricted, based on the nature of the restriction.

Irrevocable gifts in trust

- **Charitable remainder annuity trust.** With an annuity trust, the donor retains the right to a specified annuity amount for a fixed period or the lifetime of the designated income beneficiary. The donor fixes the amount payable by an annuity trust at the inception of the trust.

Idea

To set up a charitable remainder trust, a donor places cash or certain assets—such as publicly traded securities or unmortgaged real estate—in a trust that will ultimately benefit a charity. The donor collects payments from the trust and gets an immediate income tax deduction. Charities should make adequate plans before accepting the administration of a charitable remainder trust.

- **Charitable remainder unitrust.** The unitrust and annuity trust are very similar with two important differences: (1) the unitrust payout rate is applied to the fair market value of the net trust assets, determined annually, to establish the distributable amount each year, as contrasted to a fixed payment with an annuity trust, and (2) additional contributions may be made to a unitrust compared to one-time gifts allowable to annuity trusts.

- **Charitable lead trust.** The charitable lead trust is the reverse of the charitable remainder trust. The donor transfers property into a trust, creating an income interest in the property in favor of the charitable organization for a period of years or for the life or lives of an individual or individuals. The remainder interest is either returned to the donor or given to a noncharitable beneficiary (usually a family member).

- **Pooled income fund.** A pooled income fund consists of separate contributions of property from numerous donors. A pooled income fund's payout to its income beneficiaries is not a fixed percentage. The rate of return that the fund earns each year determines the annual payout.

Revocable gifts

- **Trust savings accounts.** A trust savings account may be established at a bank, credit union, or savings and loan. The account is placed in the name of the depositor "in trust for" a beneficiary, a person, or organization other than the depositor.

The depositor retains full ownership and control of the account. The beneficiary receives the money in the account either when the depositor dies or when the depositor turns over the passbook.

▶ **Insurance and retirement plan proceeds.**
A nonprofit organization may be named the beneficiary of an insurance policy or retirement plan. The owner of the policy or retirement plan completes a form naming the nonprofit as the beneficiary, and the company accepts the form in writing. The gift may be for part or all the proceeds. However, the IRS is scrutinizing life insurance arrangements in which investors share a portion of policy proceeds.

Idea

During 2006 and 2007, donors can make tax-free rollovers from a traditional or Roth Individual Retirement Account (IRA) to a charity (see pages 7-8 for a possible extension of this provision).

▶ **Bequests.** By a specific bequest, an individual may direct that, at death, a charity shall receive either a specified dollar amount or specific property. Through a residuary bequest, an individual may give to charity the estate portion remaining after the payment of other bequests, debts, taxes, and expenses.

Percentage Limitations

Charitable deductions for a particular tax year are limited by certain percentages of an individual's adjusted gross income (AGI). These are the limitations:

▶ Gifts of cash and ordinary income property to public charities and private operating foundations are limited to 50% of AGI. Any excess may generally be carried forward up to five years.

▶ Gifts of long-term (held 12 months or more) capital gain property to public charities and private operating foundations are limited to 30% of AGI. The same five-year carry-forward is possible.

▶ Donors of capital gain property to public charities and private operating foundations may use the 50% limitation, instead of the 30% limitation, where the amount of the contribution is reduced by all the unrealized appreciation (nontaxed gain) in the value of the property.

▶ Gifts of cash, short-term (held less than 12 months) capital gain property, and ordinary income property to private foundations and certain other charitable donees (other than public charities and private operating foundations) are generally limited to the item's cost basis and 30% of AGI. The carry-forward rules apply to these gifts.

▶ Gifts of long-term (held 12 months or more) capital gain property to private foundations and other charitable donees (other than public charities and private operating foundations) are generally limited to 20% of AGI. There is no carry-forward for these gifts.

▶ Charitable contribution deductions by corporations in any tax year may not exceed 10% of pretax net income. Excess contributions may be carried forward up to five years.

Gifts That May Not Qualify as Contributions

Some types of gifts do not result in a tax deduction and no contribution acknowledgment should be provided by the church:

> **Earmarked gifts.** When computing one's tax return, most Americans know that they cannot count tuition payments as a charitable deduction, even though the check is made out to a 501(c)(3) educational institution. In addition, most taxpayers know that their tuition payments are still not deductible if they are paid to a charity with instructions to forward the funds to the appropriate college or university.

Unfortunately, far too few donors and charitable institutions apply the same logic to other similar circumstances. In too many situations, it is generally accepted that when grants or gifts cannot be made directly, all one must do is "launder" the money through a convenient "fiscal agent," which is frequently the local church or other charity.

An earmarked gift is a transfer that has *not* been made to a charity in a deductible form because the recipient charity's function is as an agent for a particular noncharitable recipient.

Here are a few examples of the improper use of a charity as a *fiscal agent* in an effort to obtain a charitable deduction:

> "I want to help my friends Fred and Mary who are going through a tough financial time because of a recent hurricane. I realize they have no connection with your ministry but if I give the ministry $500, will you pass it through to them and give me a charitable receipt?"

> "I want to give $10,000 to the ministry so the funds can be passed on to a college to cover the tuition for the pastor's daughter. Will the church process this gift and give me a receipt?"

Warning

Gifts restricted for projects by donors qualify for a charitable deduction. Gifts preferenced for support under the deputized fund-raising concept (see pages 192-95) may qualify for a charitable deduction. But when a donor places too many restrictions on a gift, especially when the donor wants the gift to personally benefit a certain individual, it often does not qualify for a charitable deduction.

Examples like these are donations "earmarked" for individuals. They are also called "conduit" or "pass-through" transactions. These connotations are negative references when used by the Internal Revenue Service (IRS) and generally denote amounts that do not qualify for a charitable deduction. To be deductible, the charity must have discretion and control over the contribution without any obligation to benefit a designated individual.

▶ **Identifying an earmarked gift.** A tell-tale sign of an earmarked gift is when someone says they want to "run a gift through the ministry," "pass a gift through the ministry," or "process a gift through the ministry." Of course, it is possible the donor will not so clearly signal an earmarked gift and use more general terminology. This is why ministries should have a good understanding on the concept of earmarked gifts in addition to an awareness of tell-tale terminology.

Though the concept in tax law is well-established, it can be hard to apply to specific situations. Several issues may impact the complexities of these gifts:

☐ The donor's motivation may be loving and charitable in a broad sense; they really want to help, and the only problem is their desire for control.

☐ Many organizations are lax in monitoring this area, and the donor may well say, "If your charity won't process this gift for me, I know of another charity that will handle it."

☐ Sometimes the difference between a nondeductible conduit gift and a deductible restricted gift is not who benefits but only who determines the beneficiary.

However, savvy charity leaders will establish and follow clear policies to prohibit donors from passing money through the ministry simply to gain a tax benefit.

Though many charitable donations are based on a sense of charity, selflessness, and even love, the IRS believes that people may also have other motivations. The law prevents donors from having undue influence over charities and restricts donors from manipulating a charity into serving noncharitable interests and themselves receiving a deduction for it at the same time.

A special category of earmarked gifts is where a donor passes a gift through the charity for the donor's personal benefit. Scholarship gifts passed through a charity for the donor's children (instead of paying tuition) raise allegations of tax fraud. Gifts by a donor to purchase life insurance on the donor benefiting the donor's family resulted in a law which can cause substantial penalties for both the donor and organization. Contributions to a qualified charity earmarked for an unqualified donee may raise a question as to qualifying for a charitable deduction.

Gifts to a ministry for the support of missionaries or other workers (often called "deputized fund-raising") are subject to a different set of guidelines than those generally associated with earmarked gifts. Gifts made under a properly structured deputized fund-raising program are generally tax deductible to the donor.

▶ **Strings attached.** A gift must generally be complete and irrevocable to qualify for a charitable deduction. There is usually no gift if the donor leaves "strings attached" that can be pulled later to bring the gift back to the donor or remove it from the control of the charity.

Example: A donor makes a "gift" of $10,000 to a church. The "gift" is followed or preceded by the sale from the church to the donor of an asset valued at $25,000 for $15,000. In this instance, the $10,000 gift does not qualify as a charitable contribution. It also raises the issue of private inurement relating to the sale by the church.

▶ **Services.** No deduction is allowed for the contribution of services to a charity.

Example: A carpenter donates two months of labor on the construction of a new facility built by your church. The carpenter is not eligible for a charitable deduction for the donation of his time. The carpenter is entitled to a charitable deduction for any donated out-of-pocket expenses including mileage (14 cents per mile for 2007) for driving to and from the project. If the donated out-of-pocket expenses are $250 or more in a calendar year, the carpenter will need an acknowledgment from the church (see page 198).

Warning

When a person makes a gift of services to a charity, it may be the highest gift that can be made—a gift of one's talents. However, the gift of services does not qualify for a charitable deduction, and it should never be receipted by the charity—only express appreciation. Out-of-pocket expenses related to the gift of services qualify as a charitable gift.

▶ **Use of property.** The gift of the right to use property does not yield a tax deduction to the donor.

Example: A donor provides a church with the rent-free use of an automobile for a year. No charitable deduction is available to the donor for the value of that use. If the donor paid the taxes, insurance, repairs, gas, or oil for the vehicle while it is used by the church, these items are deductible as a charitable contribution based on their cost.

Charitable Gift Timing

When donors make gifts near the end of the year, the question often arises: "Is my gift deductible this year?" A donor's charitable deduction, assuming deductions are itemized, depends on various factors:

▶ **Checks.** A donation by check is considered made on the date the check is delivered or mailed, as evidenced by its postmark, if the check subsequently clears the donor's bank in due course. For example, a check that is mailed with a December 31 postmark and promptly deposited by the charity will be deductible by the donor in the year the check is written, even though the check clears the bank the following year. However, a postdated check is not deductible until the day of its date.

Example 1: Donor mails a check with a postmark of December 31, 2007. The charity does not receive the check until January 7, 2008. The charity deposits the check in its bank on January 7, and it clears the donor's bank on January 10. The gift is deductible by the donor in 2007.

Example 2: Donor delivers a check to the charity on December 31, 2007. The donor asks that the check be held for three months. Complying with the donor's request, the charity deposits the check on March 31, 2008. This gift is deductible by the donor in 2008.

Example 3: Donor delivers a check to the charity on January 5, 2008. The check is dated December 31, 2007. The gift is deductible by the donor in 2008.

- **Credit cards.** A contribution charged to a bank credit card is deductible by the donor when the charge is made, even though the donor does not pay the credit card charge until the next year.

- **Internet donations.** Donors can instruct their banks via phone or computer to pay contributions to your charity. If a donor uses this method to make a donation, it's deductible at the time payment is made by the bank.

- **Pledges.** A pledge is not deductible until payment or other satisfaction of the pledge is made.

- **Securities.** A contribution of stock is completed upon the unconditional delivery of a properly endorsed stock certificate to your charity or its agent. If the stock is mailed and is received by the charity or its agent in the ordinary course of the mail, the gift is effective on the date of mailing. If the donor delivers a stock certificate to the issuing corporation or to the donor's broker for transfer to the name of the charity, the contribution is not completed until the stock is actually transferred on the corporation's books.

- **Real estate.** A gift of real estate is deductible at the time a properly executed deed is delivered to the charity.

Acknowledging and Reporting Charitable Gifts

Contributors to your charity seeking a federal income tax charitable contribution deduction must produce, if asked, a written receipt from the charity if a single contribution's value is $250 or more. Strictly speaking, the burden of compliance with the $250 or more rule falls on the donor. In reality, the burden and administrative costs fall on the charity, not the donor.

The IRS can fine a charity that deliberately issues a false acknowledgment to a contributor. The fine is up to $1,000 if the donor is an individual and $10,000 if the donor is a corporation.

A donor will not be allowed a charitable deduction for single donations by check or gifts-in-kind of $250 or more unless the donor has an acknowledgment from your charity.

If a donor makes multiple contributions of $250 or more to one charity, one acknowledgment that reflects the total amount of the donor's contributions to the charity for the year

CHAPTER 7 ➤ CHARITABLE GIFTS

Sample Charitable Gift Receipt

Received from: Howard K. Auburn   Receipt #1

Cash received as an absolute gift:

Date Cash Received	Amount Received
1/2/08	$250.00
1/16/08	50.00
3/13/08	300.00
3/27/08	100.00
6/12/08	500.00
7/10/08	150.00
8/21/08	200.00
10/16/08	400.00
11/20/08	350.00
	$2,300.00

Any goods or services you may have received in connection with this gift were solely intangible religious benefits.

   (*Note:* It is very important for a religious organization to use wording of this nature when no goods or services were given in exchange for the gift.)

This document is necessary for any available federal income tax deduction for your contribution. Please retain it for your records.

Receipt issued on: January 10, 2009
Receipt issued by: Harold Morrison, Treasurer
                      Castleview Church
                      1008 High Drive
                      Dover, DE 19901

1. This sample receipt is based on the following assumptions:
   A. No goods or services were provided in exchange for the gifts other than intangible religious benefits.
   B. The receipt is issued on a periodic or annual basis for all gifts whether over or under $250.
2. All receipts should be numbered consecutively for control and accounting purposes.

Sample Letter to Noncash Donors

**Charitable Gift Receipt for Noncash Gifts
(other than for autos, boats, or airplanes)**
RETAIN FOR INCOME TAX PURPOSES

Noncash Acknowledgment #1

(All acknowledgments should be numbered consecutively for control and accounting purposes.)

Donor's name and address

Date Acknowledgment Issued

Thank you for your noncash gift as follows:
    Date of gift:
    Description of gift:
    (*Note:* No value is shown for the gift. Valuation is the responsibility of the donor.)

    To substantiate your gift for IRS purposes, the tax law requires that this acknowledgment state whether you have received any goods or services in exchange for the gift. You have received no goods or services. (*Note:* If goods or services were provided to the donor, replace the previous sentence with: In return for your contribution, you have received the following goods or services __(description)__ which we value at __(good-faith estimate)__. The value of the goods and services you received must be deducted from the value of your contribution to determine your charitable deduction.)

    If your noncash gifts for the year total more than $500, you must include Form 8283 (a copy of Form 8283 and its instructions are enclosed for your convenience) with your income tax return. Section A is used to report gifts valued at $5,000 or under. You can complete Section A on your own. When the value of the gift is more than $5,000, you will need to have the property appraised. The appraiser's findings are reported in Section B of Form 8283. The rules also apply if you give "similar items of property" with a total value above $5,000—even if you gave the items to different charities. Section B of Form 8283 must be signed by the appraiser. It is essential to attach the form to your tax return.

    You might want an appraisal (even if your gift does not require one) in case you have to convince the IRS of the property's worth. You never need an appraisal or an appraisal summary for gifts of publicly traded securities, even if their total value exceeds $5,000. You must report those gifts (when the value is more than $500) by completing Section A of Form 8283 and attaching it to your return.

    For gifts of publicly traded stock, an appraisal is not required. For gifts of closely held stock, an appraisal is not required if the value of the stock is under $10,000, but part of the appraisal summary form must be completed if the value is over $5,000. If the gift is valued over $10,000, then both an appraisal and an appraisal summary form are required.

    If we receive a gift of property subject to the appraisal summary rules, we must report to both the IRS and you if we dispose of the gift within three years. We do not have to notify the IRS or you if we dispose of a gift that did not require an appraisal summary.

    Again, we are grateful for your generous contribution. Please let us know if we can give you and your advisors more information about the IRS's reporting requirements.

                                                  Your Nonprofit Organization

is sufficient. In other words, the charity can total all of the contributions for a donor and only show the total amount on the receipt.

If a donor contributes cash, the donor must have an acknowledgment or to qualify for a charitable deduction—this is true for all cash gifts without regard to whether they are single gifts of $250 or more.

▶ **Information to be included in the receipt.** The following information must be included in the gift receipt:

- ☐ the donor's name,
- ☐ if cash, the amount of cash contributed,
- ☐ if property, a description, but not the value (if the gift is an auto, boat, or airplane, the charity must generally provide Form 1098-C to the donor—see pages 173-75 for a more detailed discussion), of the property,
- ☐ a statement explaining whether the charity provided any goods or services to the donor in exchange for the contribution,
- ☐ if goods or services were provided to the donor, a description and good-faith estimate of their value and a statement that the donor's charitable deduction is limited to the amount of the payment in excess of the value of the goods and services provided, and if services were provided consisting solely of intangible religious benefits, a statement to that effect,
- ☐ the date the donation was made, and
- ☐ the date the receipt was issued.

▶ **When receipts should be issued.** Donors must obtain their receipts no later than the due date, plus any extension, of their income tax returns or the date the return is filed, whichever date is earlier. If a donor receives the receipt after this date, the gift does not qualify for a contribution deduction even on an amended return.

If your charity is issuing receipts on an annual basis, you should try to get them to your donors by at least January 31 each year and earlier in January if possible. This will assist your donors in gathering the necessary data for tax return preparation.

Form 1098-C must be provided within 30 days after the date that the vehicle is sold or within 30 days of the donation date if the charity keeps the property.

▶ **Frequency of issuing receipts.** The receipts or acknowledgments can be issued gift-by-gift, monthly, quarterly, annually, or any other

> **Idea**
>
> Donors are only required to have receipts for single gifts of $250 or more (unless it is a gift of cash). Churches often issue gift acknowledgments on a quarterly, semiannual, or annual basis. However, most parachurch ministries issue receipts for every gift, regardless of the amount. This provides the charity a vehicle to encourage the donor to make another gift.

frequency. For ease of administration and clear communication with donors, many charities provide a receipt for all gifts, whether more or less than $250.

▶ **Form of receipts.** Except for Form 1098-C, used for gifts of autos, boats, or airplanes, no specific design of the receipt is required. The IRS has not issued any sample receipts to follow.

The receipt can be a letter, a postcard, or a computer-generated form. It does not have to include the donor's social security number or other taxpayer identification number. A receipt can also be provided electronically, such as via an email addressed to the donor.

▶ **Separate gifts of less than $250.** If a donor makes separate gifts by check during a calendar year of less than $250, there is no receipting requirement since each gift is a separate contribution. The donor's cancelled check will provide sufficient substantiation. However, most charities receipt all gifts with no distinction between the gifts under or over $250.

▶ **Donations payable to another charity.** A church member may place a check in the offering plate of $250 or more payable to a mission organization designed for the support of a particular missionary serving with the mission. In this instance, no receipting is required by your church. Since the check was payable to the mission agency, that entity will need to issue the acknowledgment to entitle the donor to claim the gift as a charitable contribution.

▶ **Donor's out-of-pocket expenses.** You may have volunteers who incur out-of-pocket expenses on behalf of your charity. Substantiation from your charity is required if a volunteer claims a deduction for unreimbursed expenses of $250 or more. However, the IRS acknowledges that the charity may be unaware of the details of the expenses or the dates on which they were incurred. Therefore, the charity must substantiate only the types of services performed by the volunteer which relate to out-of-pocket expenses.

▶ **Individuals.** Gifts made to poor or needy individuals ordinarily do not qualify as charitable contributions. Gifts made personally to employees of a charity are not charitable contributions.

▶ **Foreign organizations.** Earmarked gifts are not limited to gifts earmarked for individuals; a gift may be earmarked for an organization. It may be inappropriate to accept gifts restricted for a foreign charity even if the charitable purposes of the foreign charity are consistent with the purposes of the U.S. charity.

Example 1: An individual offers to make a $5,000 donation to a charity restricted for the Sri Lanka Relief Outreach for its relief and development purposes, a foreign charity. While the ministry provides funding for various foreign missionary endeavors, it has no connection with the Sri Lanka Relief Outreach and has no practical way to provide due diligence in relation to a gift to this entity. Based on these facts, the gift has the characteristics of an earmarked gift. The funds should generally not be accepted by the charity.

Example 2: Same fact pattern as in Example 1, except the charity regularly sponsors short term mission trips to Sri Lanka and provides funds to the Sri Lanka Relief Outreach, based on the due diligence performed by the charity's staff and volunteers on mission trips with respect to this particular foreign entity. Based on these facts, the charity is generally in a sound position to make a gift of $5,000 to the Sri Lanka-based charity as requested by the donor, avoiding the characteristics of earmarking.

Since gifts by U.S. taxpayers to a foreign charity do not produce a charitable deduction, donors may earmark a gift for a foreign charity to try to convince a charity to pass it through to the entity. When a domestic charity is empowered in such a way that it is no more than an agent of or trustee for a particular foreign organization, has purposes so narrow that its funds can go only to a particular foreign organization, or solicits funds on behalf of a particular foreign organization, the deductibility of gifts may be questioned by the IRS.

There are some acceptable situations where a U.S. charity may receive gifts for which a deduction is allowed with the money used abroad:

- ☐ The money may be used by the U.S. charity directly for projects that it selects to carry out its own exempt purposes. In this instance, the domestic organization would generally have operations in one or more foreign countries functioning directly under the U.S. entity. The responsibility of the donee organization ends when the purpose of the gift is fulfilled. A system of narrative and financial reports is necessary to document what was accomplished by the gift.

- ☐ It may create a subsidiary organization in a foreign country to facilitate its exempt operations there, with certain of its funds transmitted directly to the subsidiary. In this instance, the foreign organization is merely an administrative arm of the U.S. organization, with the U.S. organization considered the real recipient of the contributions. The responsibility of the U.S. organization ends when the purpose of the gift is fulfilled by the foreign subsidiary.

- ☐ It may make grants to charities in a foreign country in furtherance of its exempt purposes, following review and approval of the uses to which the funds are to be put. The responsibility of the U.S. organization ends when the purpose of the gift is fulfilled by the foreign organization. A narrative and financial report from the foreign organization will usually be necessary to document the fulfillment of the gift.

- ☐ It may transfer monies to another domestic entity with the second organization fulfilling the purpose of the gift. The responsibility of the first entity usually ends when the funds are transferred to the second organization.

The tax law is clear that money given to an intermediary charity but earmarked for an ultimate recipient is considered as if it has been given directly to the ultimate recipient. It is earmarked if there is an understanding, written or oral, whereby the donor binds the intermediary charity to transfer the funds to the ultimate recipient. The tax law does not allow donors to accomplish indirectly through a conduit (an intermediary charity) what the donor cannot accomplish directly.

➤ **Contingencies.** If a contribution will not be effective until the occurrence of a certain event, an income tax charitable deduction generally is not allowable until the occurrence of the event.

> **Example:** A donor makes a gift to a college to fund a new education program that the college does not presently offer and is not contemplating. The donation would not be deductible until the college agrees to the conditions of the gift.

➤ **Charitable remainders in personal residences and farms.** The charitable gift regulations are silent on the substantiation rules for remainder interests in personal residences and farms. It should be assumed that the $250 substantiation rules apply to those gifts unless the IRS provides other guidance.

➤ **Charitable trusts.** The $250 substantiation rules do not apply to charitable remainder trusts and charitable lead trusts.

➤ **Gift annuities.** When the gift portion of a gift annuity or a deferred payment gift annuity is $250 or more, a donor must have an acknowledgment from the charity stating whether any goods or services—in addition to the annuity—were provided to the donor. If no goods or services were provided, the acknowledgment must so state. The acknowledgment need not include a good-faith estimate of the annuity's value.

➤ **Pooled income funds.** The substantiation rules apply to pooled income funds. To deduct a gift of a remainder interest of $250 or more, a donor must have an acknowledgment from the charity.

Most gifts do not require any reporting by the charity to the IRS. In addition to gifts of autos, boats, and airplanes (see pages 173-75), certain gifts require IRS reporting, or execution of a form that the donor files with the IRS:

➤ **Gifts of property in excess of $5,000.** Substantiation requirements apply to contributions of property (other than money and publicly traded securities) if the total claimed or reported value of the property is more than $5,000. For these gifts, the donor must obtain a qualified appraisal and attach an appraisal summary to the return on which the deduction is claimed. There is an exception for non-publicly traded stock. If the claimed value of the stock does not exceed $10,000 but is greater than $5,000, the donor does not have to obtain an appraisal by a qualified appraiser.

The appraisal summary must be on Form 8283, signed and dated by the charity and the appraiser, and attached to the donor's return on which a deduction is claimed. The signature by the charity does not represent concurrence in the appraised value of the contributed property.

If Form 8283 is required, it is the donor's responsibility to file it. The charity is under no responsibility to see that donors file this form or that it is properly completed. However, advising donors of their obligations and providing them with the form can produce donor goodwill.

➤ **Gifts of property in excess of $500.** Gifts of property valued at $500 or more require the completion of certain information on page 1 of Form 8283. For gifts between $500 and $5,000 in value, there is no requirement of an appraisal or signature of the charity.

➤ **Charity reporting for contributed property.** If property received as a charitable contribution requiring an appraisal summary on Form 8283 is sold, exchanged, or otherwise disposed of by the charity within three years after the date of its contribution, the charity must file Form 8282 with the IRS within 125 days of the disposition.

This form provides detailed information on the gift and the disposal of the property. A copy of this information return must be provided to the donor and retained by the charity. A charity that receives a charitable contribution valued at more than $5,000 from a corporation generally does not have to complete Form 8283.

A letter or other written communication from a charity acknowledging receipt of the property and showing the name of the donor, the date and location of the contribution, and a detailed description of the property is an acceptable contribution receipt for a gift of property.

> **Caution**
>
> The IRS places certain reporting requirements on donors and charities with respect to many property gifts. They are looking for property valued at one amount on the date of the gift and sold by the charity for much less. Charities should never place a value on a gift of property. This is the responsibility of the donor.

There is no requirement to include the value of contributed property on the receipt. A tension often surrounds a significant gift of property because the donor may request the charity to include an excessively high value on the charitable receipt. It is wise for the charity to remain impartial in the matter and simply acknowledge the property by description and condition while excluding of a dollar amount.

> **Example:** A charity receives a gift of real estate. The receipt should include the legal description of the real property and a description of the improvements with no indication of the dollar value.

2008 CHURCH AND NONPROFIT TAX & FINANCIAL GUIDE

Form 8282 (Rev. January 2007)
Department of the Treasury
Internal Revenue Service

Donee Information Return
(Sale, Exchange, or Other Disposition of Donated Property)

► See instructions.

OMB No. 1545-0908

Give a Copy to Donor

What Parts to Complete:
- If the organization is an **Original Donee**, complete *Identifying Information*, Part I (lines 1a–1d and, if applicable, lines 2a–2d), and Part III.
- If the organization is a **Successor Donee**, complete *Identifying Information*, Part I, Part II, and Part III.

Identifying Information

Print or Type

Name of charitable organization (donee): **Oneonta First Church**

Employer identification number: **35 : 4829542**

Address (number, street, and room or suite no.) (or P.O. box no. if mail is not delivered to the street address): **292 River Street**

City or town, state, and ZIP code: **Oneonta, NY 13820**

Part I — Information on ORIGINAL DONOR and SUCCESSOR DONEE Receiving the Property

1a Name of original donor of the property: **Keith E. Chapman**
1b Identifying number(s): **512-40-8076**
1c Address (number, street, and room or suite no.) (or P.O. box no. if mail is not delivered to the street address):
1d City or town, state, and ZIP code:

Note. Complete lines 2a–2d only if the organization gave this property to another charitable organization (successor donee).

2a Name of charitable organization:
2b Employer identification number:
2c Address (number, street, and room or suite no.) (or P.O. box no. if mail is not delivered to the street address):
2d City or town, state, and ZIP code:

Part II — Information on PREVIOUS DONEES. Complete this part only if the organization was not the first donee to receive the property. See the instructions before completing lines 3a through 4d.

3a Name of original donee:
3b Employer identification number:
3c Address (number, street, and room or suite no.) (or P.O. box no. if mail is not delivered to the street address):
3d City or town, state, and ZIP code:

4a Name of preceding donee:
4b Employer identification number:
4c Address (number, street, and room or suite no.) (or P.O. box no. if mail is not delivered to the street address):
4d City or town, state, and ZIP code:

For Paperwork Reduction Act Notice, see page 4.   Cat. No. 62307Y   Form **8282** (Rev. 1-2007)

Form 8282 (Rev. 1-2007)   Page **2**

Part III — Information on DONATED PROPERTY

	1. Description of the donated property sold, exchanged, or otherwise disposed of and how the organization used the property. (If you need more space, attach a separate statement.)	2. Did the disposition involve the organization's entire interest in the property?		3. Was the use related to the organization's exempt purpose or function?		4. Information on use of property. • If you answered "Yes" to question 3 and the property was tangible personal property, describe how the organization's use of the property furthered its exempt purpose or function. Also complete Part IV below. • If you answered "No" to question 3 and the property was tangible personal property, describe the organization's intended use (if any) at the time of the contribution. Also complete Part IV below, if the intended use at the time of the contribution was related to the organization's exempt purpose or function and it became impossible or infeasible to implement.
		Yes	No	Yes	No	
A	Real Estate/vacant lot, 82 White Street, Oneonta, NY	X			X	
B						
C						
D						

		Donated Property			
		A	B	C	D
5	Date the organization received the donated property (MM/DD/YY)	9/1/07	/ /	/ /	/ /
6	Date the original donee received the property (MM/DD/YY)	11/10/07	/ /	/ /	/ /
7	Date the property was sold, exchanged, or otherwise disposed of (MM/DD/YY)	/ /	/ /	/ /	/ /
8	Amount received upon disposition	$ 3,780	$	$	$

Part IV — Certification

You must sign the certification below if any property described in Part III above is tangible personal property and:
- You answered "Yes" to question 3 above, or
- You answered "No" to question 3 above and the intended use of the property became impossible or infeasible to implement.

Under penalties of perjury and the penalty under Internal Revenue Code section 6720B, I certify that the property that meets the above requirements and is described above in Part III either was used to further the donee organization's exempt purpose or function, or the donee organization intended to use the property for its exempt purpose or function but the intended use became impossible or infeasible to implement.

Signature of officer: *[signed]*   ►   Date: **12-1-07**

Under penalties of perjury, I declare that I have examined this return, including accompanying schedules and statements, and to the best of my knowledge and belief, it is true, correct, and complete.

Sign Here

Signature of officer: *[signed]*   Title: **Treasurer**   Date:

Type or print name:

Form **8282** (Rev. 1-2007)

This form must generally be filed by a charity if it disposes of charitable deduction property within three years of the date the original donee received it and the items are valued at $500 or more.

CHAPTER 7 — CHARITABLE GIFTS

Form 8283
(Rev. December 2005)
Department of the Treasury
Internal Revenue Service

Noncash Charitable Contributions

► Attach to your tax return if you claimed a total deduction of over $500 for all contributed property.
► See separate instructions.

OMB No. 1545-0908
Attachment Sequence No. **155**

Name(s) shown on your income tax return: **Mark A. and Joan E. Murphy**
Identifying number: **392-83-1982**

Note. Figure the amount of your contribution deduction before completing this form. See your tax return instructions.

Section A. Donated Property of $5,000 or Less and Certain Publicly Traded Securities—List in this section **only** items (or groups of similar items) for which you claimed a deduction of $5,000 or less. Also, list certain publicly traded securities even if the deduction is more than $5,000 (see instructions).

Part I — Information on Donated Property—If you need more space, attach a statement.

	(a) Name and address of the donee organization	(b) Description of donated property (For a donated vehicle, enter the year, make, model, condition, and mileage)
A	Endless Mountain Church, 561 Maple, Rochester, NY 14623	Used bedroom furniture
B		
C		
D		
E		

Note. If the amount you claimed as a deduction for an item is $500 or less, you do not have to complete columns (d), (e), and (f).

	(c) Date of the contribution	(d) Date acquired by donor (mo., yr.)	(e) How acquired by donor	(f) Donor's cost or adjusted basis	(g) Fair market value (see instructions)	(h) Method used to determine the fair market value
A	10-1-07	4-96	Purchased	3,400	750	Sales of comparable used furniture
B						
C						
D						
E						

Part II — Partial Interests and Restricted Use Property

Complete lines 2a through 2e if you gave less than an entire interest in a property listed in Part I. Complete lines 3a through 3c if conditions were placed on a contribution listed in Part I; also attach the required statement (see instructions).

2a Enter the letter from Part I that identifies the property for which you gave less than an entire interest ► _____
If Part II applies to more than one property, attach a separate statement.

b Total amount claimed as a deduction for the property listed in Part I: (1) For this tax year ► _____
(2) For any prior tax years ► _____

c Name and address of each organization to which any such contribution was made in a prior year (complete only if different from the donee organization above):

Name of charitable organization (donee) _____

Address (number, street, and room or suite no.) _____

City or town, state, and ZIP code _____

d For tangible property, enter the place where the property is located or kept ► _____
e Name of any person, other than the donee organization, having actual possession of the property ► _____

		Yes	No
3a	Is there a restriction, either temporary or permanent, on the donee's right to use or dispose of the donated property?		
b	Did you give to anyone (other than the donee organization or another organization participating with the donee organization in cooperative fundraising) the right to the income from the donated property or to the possession of the property, including the right to vote donated securities, to acquire the property by purchase or otherwise, or to designate the person having such income, possession, or right to acquire?		
c	Is there a restriction limiting the donated property for a particular use?		

For Paperwork Reduction Act Notice, see page 6 of separate instructions.   Cat. No. 62299J   Form **8283** (Rev. 12-2005)

This form must be completed and filed with the donor's income tax return for gifts of property valued at $500 or more. There is no requirement of an appraisal or signature of the donee organization for gifts valued between $500 and $5,000.

Form 8283 (Rev. 12-2005)   Page **2**

Name(s) shown on your income tax return: Mark A. and Joan E. Murphy
Identifying number: 392-83-1982

Section B. Donated Property Over $5,000 (Except Certain Publicly Traded Securities)—List in this section only items (or groups of similar items) for which you claimed a deduction of more than $5,000 per item or group (except contributions of certain publicly traded securities reported in Section A). An appraisal is generally required for property listed in Section B (see instructions).

Part I — Information on Donated Property—To be completed by the taxpayer and/or the appraiser.

4 Check the box that describes the type of property donated:
- ☐ Art* (contribution of $20,000 or more)
- ☐ Qualified Conservation Contribution
- ☐ Equipment
- ☐ Art* (contribution of less than $20,000)
- ☒ Other Real Estate
- ☐ Securities
- ☐ Collectibles**
- ☐ Intellectual Property
- ☐ Other

*Art includes paintings, sculptures, watercolors, prints, drawings, ceramics, antiques, decorative arts, textiles, carpets, silver, rare manuscripts, historical memorabilia, and other similar objects.
**Collectibles include coins, stamps, books, gems, jewelry, sports memorabilia, dolls, etc., but not art as defined above.

Note. If your total art contribution was $20,000 or more, you must attach a complete copy of the signed appraisal. If your deduction for any donated property was more than $500,000, you must attach a qualified appraisal of the property. See instructions.

5	(a) Description of donated property (if you need more space, attach a separate statement)	(b) If tangible property was donated, give a brief summary of the overall physical condition of the property at the time of the gift	(c) Appraised fair market value
A	Residence and two lots:	Good repair	42,500
B	2080 Long Pong Road		
C	Syracuse, NY		
D			

	(d) Date acquired by donor (mo., yr.)	(e) How acquired by donor	(f) Donor's cost or adjusted basis	(g) For bargain sales, enter amount received	(h) Amount claimed as a deduction	(i) Average trading price of securities
A	7-20-06	Purchased	36,900		42,500	
B						
C						
D						

Part II — Taxpayer (Donor) Statement—List each item included in Part I above that the appraisal identifies as having a value of $500 or less. See instructions.

I declare that the following item(s) included in Part I above has to the best of my knowledge and belief an appraised value of not more than $500 (per item). Enter identifying letter from Part I and describe the specific item. See instructions. ▶ _____

Signature of taxpayer (donor) ▶ *Mark A. Murphy*   Date ▶ 2-28-07

Part III — Declaration of Appraiser

I declare that I am not the donor, the donee, a party to the transaction in which the donor acquired the property, employed by, or related to any of the foregoing persons, or married to any person who is related to any of the foregoing persons. And, if regularly used by the donor, donee, or party to the transaction, I performed the majority of my appraisals during my tax year for other persons.

Also, I declare that I hold myself out to the public as an appraiser or perform appraisals on a regular basis; and that because of my qualifications as described in the appraisal, I am qualified to make appraisals of the type of property being valued. I certify that the appraisal fees were not based on a percentage of the appraised property value. Furthermore, I understand that a false or fraudulent overstatement of the property value as described in the qualified appraisal or this Form 8283 may subject me to the penalty under section 6701(a) (aiding and abetting the understatement of tax liability). I affirm that I have not been barred from presenting evidence or testimony by the Office of Professional Responsibility.

Sign Here Signature ▶ *Andrew J. Noble*   Title ▶ President   Date ▶ 3-20-07

Business address (including room or suite no.): 1100 North Adams Street
Identifying number: 541-90-9796
City or town, state, and ZIP code: Elmira, NY 14904

Part IV — Donee Acknowledgment—To be completed by the charitable organization.

This charitable organization acknowledges that it is a qualified organization under section 170(c) and that it received the donated property as described in Section B, Part I, above on the following date ▶ 1-31-07

Furthermore, this organization affirms that in the event it sells, exchanges, or otherwise disposes of the property described in Section B, Part I (or any portion thereof) within 2 years after the date of receipt, it will file **Form 8282**, Donee Information Return, with the IRS and give the donor a copy of that form. This acknowledgment does not represent agreement with the claimed fair market value.

Does the organization intend to use the property for an unrelated use? ☐ Yes ☒ No

Name of charitable organization (donee): Fairlawn Heights Church
Employer identification number: 35-4029876
Address (number, street, and room or suite no.): PO Box 829
City or town, state, and ZIP code: Oswego, NY 13126

Authorized signature: *James A. Black*   Title: Executive Pastor   Date: 4-15-07

Section B must be completed for gifts of items (or groups of similar items) for which a deduction was claimed of more than $5,000 per item or group.

▶ Acknowledging and reporting gifts of autos, boats, and airplanes

Charities are required to provide contemporaneous written acknowledgment (generally use Form 1098-C; see page 174) containing specific information to donors of autos, boats, and airplanes. Taxpayers are required to include a copy of the written acknowledgments with their tax returns in order to receive a deduction. The donee organization is also required to provide the information contained in the acknowledgment to the IRS. The information included in such acknowledgments as well as the meaning of "contemporaneous" depends on what the charity does with the donated vehicle.

Vehicle sold before use or improvement. If the donated auto, boat, or airplane is sold before significant intervening use or material improvement of the auto, boat, or airplane by the organization, the gross proceeds received by the donee organization from the sale of the vehicle will be included on the written acknowledgment. Therefore, for donated property sold before use or improvement, the deductible amount is the gross proceeds received from the sale.

For property sold before use or improvement, a written acknowledgment is considered contemporaneous if the donee organization provides it within 30 days of the sale of the vehicle. The written acknowledgment provided by the charity should include the following information:

- the name and taxpayer identification number of the donor,
- the vehicle, boat, or airplane identification number or similar number,
- certification that the property was sold in an arm's length transaction between unrelated parties,
- the gross proceeds from the sale, and
- a statement that the deductible amount may not exceed the amount of the gross proceeds.

If a donee organization furnishes a false or fraudulent acknowledgment or fails to furnish an acknowledgment in accordance with the time and content requirements, the charity will be subject to a penalty equal to the greater of

- the product of the highest rate of tax and the sales price stated on the acknowledgment, or
- the gross proceeds from the sale of the property.

Vehicle not sold before use or improvement. Charities may plan to significantly use or materially improve a donated auto, boat, or airplane before or instead of selling the property. In such circumstances, the charity would not include a dollar amount in the written acknowledgment. Instead, the written acknowledgment (written within 30 days of the contribution of the vehicle to be considered contemporaneous) should

Form 1098-C

7878	☐ CORRECTED

DONEE'S name, street address, city, state, ZIP code, and telephone no.
Lamont Community Church
101 East Main
Lamont, KS 66855

OMB No. 1545-1959
2007
Form **1098-C**

Contributions of Motor Vehicles, Boats, and Airplanes

1 Date of contribution: 12/31/07

2 Make, model, and year of vehicle: Mazda Pickup 1996

DONEE'S federal identification number: 35-0189211
DONOR'S identification number: 514-41-8007

3 Vehicle or other identification number: 1FAFP58923V159753

DONOR'S name: Fred Wilbur

4a ☒ Donee certifies that vehicle was sold in arm's length transaction to unrelated party

Street address (including apt. no.): 512 North Main

4b Date of sale: 1-15-08

City, state, and ZIP code: Lamont, KS 66855

4c Gross proceeds from sale (see instructions): $ 3,000

Copy A
For Internal Revenue Service Center
File with Form 1096.

For Privacy Act and Paperwork Reduction Act Notice, see the 2007 General Instructions for Forms 1099, 1098, 5498, and W-2G.

5a ☐ Donee certifies that vehicle will not be transferred for money, other property, or services before completion of material improvements or significant intervening use

5b ☐ Donee certifies that vehicle is to be transferred to a needy individual for significantly below fair market value in furtherance of donee's charitable purpose

5c Donee certifies the following detailed description of material improvements or significant intervening use and duration of use

6a Did you provide goods or services in exchange for the vehicle? ▶ Yes ☐ No ☐

---

include the following information (Form 1098-C may be used as the acknowledgment):

- the name and taxpayer identification number of the donor,
- the vehicle, boat, or airplane identification number or similar number,
- certification of the intended use or material improvement of the property and the intended duration of such use, and
- certification that the property will not be transferred in exchange for money, other property, or services before completion of such use or improvement.

The deductible amount for contributed autos, boats, or airplanes that will be used or improved by the charity is the fair market value of the property, as determined by the donor, taking into consideration accessories, mileage, and other indicators of the property's general condition.

For donated autos, boats, or airplanes that a charity will use or improve, if a donee organization furnishes a false or fraudulent acknowledgment or fails to furnish an acknowledgment in accordance with the time and content requirements, the charity will be subject to a penalty equal to the greater of

- the product of the highest rate of tax and the claimed value of the property, or
- $5,000.

In certain instances, an auto, boat, or airplane may be sold at a price significantly below fair market value (or gratuitously transferred) to needy individuals in direct furtherance of the donee organization's charitable purpose (although it is difficult to imagine how a boat or an airplane would meet this definition).

For a property that meets this definition, the gift acknowledgment also must contain a certification that the donee organization will sell the property to a needy individual at a price significantly below fair market value (or, if applicable, that the donee organization gratuitously will transfer the property to a needy individual) and that the sale or transfer will be in the direct furtherance of the donee organization's charitable purpose of relieving the poor and distressed or the underprivileged who are in need of a means of transportation.

> **Example:** On March 1, 2008, a donor contributes a qualified vehicle to a qualified charity. The organization's charitable purposes include helping needy individuals who are unemployed develop new job skills, finding job placements for these individuals, and providing transportation for these individuals who need a means of transportation to jobs in areas not served by public transportation. The charity determines that, in direct furtherance of its charitable purpose, the charity will sell the qualified vehicle at a price significantly below fair market value to a trainee who needs a means of transportation to a new workplace. On or before March 31, 2008, the charity provides Form 1098-C to the donor containing the donor's name and taxpayer identification number, the vehicle identification number, a statement that the date of the contribution was March 1, 2008, a certification that the charity will sell the qualified vehicle to a needy individual at a price significantly below fair market value, and a certification that the sale is in direct furtherance of the charity's charitable purpose.

Generally, no deduction is allowed unless donors receive Form 1098-C within 30 days after the date that the vehicle is sold or within 30 days of the donation date if the charity keeps the car. If the vehicle is sold, donors must be informed of the gross selling price.

If the charity keeps the car, the private-party sale price must be used by donors to figure the charitable tax deduction for donations, not the higher dealer retail price.

Quid Pro Quo Disclosure Requirements

When a donor receives goods or services of value approximate to the amount transferred, there is no gift. This is because the person received a quid pro quo in exchange for the transfer, and thus, there is no gift at all. If the payment to a charity exceeds the approximate amount of goods or services provided to the payor, the difference qualifies as a charitable gift.

The charity is required to provide a receipt for all transactions where the donor makes a payment of more than $75 to the charity and receives goods or services (other than intangible religious benefits or items of token value).

Form of the receipt

The receipt must

➤ inform the donor that the amount of the contribution that is deductible for federal income tax purposes is limited to the difference in the amount of money and the value of any property contributed by the donor *over* the value of the goods or services provided by the organization, and

➤ provide the donor with a good-faith estimate of the value of goods or services that the charity is providing in exchange for the contribution.

Only single payments of more than $75 are subject to the rules. Payments are not cumulative. It is not a difference of $75 between the amount given by the donor and the value of the object received by the donor that triggers the disclosure requirements, but the amount actually paid by the donor.

Calculating the gift portion

It is not a requirement for the donee organization to actually complete the subtraction of the benefit from a cash payment, showing the net charitable deduction. However, providing the net amount available for a charitable deduction is a good approach for clear communication with your donors.

When to make the required disclosures

The disclosure of the value of goods or services provided to a donor may be made in the donor solicitation as well as in the subsequent receipt. However, sufficient information will generally not be available to make proper disclosure upon solicitation. For example, the value of a dinner may not be known at the time the solicitation is made.

Goods provided to donors

To determine the net charitable contribution, a gift must generally be reduced by the fair market value of any premium, incentive, or other benefit received by the donor in exchange for the gift. Common examples of premiums are books, tapes, and Bibles. For gifts of over $75, organizations must advise the donor of the fair market value of the premium or incentive and explain that the value is not deductible for tax purposes.

Donors must reduce their charitable deduction by the fair market value of goods or services they receive even when the goods or services were donated to the charity for use as premiums or gifts or when they were bought wholesale by the charity. Therefore, charities cannot pass along to donors the savings realized by receiving products at no cost or buying products at a discount.

If donors receive benefits of insubstantial value, they are allowed a full tax deduction for the donation:

- **Low-cost items.** If an item that has a cost (not retail value) of less than $8.90 and bears the name or logo of your organization is given in return for a donation of more than $44.50 (2007 inflation-adjusted amount), the donor may claim a charitable deduction for the full amount of the donation. Examples of items that often qualify as tokens are coffee mugs, key chains, bookmarks, and calendars.

- *De minimis* **benefits.** A donor can take a full deduction if the fair market value of the benefits received in connection with a gift does not exceed 2% of the donation or $89 (2007 inflation-adjusted amount), whichever is less.

Examples of the quid pro quo rules

Here are various examples of how the quid pro quo rules apply:

- **Admission to events.** Many organizations sponsor banquets, concerts, or other events to which donors and prospective donors are invited in exchange for a contribution or other payment. Often, the donor receives a benefit equivalent to the payment and no charitable deduction is available.

    But if the amount paid is more than the value received, the amount in excess of the fair market value is deductible if the donor intended to make a contribution.

- **Auctions.** The IRS generally takes the position that the fair market value of an item purchased at a charity auction is set by the bidders. The winning bidder, therefore, cannot pay more than the item is worth. That means there is no charitable contribution in the IRS's eyes, no deduction, and no need for the charity to provide any charitable gift substantiation document to the bidder.

Warning

An organization must furnish a disclosure statement in connection with either the solicitation or the receipt of a quid pro quo contribution of over $75. The statement must be in writing and must be made in a manner that is likely to come to the attention of the donor. For example, a disclosure in small print within a larger document might not meet this requirement.

However, many tax professionals take the position that when the payment (the purchase price) exceeds the fair market value of the items, the amount that exceeds the fair market value is deductible as a charitable contribution. This position also creates a reporting requirement under the quid pro quo rules. Most charities set the value of every object sold and provide receipts to buyers.

> **Example:** Your church youth group auctions goods to raise funds for a missions trip. An individual bought a quilt for $200. The church takes the position that the quilt had a fair market value of $50 even though the

bidder paid $200. Since the payment of $200 exceeded the $75 limit, the church is required to provide a written statement indicating that only $150 of the $200 payment is eligible for a charitable contribution.

▶ **Bazaars.** Payments for items sold at bazaars and bake sales are not tax deductible to donors since the purchase price generally equals the fair market value of the item.

▶ **Banquets.** Whether your organization incurs reporting requirements in connection with banquets where funds are raised depends on the specifics of each event.

> **Example 1:** Your church sponsors a banquet for missions charging $50 per person. The meal costs the church $15 per person. There is no disclosure requirement since the amount charged was less than $75. However, the amount deductible by each donor is only $35.

> **Example 2:** Your church invites individuals to attend a missions banquet without charge. Attendees are invited to make contributions or pledges at the end of the banquet. These payments probably do not require disclosure even if the amount given is $75 or more because there is only an indirect relationship between the meal and the gift.

▶ **Deduction timing.** Goods or services received in consideration for a donor's payment include goods and services received in a different year. Thus, a donor's deduction for the year of the payment is limited to the amount, if any, by which the payment exceeds the value of the goods and services.

▶ **Good-faith estimates.** A donor is not required to use the estimate provided by a donee organization in calculating the deductible amount. When a taxpayer knows or has reason to know that an estimate is inaccurate, the taxpayer may ignore the organization's estimate.

Charitable Contribution Substantiation Requirements

	Not more than $75	Over $75 and under $250	At least $250 and under $500	At least $500 and under $5,000	$5,000 and over
Canceled check acceptable for donor's deduction?	Yes	Yes	No	No	No
Contribution receipt required for deduction?	No*	No*	Yes	Yes	Yes
Charity's statement on donor's receipt of goods or services required?	No	Yes**	Yes**	Yes**	Yes**

*Generally, no if paid by check, credit card or wire transfer. Yes, if paid by cash.
**May be avoided if the charity meets the low-cost items or *de minimis* benefits exceptions described on page 177.

CHAPTER 7 ➢ CHARITABLE GIFTS

Sample Charitable Gift Receipt

Receipt #2

Received from: Charles K. Vandell

Cash received:

Date Cash Received	Gross Amount Received	Value of Goods or Services	Net Charitable Contribution
1/23/08	$80.00	$25.00 [1]	$ 55.00
3/20/08	300.00		300.00
4/24/08	60.00		60.00
6/19/08	500.00	100.00 [2]	400.00
9/04/08	275.00		275.00
10/30/08	200.00		200.00
12/18/08	1,000.00		1,000.00
			$2,290.00

Property received described as follows:
Received on October 22, 2008, 12 brown Samsonite folding chairs.

In return for certain gifts listed above, we provided you with the following goods or services (our estimate of the fair market value is indicated):

   (1) Christian music tapes $25.00
   (2) Limited edition art print $100.00

You may have also received intangible religious benefits, but these benefits do not need to be valued for tax purposes.

The deductible portion of your contribution for federal income tax purposes is limited to the excess of your contribution over the value of goods and services we provided to you.

This document is necessary for any available federal income tax deduction for your contribution. Please retain it for your records.

Receipt issued on: January 15, 2009
Receipt issued by: Harold Morrison, Treasurer
                          Castleview Church
                          1008 High Drive
                          Dover, DE 19901

1. This sample receipt is based on the following assumptions:
   A. Goods or services were provided in exchange for the gifts.
   B. The receipt is issued on a periodic or annual basis for all gifts whether over or under $250.
2. All receipts should be numbered consecutively for control and accounting purposes.

➤ **Rights of refusal.** A donor can claim a full deduction if he or she refuses a benefit from the charity. However, this must be done affirmatively. Simply not taking advantage of a benefit is not enough. For example, a donor who chooses not to make use of tickets made available by your organization must deduct the value of the tickets from his or her contribution before claiming a deduction. However, a donor who rejects the right to a benefit at the time the contribution is made (*e.g.*, by checking off a refusal box on a form supplied by your charity) can take a full deduction.

Remember

Many charities offer products and suggest a donation amount with respect to the products. For example, a charity may offer a book with a suggested donation amount of $30. If the fair market value of the book is $30 and the individual sends $30 to the charity, no charitable donation has been made. However, if the charity receives $50, a $20 charitable deduction is available.

➤ **Sale of products or a service at fair market value.** When an individual purchases products or receives services approximate to the amount paid, no part of the payment is a gift.

Example 1: An individual purchases tapes of a series of Sunday morning worship services for $80. The sales price represents fair market value. Even though the amount paid exceeds the $75 threshold, the church is not required to provide a disclosure statement to the purchaser because the value of the products is approximate to the amount paid to the church.

Example 2: The Brown family uses the fellowship hall of the church for a family reunion. The normal rental fee is $300. The Browns give a check to the church for $300 marked "Contribution." No receipt should be given because no charitable contribution was made. The Browns received a benefit approximate to the amount of their payment.

Example 3: The Brown family uses the church sanctuary and fellowship hall for a wedding and the reception. The church does not have a stated use fee but asks for a donation from those who use the facility. The comparable fee to rent similar facilities is $250. The Browns give a check to the church for $250 marked "Contribution." No receipt should be given because no charitable contribution was made. The Browns received a benefit approximate to the amount of their payment. *Note:* It is inappropriate for the church to try to mask a fee by calling it a donation.

Example 4: Your church operates a Christian school. The parent of a student at the school writes a check payable to the church for his child's tuition. No receipt should be given because a payment of tuition does not qualify as a charitable contribution.

Deputized Fund-Raising

Donations may be received, payable to your charity, for the support of a particular missionary (often called deputized fund-raising). These gifts may qualify as a charitable contribution if the charity exercises sufficient discretion and control over the gift. If so, the charity should include the amounts in acknowledgments issued to donors. Then the funds should be remitted as a gift or a grant to the missionary-sending organization for their disbursement in relation to the individual missionary or directly to the missionary, if the missionary is independent of a missionary-sending organization.

Even the IRS has acknowledged that deputized fund-raising is a widespread and legitimate practice, and the contributions properly raised by this method are tax-deductible.

How does a charity properly raise funds using the deputized concept? The IRS outlines two general tests to determine whether a tax-deductible contribution was made to or for the use of a charitable organization or whether a gift is a nondeductible pass-through to a particular individual who ultimately benefited from the contribution:

> **Key Issue**
>
> There is an extremely fine line between a personal nondeductible gift to a missionary (or other religious worker) and a tax-deductible gift to a charity to provide funding for the ministry of a particular employee of the charity. The key is the intention of the donor to benefit the charity and the charity's discretion and control over the gift.

> **Intended benefit test.** The IRS has provided the following suggested language for use in donor receipts to help clarify the record of the true intentions of a donor at the time of the contribution:
>
> > "This contribution is made with the understanding that the donee organization has complete control and administration over the use of the donated funds."
>
> Thus, use of this language should provide strong evidence of both donor intent and organizational control in the deputized fund-raising context.
>
> But when should a donor understand that making a gift to a charity gives the charity complete control and administration over his or her gift? The best time for this understanding to occur is at the point of solicitation—before the gift is ever made, underscoring the principle of truthfulness in fund-raising. And using the suggested wording at the point of solicitation is the best way to communicate the pertinent facts to the prospective donor before the donation is made.
>
> The IRS formally indicated that the following language in solicitations for contributions, with no conflicting language in the solicitations and no conflicting understandings between the parties, will help show that the qualified donee has exercised the necessary control over contributions, that the donor has reason to know that the

qualified donee has the necessary control and discretion over contributions, and that the donor intends that the qualified donee is the actual recipient of the contributions:

> "Contributions are solicited with the understanding that the donee organization has complete discretion and control over the use of all donated funds."

➤ **Control test.** The IRS uses the phrase "discretion and control" with respect to a charity's obligation over deputized funds. Informally, the IRS has stated that discretion and control may be evidenced by such factors as adequate selection and supervision of the self-supported worker (a worker who raises part or all of his or her support) and formalizing a budget that establishes the compensation and expenses of each deputized individual. Establishing compensation and expense reimbursements with reference to considerations other than an amount of money a deputized fundraiser collects is very important. For a complete list of the factors indicating adequate discretion and control, see the box on page 183.

But how does a charity know if the "intended benefit" and "control" tests have been met? Unfortunately, the IRS provides little guidance for these tests. Charities, with advice from their CPAs and attorneys, have no choice but to design their action plan without any bright-line test or else clear safe harbors with two tests as a guide. (Note: In the fall of 1999, the author participated in the last significant meeting conducted with the IRS National Office on the deputized fund-raising topic.) The following is a review of issues that should be considered by ministries using the deputized fund-raising approach:

➤ Determine how to put donors on notice that you will exercise discretion and control over the donations. Using the IRS-recommended language in solicitations—written or verbal—*and* on receipts is wise.

➤ Be sure your organization consistently communicates with your donors. Eliminating written conflicts between solicitation letters (including "prayer" letters), donor response forms, deputized worker training materials, receipts, and other related documents can be accomplished by a careful review of your current documents. It is also important to establish procedures to ensure that the reviews are ongoing. The more daunting task is the proper training and continuing reinforcement to self-supported workers of the need to clearly and consistently communicate the discretion and control concept to donors.

➤ Use appropriate terminology when communicating with donors. Since the charity should not infer that contributions will be paid as salary, fringe benefits, and expense reimbursements to a particular person, communication to donors from the charity or self-supported workers should consistently underscore the charity's discretion and control over donations. A donor may indicate a preference that a gift to a charity be used to support the ministry of a certain individual, and the charity may track the dollars based on the preference. But the charity and the deputized worker should refrain from any inference that the contributions will be paid as salary or expense reimbursements to the worker. This is a fine line but one that should be observed.

Factors Demonstrating Control and Discretion Over the Deputized Fund-Raising Process

According to the IRS, charities that receive revenues through deputized fund-raising—through individual missionaries, staff members, or volunteers conducting grassroots fund-raising to support the organization—can demonstrate control and discretion by the following factors:

➤ Control by the governing body of donated funds through a budgetary process;

➤ Consistent exercise by the organization's governing body of responsibility for establishing, reviewing, and monitoring the programs and policies of the organization;

➤ Staff salaries set by the organization according to a salary schedule approved by the governing body. Salaries must be set by reference to considerations other than an amount of money a deputized fund-raiser collects. There can be no commitments that contributions will be paid as salary or expenses to a particular person;

➤ Amounts paid as salary, to the extent required by the Internal Revenue Code, reported as compensation on Form W-2 or Form 1099-MISC;

➤ Reimbursements of legitimate ministry expenses approved by the organization, pursuant to guidelines approved by the governing body. Reimbursement must be set by considerations other than the amount of money a deputized fund-raiser collects;

➤ Thorough screening of potential staff members pursuant to qualifications established by the organization that are related to its exempt purposes and not principally related to the amount of funds that may be raised by the staff members;

➤ Meaningful training, development, and supervision of staff members;

➤ Staff members assigned to programs and project locations by the organization based upon its assessment of each staff member's skills and training, and the specific needs of the organization;

➤ Regular communication to donors of the organization's full control and discretion over all its programs and funds through such means as newsletters, solicitation literature, and donor receipts; and

➤ The financial policies and practices of the organization annually reviewed by an audit committee, a majority of whose members are not employees of the organization.

Clear communication with donors about the discretion and control issue not only places the donor on notice, but also serves to reinforce this concept in the mind of the deputized worker. Too often, self-supported workers assume they have an element of personal ownership of funds that they raise for the charity. For example, when the worker leaves the employment of charity A, he may mistakenly believe that the balance in his account will be transferred to charity B, where he will be employed. While a transfer to charity B may be appropriate, it is not required.

Short-Term Mission Trips

Many churches and parachurch organizations sponsor individuals and/or teams of individuals that serve on short-term mission trips, domestically and internationally. The proper handling of funds raised and expended for short-term mission trips often raises some challenging issues.

The definition of "short-term" varies from one sponsoring organization to another. For church-sponsored trips, a short-term mission trip often means a trip of a week or two in duration. However, for a missions organization, a short-term trip may last as long as two years. Short-term mission trips sometimes only involve adults. Other times, participants are minors, supervised by adults, or some combination of adults and minors.

Funding options for short-term mission trips. Short-term mission trips may be funded in a variety of ways. For example, the sponsoring organization may pay part or all of the expenses of the trip from the organization's general budget. Or a donor may give funds restricted for short-term mission trips without any preference or reference as to particular mission trip participants—the donor simply wishes to support the program of sending short-term missionaries. However, most organizations sponsoring short-term mission trips seek gifts that are preferenced for particular trip participants.

> **Funding from the sponsoring organization's general budget.** Expenses relating to short-term mission trips may be funded in full by the sponsoring organization, a church, or parachurch organization. The use of funds from the general budget of a nonprofit organization is appropriate if short-term mission trips are consistent with the tax-exempt purposes of the sponsoring charity.

> **Funds directly expended by the trip participant with no financial involvement of the sponsoring organization.** A participant in a short-term mission trip may partially or totally fund trip expenses by making direct payments for airfare, lodging, meals, and other expenses. If a trip is sponsored or approved by a charity, the trip is consistent with the tax-exempt purposes of the charity, and there is no significant element of personal pleasure, recreation or vacation, expenses related to the trip are generally deductible as charitable contributions on the taxpayer's Schedule A. Personal expenses relating to "side-trips" or vacation days included in the trip are generally not deductible.

A taxpayer can claim a charitable contribution deduction for travel expenses necessarily incurred while away from home performing services for a charitable organization only if there is no significant element of personal pleasure, recreation, or vacation in such travel. This applies whether a taxpayer pays the expenses directly or indirectly. Expenses are paid indirectly if a taxpayer makes a payment to the charitable organization and the organization pays the travel expenses. The deduction will not be denied simply because the taxpayer enjoys providing services to the charitable organization.

If a donor makes a single contribution of $250 or more in paying short-term mission trip expenses, the donor must have—and the charity should provide—a written acknowledgment (see example on page 190). The acknowledgment must include:

1. A description of the services provided by the donor (such as built church building, shared the gospel on the beach);

2. A statement of whether or not the sponsoring organization provided the donor with any goods or services to reimburse the donor for the expenses incurred;

3. A description and a good faith estimate of the value of any goods or services (other than intangible religious benefits) provided to reimburse the donor; and

4. A statement of any intangible religious benefits provided to the donor.

▶ **Funding based on donor-restricted gifts for the trip but with no preference in relation to any trip participant.** Donors may make gifts restricted for a short-term mission trip project or fund. Gifts for the project could be solicited by the charity or the donor might make an unsolicited gift. These gifts generally qualified as charitable contributions and it is appropriate for the sponsoring charity to provide a charitable gift acknowledgment.

If a charity accepts gifts that are donor-restricted for a short-term mission trip project or fund, the charity is obligated to spend the funds for the intended purpose. The only exceptions are generally if the donor releases the restriction, excess funds are carried over for future trips, or if the excess funds are minimal.

▶ **Funding based on gifts preferenced for particular trip participants.** Mission trip participants generally are responsible for soliciting gifts to cover part or all of the expenses necessary for the particular trip (see pages 188-89 for a sample letter from a potential short-term mission trip participant to a potential donor).

When mission trip participants raise part or all of the funds required for a trip, the sponsoring organization generally records the amounts raised in separate accounts for each participant as a way of monitoring whether sufficient funds have been raised to cover the expenses of each individual's trip. Charges are then made against the particular account for expenses incurred for the trip. Occasionally, charges will be made to the accounts for the particular short-term mission trip participants in relation to the charity's overhead expenses for the trip.

Gifts preferred for particular trip participants should not be refunded to donors if the preferred individual does not go on the trip. Refunding these gifts is a strong indication that the sponsoring charity does not have adequate discretion and control over the gifts and the issue of earmarked gifts is raised.

When funds are raised for a short-term mission trip on a participant-by-participant basis, the deputized fund-raising guidelines generally apply (see pages 181-84). When a worker or a volunteer (a short-term mission trip participant typically fits the definition of a "volunteer") raises some of his or her own support, the IRS has proposed the following two general tests to determine whether a tax-deductible contribution was made to or for the use of a charitable organization, or whether the gift was a nondeductible, pass-through gift to a particular individual who ultimately benefited from the contribution.

1. **The intended benefit test.** The purpose of this test is to determine whether the contributor's intent in making the donation was to benefit the organization or the individual.

    The IRS has formally indicated that organizations are to avoid the use of conflicting language in their solicitations for contributions, and to avoid conflicts in understandings between the parties. This is to demonstrate that the:

    a. qualified donee has exercised the necessary control over contributions;

    b. donor has reason to know that the qualified donee will have the necessary discretion and control over contributions; and

    c. donor intends for the qualified donee to be the actual recipient of the contributions.

    The following statement should be used in solicitations for contributions:

    > *Contributions are solicited with the understanding that the donee organization has complete discretion and control over the use of all donated funds.*

2. **The discretion and control test.** The IRS uses the phrase "discretion and control" to indicate a charity's obligation regarding deputized funds. The IRS stated that charities receiving revenues from fund-raising for the support of career or short-term mission endeavors can demonstrate control and discretion with the following directives:

    a. Reimbursement of legitimate ministry expenses are approved by the organization, pursuant to the governing body's guidelines. Reimbursement must be set by considerations other than the amount of money collected by the individuals who raise funds.

    b. Potential trip members are screened according to qualifications established by the organization.

    c. Trip members are given meaningful training, development, and supervision.

d. The organization assigns trip members to programs and project locations based upon its assessment of each individual's skills and training, and the specific needs of the organization.

e. Donor receipts inform donors of the organization's full control and discretion over its programs and funds.

f. Since the organization should not commit contributions to a particular person, potential trip participants should never imply the opposite, verbally or in writing. A donor may indicate a preference that the charity use a gift to support the trip of a certain individual, and the charity may track the dollars based on that preference. However, the organization and the potential trip participant should refrain from any inference that the contributions will be paid as expenses to or for a particular worker. This is a fine line, but one that should be carefully observed.

Assuming the intended benefit and control tests are met, the tax deductibility issues of contributions for short-term mission trips are based on age, charity authorization, and the pursuit of pleasure or personal gain. Two potentially tax-deductible scenarios follow:

Example 1: **The trip participants are adults.**

a. **Participants contribute to the charity to cover the entire amount of the trip expenses.** The payments by the participants to the charity are deductible as charitable contributions if the trip involves no significant element of personal pleasure, recreation, or vacation. These trip contributions may be receipted by the charity as charitable contributions.

b. **All trip expenses are paid by the charity, and non-participants make contributions to cover trip expenses of participants who cannot afford to pay all of their own expenses.** If the charity has preauthorized the mission trip, the trip furthers the exempt purposes of the charity, and if the trip involves no significant element of personal pleasure, recreation, or vacation, gifts to cover the travel expenses of participants who cannot afford to pay all travel expenses are generally tax deductible, even if the donors indicate a preference that gifts be applied to the trip expenses of a particular participant.

Example 2: **Trip participants are minors.** If a trip participant is a minor, the minor must actually provide services to carry out the tax-exempt purposes of the trip. The age of the minor and the minor's development may be important factors in determining the minor's capability of providing services to the charity.

If parents, relatives, and/or friends contribute to the charity with a preference for their children's trip expenses, and the charity pays the trip expenses, these

Sample Short-Term Mission Trip Fund-Raising Letter

This short-term mission trip fund-raising letter demonstrates elements which follow IRS guidance. The notes in the letter relate to accounting for the gift and qualifying it for a tax deduction.

1232 Main Street
Yakima, WA 98904
509/248-6739

Date

Dear Mr. and Mrs. Donor,

> *This paragraph confirms it is a church-sponsored mission trip.*

This summer, I have an exciting opportunity to serve the Lord on a mission trip sponsored by our church (Yakima Fellowship) to East Africa. Fifteen members of my church youth group plan to participate in a 10-day trip. We will fly into Nairobi, Kenya on July 21.

Our ministry during this trip is in Nairobi at an orphanage where most of the children have AIDS. Our team will lead a Vacation Bible School, distribute clothes we will take with us, and be available to work with and support the children in the orphanage. Sponsors from our church will accompany our team and provide ministry oversight.

> *This paragraph confirms that ministry will be performed on the trip.*

One of the ways you can help me is to pray for the trip, for the ministry we will perform, and for me personally. Only with a prayer support will I be able to bless the children in the orphanage.

Yes, there are financial needs. The cost of the trip is $2,100, which each team member is responsible to raise in gifts for our church. Please pray with me that the funds to cover my trip expenses will be provided.

> *This paragraph confirms that gifts are preferenced for Jodi's trip expenses. (For accounting purposes, gifts are temporarily restricted for the mission trip.)*

Gifts to the church, with an expression of a preference for my trip expenses, are tax deductible to the extent allowed by law.

CHAPTER 1 ➤ CHARITABLE GIFTS

If you will commit to pray, please check the appropriate box on the enclosed card. If you are able to make a gift to the church to assist with my expenses, please check the appropriate box on the card, indicating your interest in helping fund my portion of the trip expenses, and make your check payable to the sponsoring church, Yakima Fellowship.
If I am unable to participate in the trip, your gifts will be used to support the short-term mission program of the church.

> This paragraph confirms the church will exercise discretion and control over the funds, implied is: "There are no refunds to donors if I don't go."

May God bless you richly as you consider your involvement in this mission trip!

Sincerely,

Jodi Hunter

Sample Short-Term Mission Trip
Response Form (Trip Expenses Paid by the Charity)

We want to support the missions outreach of Yakima Fellowship and are sending our gift of $_____.

Our preference is that this gift be used to support the short-term mission trip of Jodi Hunter. We understand that the use of the gift is subject to the discretion and control of Yakima Fellowship.

These paragraphs make it clear that the donor's intent is to benefit the charity. Their financial support of Jodi Hunter is simply a desire.

Donor(s):
Bill and Karen Smith
2315 Main
Wenatchee, WA 98801

189

Sample Short-Term Mission Trip
Gift Acknowledgment (Trip Expenses Paid by the Charity)

Official Receipt • Please keep this receipt for your tax records

Receipt #2675 Date: 01/02/08 Bill and Karen Smith 2315 Main Wenatchee, WA 98801	Preferenced for the mission trip of: Jodi Hunter	Total Amount $100	Gift Amount $100	Other Amount 0

Thank you for your contribution which is tax-deductible to the extent allowed by law. While every effort will be made to apply your gift according to an indicated preference, if any, **Yakima Fellowship** has complete discretion and control over the use of the donated funds. We thank God for you and appreciate your support.

No goods or services, in part or in whole, were provided in exchange for this gift.

Yakima Fellowship
PO Box 4256
Yakima, WA 98904
509/248-5555

Sample Short-Term Mission Trip
Gift Check (Trip Expenses Paid by the Charity)

Bill and Karen Smith
2315 Main
Wenatchee, WA 98801

Date: December 31, 2008

Pay To The Order Of: Yakima Fellowship $ 200.00

Two Hundred and no/100 -------------------------------- Dollars

For: Missions Work

Bill Smith

Note: If a donor wishes to identify the preferenced participant on the check, the "preferential" or "to support the trip of" terminology should be used to avoid communicating the gift is earmarked for a particular participant. It is generally more advisable for the donor to check an appropriately-worded box on the response form indicating a preference to support the ministry of a particular trip participant.

Sample Short-Term Mission Trip
Gift Acknowledgment (Trip Expenses Paid by the Participant)

Official Receipt • Please keep this receipt for your tax records

Receipt #4575
Date: 08/15/08
Bill and Karen Smith
2315 Main
Wenatchee, WA 98801

Description of Services Provided

Built church building in Nairobi, Kenya, on July 21-28, 2008

Thank you for your contribution which are tax-deductible to the extent allowed by law. While every effort will be made to apply your gift according to an indicated preference, if any, **Yakima Fellowship** has complete discretion and control over the use of the donated funds. We thank God for you and appreciate your support.

No goods or services, in part or in whole, were provided in exchange for this gift.

Yakima Fellowship
PO Box 4256
Yakima, WA 98904
509/248-5555

contributions are generally tax deductible (assuming the minor significantly contributes to the charity's trip purposes).

▶ **Funding based on gifts restricted for particular trip participants.** Although a donor may express a preference for a particular trip recipient, if a donor expresses a restriction for a certain trip recipient, the gift may be considered earmarked. Therefore, the gift may not qualify for a charitable deduction and should generally not be accepted (or acknowledged as a gift if accepted) by a charity sponsoring a short-term mission trip.

An earmarked gift is a transfer that is intended to benefit an individual, not the charity. It is a transfer over which the charity does not have sufficient discretion and control. In the short-term mission trip context, if the charity accepted a gift restricted for a particular trip participant, the charity would not have the freedom to use the funds for a trip participant who fell short of the financial goal for the trip.

Sponsors of short-term mission trips generally should not accept gifts earmarked for individuals because the gifts are not consistent with the charity's tax-exempt purposes.

Other Special Charitable Contribution Issues

Gifts of inventory

Donors may give some of their business inventory to a charity and ask for a charitable contribution receipt for the retail value of the merchandise. A charity should never provide such a receipt. Acknowledgments issued by a charity for inventory contributions should not state the value of the gift—only the date of the gift and a description of the items donated should be noted.

Caution

What is the bottom line of inventory contributions? An inventory item can only be deducted once—there is no contribution deduction and also a deduction as a part of cost of goods sold. The tax benefit to the donor is generally equal to the donor's cost of the items, not their retail value.

Example: Bill owns a lumberyard. The charity is constructing a building, and Bill donates some lumber for the project. Bill's company purchased the lumber during his current business year for $10,000. The retail price of the lumber is $17,000, and it would have generated a $7,000 profit if Bill's company had sold it. What is the tax impact for Bill's company? Since Bill's company acquired the item in the same business year that the lumber was donated, there is no charitable contribution for his company. The cost of the lumber, $10,000, is deducted as part of the cost of goods sold on the company books.

There are temporary rules relating to donations of books to public schools and food approved as part of the Pension Protection Act of 2006.

Payments to private schools

Tuition payments to private schools are generally nondeductible since they correspond to value received. The IRS has ruled that payments to private schools are not deductible as charitable contributions if

➤ a contract exists under which a parent agrees to make a "contribution" and that contains provisions ensuring the admission of the child;

➤ there is a plan allowing a parent either to pay tuition or to make "contributions" in exchange for schooling;

Remember

Tuition payments are personal expenses. However, taxpayers often attempt to construe tuition payments as charitable deductions. The IRS is particularly alert to arrangements that require a certain amount of contributions from a parent in addition to some tuition payments or where education is provided tuition-free.

- there is the earmarking of a contribution for the direct benefit of a particular individual; or

- there is the otherwise unexplained denial of admission or readmission to a school for children of individuals who are financially able to, but do not contribute.

Some churches operate related private schools on a "tuition-free" basis. These churches typically request that families with children in the school increase their contributions by the amount that they would otherwise have paid as tuition. In reviewing "tuition-free" situations, the IRS often questions the deductibility of gifts to the church if

- contributions of several families increased or decreased markedly as the number of their children enrolled in the school changed;

- the contributions of parents of students dropped off significantly in the summer months when the school was not in session; and

- the parents were not required to pay tuition out of their pockets.

Generally, contributions to a church by parents are not deductible as charitable contributions to the extent that the church pays the parent's tuition liabilities.

Gifts designated for employees of a charity

What should be a charity's response if a donor desires to donate a personal computer, some other asset, or money, and specifies that the donation be given to a particular employee of a charity? The donor may expect a charitable contribution receipt and want the specified employee to have the gift without incurring any taxes on the gift. Should the charity accept the gift? What are the consequences of such a gift?

Before accepting a one-time specified gift of this type, the charity must determine if it can exercise adequate control over the gift and if the specified use of the gift will result in appropriate compensation for services rendered to the charity. If the charity does not feel comfortable with these issues, the gift should be declined. If the charity feels that it can properly accept the gift, then the fair market value of the assets or amount of cash distributed to the employee(s) must be reported as compensation on their Form W-2.

> **Caution**
>
> Prayer or support letters should clearly communicate that gifts are being solicited for the charity. It is permissible to request that the gift be designated for the ministry of John Doe, who is a missionary employed by the charity. But letters should not request gifts "for a certain missionary" because of the implication it is a nondeductible conduit transaction.

A pattern of recurring gifts specified for certain employees generally should not be accepted by the charity because of the difficulty in demonstrating discretion and control over the gifts.

Gifts to a charity to support the ministry under the deputized fund-raising concept (see pages 181-84) are a separate issue. Such gifts are generally tax-deductible.

Contributions that benefit specific individuals other than staff members and other than the needy

Occasionally individuals give money to a charity but request that it be sent to a particular recipient who is not on the staff of the organization, not a missionary related to the organization, and does not qualify as a "needy" individual. When told that this "conduit" role is improper, the donor usually responds, "But I can't get a tax deduction otherwise!" The donor is absolutely correct.

The general rule in a conduit situation is that the donor is making a gift to the ultimate beneficiary. The IRS will look to the ultimate beneficiary to decide whether the gift qualifies for a charitable contribution deduction.

There are certain limited circumstances in which an organization may serve as an intermediary with respect to a gift that will be transferred to another organization or to a specific individual. In such circumstances, it is essential that the organization first receiving the monies has the right to control the ultimate destination of the funds.

> **Example:** Frank Lee makes a gift of $5,000 to Shady Lane Church. Mr. Lee stipulates that the gift must go to a particular music group of which his son is a member. The money will be used to purchase sound equipment. The group will go on tour to present religious music in churches. The group is not an approved ministry of Shady Lane Church. This gift would generally be termed a personal gift to the music group and would not be deductible as a charitable contribution. It is best if the church returns the gift to Mr. Lee. If the church accepts the gift and passes the money on to the music group, the church should advise Mr. Lee that the gift is not deductible and should not provide a charitable receipt.

Donor intent is also a key factor. If the donor intends for a gift to benefit a specific individual instead of supporting the ministry of the charity, the gift is generally not deductible.

Contributions to needy individuals and benevolence funds

Contributions made directly by a donor to needy individuals are not deductible. To qualify for a charitable deduction, contributions must be made to a qualified organization.

Contributions to benevolence funds may be claimed as charitable deductions if they are not earmarked for particular recipients.

A gift to a charitable organization involved in helping needy people marked "to aid the unemployed" is generally deductible. Yet if the gift is designated or restricted for the "Brown family" and the organization passes the money on to the Browns, the gift is generally not tax-deductible.

CHAPTER 7 > CHARITABLE GIFTS

Suggested Benevolence Fund Policy

Whereas, New Haven Church has a ministry to needy individuals; and

Whereas, The church desires to establish a Benevolence Fund through which funds for the support of needy individuals may be administered; and

Whereas, The church desires to operate the Benevolence Fund according to the highest standards of integrity;

Resolved, That New Haven Church establish a Benevolence Fund to help individuals in financial need and will develop written procedures to document the need, establish reasonable limitations of support per person during a specified time period, and obtain external verification of the need; and

Resolved, That the church will accept only contributions to the Benevolence Fund that are "to or for the use" of the church, and their use must be subject to the control and discretion of the church board. Donors may make suggestions but not designations or restrictions concerning the identity of the needy individuals; and

Resolved, That the church will provide a charitable contribution receipt for gifts that meet the test outlined in the previous resolution. The church reserves the right to return any gifts that do not meet the test.

If a donor makes a suggestion about the beneficiary of a benevolent contribution, it may be deductible if the recipient organization exercises proper control over the benevolence fund. The suggestion must only be advisory in nature, and the charity may accept or reject the suggestion. However, if every "suggestion" is honored by the organization, the earmarking could be challenged by the IRS.

A church or nonprofit organization may want to help a particular individual or family that has unusually high medical bills or other valid personal financial needs. To announce that funds will be received for the individual or family and receipt the monies through the church or nonprofit organization makes the gifts personal and not deductible as charitable contributions. An option is for the charity to set up a trust fund at a local bank. Contributions to the trust fund would not be deductible for tax purposes. Payments from the trust fund would not represent taxable income to a needy individual or family. This method of helping the needy person or family is clearly a legal approach and would represent personal gifts from one individual to another.

Warning

An area of frequent abuse involves a monetary donation that the donor specifies must go to a particular individual (or family) to assist their financial needs. Before accepting such a gift, a charity must exercise due diligence to ensure the transaction does not actually constitute earmarking of the funds by a donor, which is not deductible as a charitable contribution.

Granting of scholarships

When scholarship assistance is provided by a charity, it requires careful compliance with tax laws and regulations. Three distinct areas of the tax law must be addressed:

➤ **Protecting the contributor's tax deduction.** The contribution deduction requires the gift be "to or for the use of" a charitable entity, not an individual. To qualify, the gift must be to a church or other qualified not-for-profit organization, knowing it will be used for scholarships, but without knowing who will receive the scholarship. A gift designated for a specific individual will not qualify.

Five guidelines for protecting the contribution deduction are that

- The charity determines all scholarship recipients through the use of a scholarship committee.
- The charity has a well-published policy stating that it determines the recipients according to its own policies and that it expressly rejects any effort to honor a donor's recommendation(s).

> **Key Issue**
>
> Too often, well-meaning people want to help a relative or a friend pay their school bills; plus they want a tax deduction for the assistance. So, instead of making a personal nondeductible gift to the intended beneficiary, they make a "gift" to a charity with a request to provide a scholarship for a designated individual. This transfer of funds is not a charitable contribution and the funds should not be accepted by the charity.

- All scholarship policies contain the following statement: "Scholarships are awarded without regard to sex, race, nationality or national origin."
- Recipients of scholarships and the amount they are to receive will be based on funds already received.
- At a minimum, the criteria for scholarship qualification are in writing.

➤ **Protecting the status of the payments to the scholarship recipient.** Only a candidate for a degree can exclude amounts received as a scholarship. A qualified scholarship is any payment to or for the student if it is for "tuition and fees" or for enrollment or "fees, books, supplies and equipment" required for specific courses. It is not necessary for an organization granting a scholarship to confirm that it will be used only for qualified uses. The person receiving the scholarship must report excess amounts as taxable income.

➤ **Employee dependent scholarship programs.** Generally, scholarships for employee's dependents will be considered taxable compensation to the employee unless they meet the following precise guidelines. A few of the requirements include:

1. The existence of the program must not be presented as a benefit of employment by the organization.
2. Selection of beneficiaries must be made by an independent committee.

3. Selection must be based solely upon substantial objective standards that are completely unrelated to the employment of the recipients or their parents and to the employer's line of business.
4. Generally, not more than 25% of eligible dependents may be recipients of scholarships.

Donated travel and out-of-pocket expenses

Unreimbursed out-of-pocket expenses of a volunteer performing services for a charity are generally deductible (volunteers may not be reimbursed using the per diem method). The expenses must be directly connected with and solely attributable to the providing of the volunteer services.

The type of expenses that are deductible include transportation; travel (mileage at 14 cents per mile for 2007—special exception for certain Katrina-related mileage), meals, and lodging while away from home if there is no significant element of personal pleasure, recreation, or vacation associated with the travel; postage; phone calls; printing and photocopying; expenses in entertaining prospective donors; and required uniforms without general utility.

It is generally inappropriate to provide a volunteer with a standard charitable receipt because the charity is usually unable to confirm the actual amount of a volunteer's expenses. But a letter of appreciation may be sent to the volunteer thanking the individual for the specific services provided. The burden is on the volunteer to prove the amount of the expense.

Volunteers who incur $250 or more in out-of-pocket expenses in connection with a charitable activity are subject to the acknowledgment rules. The acknowledgment should identify the type of services or expenses provided by the volunteer and state that no goods or services were provided by the charity to the donor in consideration of the volunteer efforts (see page 198 for a sample letter to volunteers).

Gifts of frequent-flyer miles

Frequent-flyer miles are deductible as charitable donations at fair market value only if the miles are a capital asset held for long term. There are no pronouncements by the IRS that address the question of whether frequent-flyer miles are ordinary income property or capital gains property.

Frequent-flyer miles must be a capital asset held long-term (a year and a day) to be deductible at fair market value. The holding period may be difficult to prove in some instances. However, for some airlines, the periodic mileage reports could be used as documentation for the holding period.

If the miles are considered ordinary gain property, the value must be reduced by the gain that would be reported if sold at fair market value. Then the deduction is limited to basis, which normally is zero. If miles are transferred at fair market value, they produce

Sample Letter to Volunteers

Date _____

Dear Volunteer:

We appreciate the time, energy, and out-of-pocket costs you devote to our cause as follows:

Description of Services/Expenses Provided/Date Provided

_____

_____

_____

No goods or services were provided to you by our church, except intangible religious benefits, in consideration of your volunteer efforts.

You may deduct unreimbursed expenses that you incur incidental to your volunteer work. Transportation costs (travel from home to our church or other places where you render services), phone calls, postage stamps, stationery, and similar out-of-pocket costs are deductible.

You can deduct the IRS approved charitable mileage rate in computing the costs of operating your car while doing volunteer work as well as unreimbursed parking and toll costs. Instead of using the cents-per-mile method, you can deduct your actual auto expenses, provided you keep proper records. However, insurance and depreciation on your car are not deductible.

If you travel as a volunteer and must be away from home overnight, reasonable payments for meals and lodging as well as your travel costs are deductible. Your out-of-pocket costs at a convention connected with your volunteer work are deductible if you were duly chosen as a representative of our church.

You cannot deduct travel expenses as charitable gifts if there is a significant element of personal pleasure, recreation, or vacation in the travel.

You cannot deduct the value of your services themselves. If you devote 100 hours during the year to typing for us and the prevailing rate for these services is $8.00 per hour, you can't deduct the $800 value of your services. Although deductions are allowed for property gifts, the IRS doesn't consider your services "property." Nor is the use of your home for meetings a "property contribution."

Finally, you may be required to substantiate your deduction to the IRS. Be prepared to prove your costs with cancelled checks, receipted bills, and diary entries. If your expenses total $250 or more for the calendar year, you must have this acknowledgment in hand before you file your income tax return.

Again, thank you for furthering our cause with that most precious commodity: your time.

Castleview Church

either ordinary income or perhaps short-term capital gain (if they are a capital asset), and the taxpayer's deduction is limited to basis, which is zero.

Charities should simply express appreciation for the gift of frequent-flyer miles, advising the donor to consult their tax advisor concerning tax-deductibility issues.

Tithing ministry funds

Some charities desire to give a tithe of what they receive to another charity. This is often based on their sincere belief that the scriptural principles of tithing extend to their ministry income. Before a charity adopts a tithing policy, it should consider certain issues.

When a donor makes a gift to a charity, the gift must be used by the charity in the furtherance of its tax-exempt purposes—whether or not the gift is restricted.

If a charity tithes from unrestricted or restricted funds, care must be taken to assure that funds expended by charity B are not for charitable purposes more broad than the charitable purposes communicated by charity A to its donors.

Non-gift income such as product sales, rental income, and investment income are not tied to donor expectations. Thus, a charity may have more flexibility to use these funds as the source of a tithe as long as charity B expends the funds within charity A's tax-exempt purpose.

Tithing on donor-restricted gifts is inappropriate unless the charity has clearly communicated the tithing policy will be applied to restricted gifts. Otherwise, when a donor gives a gift for a specific purpose, it becomes a restriction that those funds be spent for the stated purpose only.

If a charity decides to adopt a tithing policy that includes donor's gifts, it is important that the charity properly communicate this policy to its donors. This should be done at least annually through venues such as annual reports, fund-raising appeals, or gift receipts.

Prohibiting the acceptance of restricted gifts

Occasionally a charity will adopt a policy prohibiting restricted gifts to the charity. The prohibition may be stated in a policy by the governing board or other administrative policy. What impact does this type of policy have on a donor's gift? It depends on the understanding between the donor and the donee.

The mere fact the charity has a policy not to honor restricted gifts does not supercede the donor's gift restriction unless the charity's policy is clearly communicated to donors. A "Yes" answer to all of the following questions would be helpful to support a charity's policy on prohibiting restricted gifts:

- ➤ Do all appeals for fund gifts (from the pulpit, in written solicitations, etc.) clearly and explicitly express the charity's policy that it will not accept any restricted gifts?

- ➤ Are offering envelopes and other response vehicles devoid of any option to restrict gifts for missions, buildings, etc.?

➤ Are charitable gift receipts devoid of any indication of restriction limitations?

➤ If the charity receives a gift with a donor restriction, do they refund the money or offer to refund it unless the donor agrees to remove the gift restriction?

It generally is difficult to adequately communicate a "no restricted gifts" policy to all donors. Additionally, the charity's communication is simply part of the equation; a donor's intent relates both to what is communicated in an appeal and to any donor instructions accompanying the gift. On balance, charities are better served to proactively approve projects to which donors can restrict their gifts.

Refunding gifts or sending contributions to another charity

Since contributions must be irrevocable to qualify for a charitable deduction, there generally is no basis to return an undesignated gift to a donor. Requests from donors to return undesignated gifts should be denied under nearly any circumstance.

However, donors may contribute designated funds based on the anticipation that a certain event will occur. Their intent is to make an irrevocable gift. For example, a church raises money to buy new pews. However, an insufficient amount is raised and the church board abandons the project. What happens to the money that was designated by donors for the pews? If the donors can be identified, they should be asked whether they would like to remove the designation related to their gift. Otherwise, the money should be returned to the donors. If contributions are returned to donors, a written communication should accompany the refund advising donors of their responsibility to file amended tax returns if a charitable deduction was claimed. If the donors cannot be identified, the congregation could redirect use of the funds.

> **Idea**
>
> Ministries should have policies and procedures in place to address requests for the return of charitable donations. Significant gifts should ordinarily be returned only after a thorough review by knowledgeable advisors and perhaps after approval by the governing board.

In some instances, after a donor makes a restricted gift to a charity, the donor requests that the funds be transferred to a second charity. This sometimes occurs when a deputized worker moves from one charity to a second charity and a donor who has given funds to charity A asks that the money be transferred to charity B. It is within the discretion of charity A to determine whether the funds are retained by charity A or a gift/grant is made to charity B. A gift/grant by charity A to charity B is appropriate only if charity B is qualified to carry out the donor's restrictions. Each case must be reviewed on its own merits.

Charities should have policies and procedures in place to address requests for the return of charitable donations. Significant gifts should ordinarily be returned only after a thorough review by knowledgeable advisors and perhaps after approval by the governing board.

Request to receipt a taxpayer other than the donor

Donors or prospective donors often present challenging requests to charities. Some requests relate to the receipting of a gift or potential gift.

If a donor asks a charity to issue a gift receipt to a taxpayer other than the one making the gift, what should a charity do?

➤ Should the charity automatically issue the receipt as requested by the donor?

➤ Should the charity ask for an explanation?

➤ If the donor provides an explanation that evidences an attempt to understate income or social security taxes, what should the charity do?

➤ If the charity provides a receipt to a taxpayer other than the donor, is the charity aiding tax evasion?

➤ Even if the law does not cover these issues, is there a position of "high ground" for the charity?

Donor privacy

While donor information is treated with the utmost confidentiality by most nonprofit organizations, there is no federal law that mandates donor privacy.

Is it acceptable for a church pastor, parachurch chief executive officer, or fund-raising consultant to be given a list of donors, identified either within dollar ranges or with actual

---

Policy on Issuing Receipts to Someone Other Than the Remitter of the Funds

When the charity receives requests for receipts to be issued to a taxpayer other than the remitter of the funds, receipts will be issued only to the taxpayer making the gift.

➤ For a cash gift, the person or entity named on the check (or the individual delivering the cash) is the one to whom the receipt is addressed.

➤ The person or entity transferring ownership of non-cash assets to a charity is the donor.

The following exceptions to this policy may be permitted:

➤ If the donor documents the appropriateness of issuing a receipt to a taxpayer other than the donor, an exception may be made to the policy.

➤ To facilitate the processing of modest gifts, an exception may be made for small gifts where the risk of significant fraud is diminished.

Sample Donor Privacy Policy

XYZ Charity is committed to respecting the privacy of our donors. We have developed this privacy policy to ensure our donors that donor information will not be shared with any third party.

Awareness. This policy is shared to make you aware of our privacy policy and to inform you of the way your information is used. We also provide you with the opportunity to remove your name from our mailing list, if you desire to do so.

Information collected. Here are the types of donor information that we collect and maintain:

- contact information: name, organization/church, complete address, phone number, email address;
- payment information: credit card number and expiration date, and billing information;
- shipping information: name, organization/church, complete address;
- information concerning how you heard about XYZ Charity;
- information you wish to share: questions, comments, suggestions; and
- your request to receive periodic updates: *e.g.*, to individuals who request them, we will send periodic mailings related to specific fund-raising appeals, prayer concerns, and newsletters.

How information is used. XYZ Charity uses your information to understand your needs and provide you with better service. Specifically, we use your information to help you complete a transaction, communicate back to you, and update you on ministry happenings. Credit card numbers are used only for donation or payment processing and are not retained for other purposes. We use the comments you offer to provide you with information requested, and we take seriously each recommendation as to how we might improve communication.

No sharing of personal information. XYZ Charity will not sell, rent, or lease your personal information to other organizations. We assure you that the identity of all our donors will be kept confidential. Use of donor information will be limited to the internal purposes of our charity and only to further our ministry activities and purposes.

Removing your name from our mailing list. It is our desire to not send unwanted mail to our donors. Please contact us if you wish to be removed from our mailing list.

Contacting us. If you have comments or questions about our donor privacy policy, please send us an email at info@XYZCharity.org or call us at (800) 323-0909.

contribution amounts? This practice is not prohibited or considered unethical if this information is used within a limited context on a "need to know" basis for a specific function. However, circulating this information outside the church or parchurch organization would be considered unethical.

It is wise and prudent for a ministry to maintain a donor privacy policy to help assure its donors of their privacy in contributing to the ministry. Charities should consider including several components in developing donor privacy policies:

➤ **How the donor information is used.** The donor privacy policy should explain how donor information will be used. Common uses are to process contributions, communicate with donors, and update them about charity events or programs.

➤ **Who the donor information is shared with.** The privacy policy should specify whether the charity will share donor information with other organizations. Most ministries have a policy not to share any form of donor information. If, however, a nonprofit does share donor information with other organizations, it is important that they disclose that fact in the donor privacy policy. Doing so allows donors to be aware that any personal information given may be passed on to another organization.

➤ **Removal from the mailing list.** A good donor privacy policy will also include instructions that persons may follow to remove their name from the mailing list.

Charities may communicate their policy on donor privacy in several different places. The policy may be included in fund-raising appeals, response vehicles, contribution receipts, annual reports, and on the ministry's website. Charities can publish their entire donor privacy policy or create a simplified donor privacy statement to be used on documents and websites.

Charitable solicitation registration

More than 40 states have laws regulating the solicitation of funds for charitable purposes. These statutes generally require organizations to register with a state agency before soliciting the state's residents for contributions, providing exemptions from registration for certain categories of organizations. In addition, organizations may be required to file periodic financial reports. State laws may impose additional requirements on fund-raising activity involving paid solicitors and fund-raising counsel. Charitable organizations may wish to contact the appropriate state agency to learn more about the requirements that may apply in their state, before soliciting contributions. In some states, municipal or other local governments may also require organizations soliciting charitable contributions to register and report.

To determine in what state(s) you may be required to register to solicit charitable contributions or hold assets subject to a charitable trust, see the website of the National Association of State Charity Officials: www.nasconet.org/agencies/document_view.

Child adoption gifts

It is not surprising that charities and donors often seek ways to provide financial support to couples involved in the adoption process. The cost to adopt a child often exceeds the financial resources of the adopting couple.

While there are a few ways charities can legitimately assist adoptive parents, these options are very limited. A charity should carefully scrutinize any gifts that are designated for a particular adoptive family. The IRS may consider such gifts as conduit or pass-through transactions which do not qualify for a charitable receipt by a charity or a charitable deduction by a donor and could endanger the tax status of a charity.

The following are some considerations for providing support for adoptive parents:

➤ **Personal gifts to the adoptive parents.** An individual may make a personal gift to adoptive parents to assist with adoption expenses. Personal gifts are not deductible as charitable gifts and are not taxable to the adoptive parents.

➤ **Gifts for adoptive parents by a charity whose purpose and nature are not consistent with such gifts.** If gifts by a charity to adoptive families are not consistent with the broad limits imposed by the charity's purpose and nature, the gifts are generally not a proper use of tax-exempt funds.

➤ **Gifts for adoptive parents from the operating fund of a charity.** If adoption assistance is consistent with the charity's purpose and nature, a charity generally has a sound basis to provide assistance for adoptive parents from the charity's general funds (budgeted or unbudgeted); *e.g.*, the charity has available funds that were not designated by a donor for a particular adoptive family. Payments for adoptive families are often made on the basis of financial need and paid directly to the adoption agency to assure that the funds are properly used. These payments are tax-free to the adopted parents.

➤ **Gifts to a charity's adoption fund not preferenced for a particular adoptive family and gifts for an adoptive family from the fund.** If adoption assistance is consistent with the charity's purpose and nature, a charity generally has a sound basis to establish a restricted fund (either temporarily restricted or permanently restricted) to accept gifts that are not designated by a donor for a particular adoptive family. Gifts to such a fund will generally qualify as charitable gifts. Payments for adoptive families are often made on the basis of financial need. Payments should typically be made directly to the adoption agency or reimbursed to the adoptive parents based on adequate documentation to assure that the funds are properly used.

➤ **Gifts to a charity preferenced for a particular adoptive family and gifts for the adoptive family from the fund.** Even if adoption assistance is consistent with the charity's governing documents, gifts that are preferenced by a donor for a particular adoptive family may raise conduit or pass-through transaction issues. To be deductible, the charity must generally have control and discretion over the contribution without any obligation to benefit a preferred individual, obtain adequate information about the potential recipient of the funds (including financial resources), avoid refunding gifts to donors if a particular adoption is not completed, and avoid conflicts of interest between those approving and receiving a loan or a grant. Before considering accepting gifts of this nature and making related gifts to adoptive parents, a charity should seek qualified legal counsel.

Providing Assistance to or for Adoptive Parents
Implications for Charitable Deduction Purposes

Type of Gift	Qualifies as a Charitable Deduction
Gift from a charity to/for an adoptive family based on need[1] [2] – not based on gifts designated by the donor(s), *e.g.*, from the charity's general fund.	Yes
Gift from a charity to/for an adoptive family based on gifts restricted for the charity's adoption fund but not restricted or preferenced for a particular adoptive family.	Yes
Personal gifts from one individual to/for another individual to assist in an adoption.	No
Gift from a charity to/for an adoptive family based on gifts preferenced for a particular adoptive family and the donor's intent is to benefit the adoptive family, not the charity.	No
Gift from a charity to/for an adoptive family based on gifts restricted for a particular adoptive family. *The charity is unable to provide adequate control and discretion over the payment because of the donor(s) restriction.*	No
Gift from a charity to/for an adoptive family based on gifts restricted for a particular adoptive family – the adoptive family and the donor are the same taxpayer.	Generally, no. May be tax fraud because of the circular nature of the transaction
Gift from a charity to/for an adoptive family based on gifts preferenced for a particular adoptive family. *The charity exercises adequate control and discretion over the gift.*	Based on facts and circumstances

[1] As a best practice, the payments should either be made directly to the adoption agency or reimbursed to the adoptive parents based on adequate documentation to assure that the funds are properly used.

[2] Personal gifts from an individual to another individual may have estate tax implications if the gifts to an individual exceed the annual gift tax limitation.

- **Crossing the line from a restricted to an earmarked gift.** Donors may restrict gifts either as to purpose or to time. When the restriction only relates to a project (such as a capital campaign, the mission budget of a church, or the benevolence fund) the issue of earmarked gifts does not arise. When gifts are preferred for the support of a particular missionary or a benevolent recipient and the preferencing is only an expression of a desire, not a restriction, the gift is restricted and the earmarking line generally has not been crossed.

  However, when the gift is not preferenced, but restricted for an individual, the earmarked transaction issue arises. This generally denies a charitable deduction and represents a gift that should not be received by the charity. Integrity requires carefully monitoring the restricted, preferenced, and earmarked issues.

- **Raising money for a mission trip.** The deputized fund-raising concept applies to raising money for career and short-term missionaries. When an organization accepts gifts under this concept, it assumes the responsibility for the discretion and control of the gifts. Additionally, the charity must be precise in its proper communication with the supported missionary and the donors. It is very easy to cross the line from a gift restricted for missions, perhaps even in a particular region of the world, or a specific country, to a gift earmarked (see above discussion) transaction.

  Sponsors of short-term mission trips most often cross the restricted to earmarked line when refunds are provided in relation to individuals who planned to go on a mission trip but were unable to make the trip.

- **Transactions which are part gift/part purchase.** These transactions trigger the quid pro quo rules and require churches and other charities to demonstrate integrity. Unless the charity steps up and fulfills its responsibility to report to the donor the fair market value of the goods or services provided, the donor lacks the necessary information to claim the correct charitable contribution amount.

Citations

Chapter 1, Financial Accountability

- **Expenses of spouses of board members**
  INFO 2000-0236

- **Per diem expense payments to board members**
  Rev. Rul. 67-30

Chapter 2, Tax Exemption

- **Criteria for qualifying as a church**
  Spiritual Outreach Society v. Commissioner, T.C.M. 41 (1990)

  Joseph Edward Hardy v. Commissioner, T.C.M. 557 (1990)

- **Exemption from filing Form 990 for certain missions organizations**
  Treas. Reg. 1.6033-2(g)(1)(iv)

- **General**
  501(c)(3) organization established for religious purposes
  Treas. Reg. 1.511-2(a)(3)(ii)

- **Local sales taxes**
  Thayer v. South Carolina Tax Commission, 413 S.E. 2d 810 (S.C. 1992)

  Quill Corp. v. North Dakota, S. Ct. No. 91-194

  Jimmy Swaggart Ministries v. Board of Equalization of California, 110 S. Ct. 688 (1990)

- **Private benefit/private inurement**
  Treas. Reg. 1.501(a)-1(c)
  G.C.M. 37789

- **Property taxes**
  Trinity Episcopal Church v. County of Sherburne, 1991 WL 95745 (Minn. Tax 1991)

- **Public Disclosure of Information Returns**
  P.L. 100-203

- **Tax-exempt status revoked for excessive UBI**
  United Missionary Aviation, Inc. v. Commissioner, T.C.M. 566 (1990)

  Frazee v. Illinois Department of Employment, 57 U.S.L.W. 4397, 108 S. Ct. 1514 (1989)

  Hernandez v. Commissioner, 819 F.2d 1212, 109 S. Ct. 2136 (1989)

- **Unrelated business income: general**
  Code Sec. 511-13

- **Unrelated business income: affinity credit card programs**
  T.C.M. 34 (1996)
  T.C.M. 63 (1996)

- **Unrelated business income: jeopardy to exempt status**
  Ltr. Rul. 7849003

- **Unrelated business income: organization's tour programs**
  Ltr. Rul. 9027003

- **Unrelated business income: affinity card programs**
  Ltr. Rul. 9029047
  G.C.M. 39827, July 27, 1990

- **Unrelated business income: mailing list profits**
  Disabled American Veterans v. U.S., 94 TC No. 6 (1990)

  American Bar Endowment v. U.S., 477 U.S. 105 (1986)

- **Unrelated business income: rental income**
  Ltr. Rul. 200222030

- **Unrelated business income: other**
  Hope School v. U.S., 612 F.2d 298 (7th Cir. 1980)
  Rev. Rul. 64-182

Chapter 3, Compensating Employees

- **Accountable expense reimbursement plans**
  Treas. Reg. 1.62-2
  Treas. Reg. 1.274-5(e)
  Ltr. Rul. 9317003

- **Deferred compensation**
  Code Sec. 409A
  IRS Notice 2005-1

- **Documenting employee expenses**
  T.A.M. 200435018-22

- **Fair Labor Standards Act**
  DeArment v. Harvey, No. 90-2346 (8th Cir. 1991)

  U.S. Department of Labor v. Shenandoah Baptist Church, 899 F.2d 1389 (4th Cir.) cert. denied, 111 S. Ct. 131 (1990)

  Shaliehsabou v. Hebrew Home of Greater Washington, 363 F.3d 299 (4th Cir. 2004)

- **Flexible spending accounts**
  Rev. Rul. 2003-102
  Code Sec. 125

- **Health reimbursement arrangements**
  Code Sec. 105
  Rev. Rul. 2002-41
  Notice 2002-45
  IRP 80,600

- **Health savings accounts**
  Code Sec. 233
  IRS Notice 2004-2
  Rev. Proc. 2004-22
  IRS Notice 2004-23
  Rev. Rul. 2004-38
  Rev. Rul. 2004-45
  IRS Notice 2004-50
- **Healthcare flexible spending accounts**
  Code Sec. 105(b), (e)
  IRS Notice 2004-42
- **Tax-sheltered annuities**
  Code Sec. 403(b)
  Code Sec. 1402(a)
  Code Sec. 3121(a)(5)(D)
  Rev. Rul. 78-6
  Rev. Rul. 68-395
  Azad v. Commissioner, 388 F. 2d74(8th Cir.1968)
  Rev. Rul. 66-274

Chapter 4, Employer Reporting

- **Classification of workers**
  Rev. Proc. 85-18
  Sec. 530 of the Revenue Act of 1978
- **Employee v. self-employed for income tax purposes**
  Rev. Rul. 87-41
- **Moving expenses**
  Code Sec. 82
  Code Sec. 3401(a)(15)

- **Noncash remuneration**
  Code Sec. 3401(a)
- **Payment of payroll taxes**
  Triplett 115 B.R. 955 (N.D. Ill. 1990)
  Carter v. U.S., 717 F. Supp. 188 (S.D. N.Y. 1989)
- **Per diem allowances**
  IRS Publication 1542
  T.D. 9064
- **Personal use of employer-provided auto**
  Temp. Reg. Sec. 1.61-2T
  IRS Notice 91-41
- **Rabbi trusts**
  Rev. Proc. 92-64
- **Reasonable compensation**
  Truth Tabernacle, Inc. v. Commissioner of Internal Revenue, T.C.M. 451 (1989)
  Heritage Village Church and Missionary Fellowship, Inc., 92 B.R. 1000 (D.S.C. 1988)
- **Taxability of benefits paid under cafeteria plans**
  Ltr. Rul. 8839072
  Ltr. Rul. 8839085
- **Temporary travel**
  Rev. Rul. 93-86
  Comprehensive National Energy Policy Act of 1992
- **Unemployment taxes**
  Code Sec. 3309(b)
  St. Martin Evangelical Lutheran Church v. South Dakota, 451 U.S. 772 (1981)
  Employment Division v. Rogue Valley Youth for Christ, 770 F.2d 588 (Ore. 1989)

- **Voluntary withholding for ministers**
  Rev. Rul. 68-507

Chapter 5, Information Reporting

- **Backup withholding**
  Code Sec. 3406
- **Cash reporting rules for charities**
  T.D. 8373
  G.C.M. 39840
- **Issuing Forms 1099-MISC**
  Rev. Rul. 84-151
  Rev. Rul. 81-232
- **Moving expense reporting**
  IRS Announcement 94-2
- **Nonresident alien payments**
  Code Sec. 1441
  Code Sec. 7701(b)
- **Volunteer fringe benefits**
  Prop. Reg. 1.132-5(r)
- **Withholding of tax on non-resident aliens**
  Pub. 515

Chapter 7, Charitable Gifts

- **Charitable remainder unitrusts**
  IRS Notice 94-78
- **Church school gifts**
  Rev. Rul. 83-104
- **Contribution denied/indirectly related school**
  Ltr. Rul. 9004030
- **Contribution designated for specific missionaries**
  Hubert v. Commissioner, T.C.M. 482 (1993)

CITATIONS

- **Contribution earmarked for a specific individual**
  Ltr. Rul. 9405003
  IRS Announcement 92-128
  Ltr. Rul. 8752031
  Rev. Rul. 79-81

- **Contribution of autos**
  IRS Publication 4302
  American Jobs Creation Act of 2004

- **Contribution of church bonds**
  Rev. Rul. 58-262

- **Contribution of promissory note**
  Allen v. Commissioner, U.S. Court of Appeals, 89-70252 (9th Cir. 1991)

- **Contribution of services**
  Rev. Rul. 67-236
  Grant v. Commissioner, 84 T.C.M. 809 (1986)

- **Contribution of unreimbursed travel expenses**
  Tafralian v. Commissioner, T.C.M. 33 (1991)
  Rev. Rul. 84-61
  Rev. Rul. 76-89

- **Contribution sent to children who are missionaries**
  Davis v. U.S., 110 S. Ct. 2014 (1990)

- **Contribution that refers to donor's name**
  IR-92-4

- **Contribution to needy individuals**
  Stjernholm v. Commissioner, T.C.M. 563 (1989)
  Ltr. Rul. 8752031
  Rev. Rul. 62-113

- **Criteria used to determine deductibility of payments to private schools**
  Rev. Rul. 83-104
  Rev. Rul. 79-99

- **Deductibility of gifts to domestic organizations for foreign use**
  Ltr. Rul. 9211002
  Ltr. Rul. 9131052
  Ltr. Rul. 9129040
  Rev. Rul. 75-65
  Rev. Rul. 63-252

- **Deductibility of membership fees as contributions**
  Rev. Rul. 70-47
  Rev. Rul. 68-432

- **Deductibility of payments relating to fund-raising events**
  Pub. 1391
  Rev. Rul. 74-348

- **Deduction of out-of-pocket transportation expenses**
  Treas. Reg. 1.170A-1(g)
  Rev. Rul. 76-89

- **Determining the value of donated property**
  IRS Pub. 561
  Rochin v. Commissioner, T.C.M. 262 (1992)

- **Gift of inventory**
  Code Sec. 170(e)
  Reg. 1.161-1
  Reg. 1.170A-1(c)(2), (3), (4)
  Reg. 1.170A-4A(c)(3)
  Rev. Rul. 85-8

- **Gift of life insurance**
  Ltr. Rul. 9147040
  Ltr. Rul. 9110016

- **Incentives and premiums**
  IRS. Pub. 1391
  Rev. Proc. 96-59
  Rev. Proc. 92-102
  Rev. Proc. 92-49
  Rev. Proc. 90-12

- **IRA rollovers**
  Pension Protection Act of 2006

- **Payments in connection with use of ministry services**
  Rev. Rul. 76-232

- **Payments to a retirement home**
  T.A.M. 9423001
  U.S. v. American Bar Endowment, 477 U.S.105 (S. Ct. 1986)

- **Scholarship gifts**
  Ltr. Rul. 9338014
  Rev. Rul. 83-104
  Rev. Rul. 62-113

- **Substantiation rules**
  Omnibus Budget Reconciliation Act of 1993
  T.D. 8690

- **Travel tours**
  Ltr. Rul. 9027003

Federal Tax Regulation (Reg.)
Treasury Decision (T.D.)
Private Letter Ruling (Ltr. Rul.)
Field Service Advice (F.S.A.)
Revenue Ruling (Rev. Rul.)
Revenue Procedure (Rev. Proc.)
Tax Court Memorandum (T.C.M.)
Technical Advice Memorandum (T.A.M.)

Index

A

Accountability to donors, *19-23*
Accountable expense reimbursement plans, *75-76, 77*
Accounting method,
    Cash and accrual, *128*
    Change in methods, *48-49*
    Modified cash, *129*
Accounting records, *127-29*
Accrual method of accounting, *128*
Aliens, nonresident, *111-12*
Annual returns, *42*
Annuity,
    Acknowledgments, *168*
    Gift, general, *156*
    Payments to annuitants, *110-11*
    Tax-sheltered (*see* Tax-sheltered annuities)
    Trust, *157*
Application for recognition of tax-exempt status, *28-29, 31-32*
Assignment of ministers, *56, 58, 88*
Auctions, *177-78*
Audits, *13, 143-49*
Autos (*see* Vehicles)

B

Backup withholding, *109*
Bank deposits, *121*
Bargain sale, *156*
Benevolence fund, *194-95*
Board,
    Conflicts of interest, *14-17, 20, 22*
    Governance, *12*
    Minutes, *12-13*
    Resolutions (*see* Resolutions)
Budgeting, *14, 143*
Bulk mailing, *50, 51*

C

Cafeteria plans, *68*
Cash,
    Disbursements, *123-27*
    Method of accounting, *128*
    Receipts, *119-23*
Cellular phones, *5*
Charitable contributions,
    Annuity trust, *157*
    Auctions, *177-78*
    Bargain sale, *156*
    Benevolence fund, *194-95*
    Conduit transactions, *159-60*
    Checks, *161-62*
    Child adoption, *204-5*
    Credit cards, *162*
    Deputized fund-raising, *181-84*
    Donor advised, *156-57*
    Donor privacy, *201-3*
    End-of-year, *161-62*
    Foreign use, *166-68*
    Frequent-flyer miles, *197, 199*
    Gift annuity, *110-11, 156, 168*
    Gifts-in-kind, *164, 197, 199*
    Incentives/premiums, *10, 20, 176-77*
    Insurance, *156, 158*
    Individual Retirement Account rollover, *7-8*
    Internet donations, *162*
    Inventory, *192*
    Lead trust, *157*
    Mileage rate, *10*
    Missionaries, *181-84*
    Needy individuals, *194-95*
    Nondeductible, *159-31*
    Out-of-pocket expenses, *166, 197, 199*
    Overfunding of projects, *200*
    Paid to another charity, *200*
    Percentage limitations, *158*
    Pooled income fund, *157, 168*
    Private schools, *192-93*
    Property, *156, 161, 162*
    Qualified donees, *151*
    Quid pro quo disclosures, *175-80*
    Real estate, *153-55, 161, 162*
    Receipting, *162-75*
    Receipting a taxpayer other than the donor, *201*
    Refunding, *200*
    Remainder interest, *156, 168*
    Restricted, *20-21, 152-55*
    Scholarships, *196-97*
    Securities, *155, 162*
    Services, *161*
    Short-term missions trips, *184-91*
    Solicitation laws, *203*
    Supporting specific individuals, *181-91*
    Tax deductible, *151-58*
    Timing of gifts, *161-62*
    Token limitations, *10, 20, 176-77*
    Unitrust, *157*
    Use of property, *161*
    Vehicles, *173-75*
    Volunteers, *114, 197, 199*
Charitable solicitation filing, state, *203*
Charity control, *152-53*
Chart of accounts, *138*
Check, gift by, *161-62*
Child adoption, *204-5*
Child care assistance plan, *65-66*
Church Audit Procedures Act, *28*
Church management software, *131-32, 133-36*
Churches,
    Exempt from FICA, *90*
    Exempt from filing Form 990, *5, 28*
    Tax-exempt status, *27-28*
COBRA, *67-68*
Common-law rules, *87*
Compensation,
    Executives, *6-7, 13-4, 55*
    General, *6, 55-84*
    Gift planners, *23*
    Reasonable, *55*
    Review, *13-14*
Compensation of executives, *6-7, 13-14, 55*
Compilation, *13, 143-44*
Conduit transactions, *159-60*
Conflicts of interest, *14-17, 20, 22*
Consumer's Price Index, *55*
Counting money, *120-23*
CPAs, *13, 143-49*
Credit cards, *82-83, 162*

D

Deferred compensation,
    403(b), *9, 61-63*
    401(k), *9, 61-63*
    In general, *61*
Dependent care assistance plan, *65-66*
Depreciation, *131*
Deputized fund-raising, *181-84*
Determination letter request, *31*
Disability insurance, *69*
Disclosure of Forms 1023 and 990, *42, 48*
Discrimination,
    Fringe benefits, *74-75*
    Immigration, *115-16*
    Racial, *49, 114-15*
Donor,
    Communication, *19-20*
    Expectations, *23*
    Intent, *23*

INDEX

Privacy, *201-3*
Preferences, *153-55*
Reporting to, *21, 23, 162-75*
Restrictions, *152-55*
Donor-advised funds, *3-4, 156-57*

E

Earmarked gifts, *159-60*
Earned income tax credit, *91, 92*
ECFA, *11, 22-23*
Employee vs. independent contractor,
    Classification of,
        Ministers, *88-89*
        Workers, *85-89*
        Common-law rules, *87*
Employer identification number, *29, 30*
Employer-provided vehicles, *63-65*
Expense reimbursements, *75-83*
Expense substantiation, *75, 77*

F

Family and Medical Leave Act, *2*
Fair Labor Standards Act, *2-3, 10, 73-74, 84*
Federal income tax, *90, 91*
Federal unemployment tax, *2, 103, 105*
FICA, *9, 89-90*
Finances,
    Accounting records, *127-43*
    Bank deposits, *131*
    Budgeting, *14, 143*
    Counting money, *120-23*
    Disbursements, *123-27*
    Petty cash, *127*
    Receipts, *119-23*
    Reports, *132, 137-43*
Financial accountability, *11-24*
Financial advice, *23*
Financial reports, *132, 137-43*
Fiscal year change, *49*
Flexible spending account, *68-69*
Foreign use, *166-68*
Forms (explained and/or reproduced)
    I-9, *115-16*
    SS-4, *29, 30*
    W-2, *97-103*
    W-2c, *103, 104*
    W-3, *103, 104*
    W-3c, *103*
    W-4, *91, 92*
    W-4P, *111*
    W-5, *91, 92*
    W-7, *91*
    W-9, *108, 109*

940, *103, 105*
941, *3, 94-95, 97*
941c, *3, 96*
941x, *3*
990, *1-2, 42-48*
990-EZ, *42*
990-N, *4*
990-T, *36*
1023, *28-29, 31-32*
1042, *111-12*
1042-S, *111-12*
1096, *107, 108*
1098, *109*
1098-C, *165, 173-75*
1099-INT, *109-10*
1099-MISC, *112-13*
1099-R, *110-11*
1120, *42*
1128, *49*
3115, *49*
3624, *50, 51*
5500, *42*
5578, *49, 114-15*
8109, *93*
8109-B, *93-94*
8274, *90*
8282, *49, 169-70*
8283, *49, 169, 171-72*
8717, *49*
8718, *31, 49*
401(k) plans, *9, 62, 63*
403(b) plans, *9, 61-63*
Frequent-flyer miles, *197, 199*
Fringe benefits,
    Dependent care, *65-66*
    Flexible spending accounts, *69,*
    Health reimbursement arrangement, *69*
    Health savings account, *69*
    Social security tax reimbursement, *70-71*
Fund accounting, *129*
Fund-raisers,
    Compensation, *21*

G

Gift annuity, *110-11, 156, 168*
Gifts-in-kind, *164, 197, 199*
Gift planners, *21*
Gifts to employees, *72*
Group exemption, *29, 32*

H

Health insurance, *66-67*

Health reimbursement arrangement, *69*
Health savings accounts, *69*
Highly compensated employees, *9, 74-75*
Honoraria, *17-18*
Housing,
    Allowance, *56-60*
    Resolutions, *57*

I

Immigration control, *115-16*
Incentives, *10, 20, 176-77*
Incorporation, *28*
Independent contractors, *86-87*
Individual Retirement Account
    rollover, *7-8*
Insurance,
    COBRA, *67-68,*
    Disability, *69*
    Health, *66-67*
    Life, *156, 158*
    Workers' Compensation, *2, 72*
Intellectual properties, *18-19*
Interest,
    Paid, *109-10*
    Received, *109*
Inurement, *39-41*
Inventory, *192*

L

Lead trust, *157*
Lease value, autos, *64-65*
Life estate, *156, 168*
Life insurance, *156, 168*
Loans to employees, *70*
Lodging *(see Housing)*

M

Magnetic media reporting, *107*
Mailing lists, *201-3*
Mailing rates, *50, 51*
Medical expenses,
    Health reimbursement arrangement, *69*
    Flexible spending account, *69*
    Health savings account, *69*
Mileage rates, *10*
Minimum wage, *2-3, 10, 73-74, 84*
Ministers,
    Assignment, *56, 58, 88*
    Classification, *88-89*
    Housing allowance, *56-60*
    Special tax provisions, *89*

Missionaries, gifts designated for, *181-84*
Missions trips, short-term, *184-91*
Modified cash method of accounting, *129*
Mortgage, interest received, *109*
Moving expenses, *71-72, 114*

N

Needy, gifts for/to, *194-95*
Newsletter plans, *66*
Nondiscrimination rules, *74-75*
Nonresident aliens, *112*

O

Offering envelopes, *121, 124*
Organizational change, *48*
Out-of-pocket expenses, *166, 197*
Overfunding of projects, *200*
Overtime, payment of, *2-3, 10, 73-74, 84*

P

Payroll taxes,
    Depositing withheld taxes, *93-94*
    Filing annual returns, *97-105*
    Filing quarterly returns, *94-97*
    Personal liability, *91, 92*
    Unemployment taxes, *2, 103, 105*
    Withholding, *89-93*
Pension limitations, *9*
Per diem allowance, *10, 76*
Petty cash, *127*
Pledge, *162*
Political activity, *53*
Pooled income fund, *157, 168*
Postal regulations, *50, 51*
Premiums *(see Incentives)*
Privacy, donor, *201-3*
Private benefit/inurement, *39-41*
Private schools, *192-93*
Property taxes, *50, 51*
Property transferred to employees, *71*
Public inspection of information returns, *42, 48*

Q

Quid pro quo disclosures, *10, 20, 175-80*

R

Rabbi trust, *61*
Racial discrimination, *114-15*
Real estate, *156, 161, 162*
Reasonable compensation, *55*
Records retention, *130*

Refunds, to donors, *200*
Reimbursement,
    Business expenses, *75-83*
    Health, *68-79*
    Mileage, volunteers, *114, 197, 199*
    Social security tax, *70-71*
Related-party transactions, *14-17, 20, 22*
Religious purposes, *27-28*
Resolutions,
    Accountable expense reimbursement, *77*
    Assignment of a minister, *88*
    Benevolence fund, *195*
    Conflicts of interest, *16-17*
    Housing allowance, *57*
Restricted contributions, *20-21, 152-55, 199-200*
Retirement plan
    Informal, *8-9*
    Limits, *9, 61-63*
Roth 401(k) and 403(b), *9*
Royalties,
    Paid to insiders, *23*
    Reporting of payments, *112-13*

S

Sales tax, *52-53*
Scholarships, *196-97*
Securities, *155, 162*
Self-employment tax, *70-71*
Services, gifts of, *161*
Short-term missions trips, *184-91*
Social security tax, FICA, *9, 89-90*
Social security tax reimbursement, *70-71*
Software,
    Church and nonprofit, *131-32, 133-36*
Specified contributions *(see Restricted contributions)*
Start-up of a nonprofit, *28-31*
State filing requirements, *50, 52-53, 206*
Statement of activity, *137, 139-40*
Statement of financial position, *137, 141*

T

Taxes, state,
    Exemption, *50, 52*
    Property, *50, 51*
    Sales, *52-53*
    Unemployment, *2, 103, 105*
Tax-exempt status,
    Advantages, *25-26*

Application, *29, 31-32*
Churches, *27-28, 31*
Granting, *31-32*
Group, *29, 32*
Limitations, *26-27*
Taxpayer identification number, *29, 30, 108, 109*
Tax-sheltered annuities, *9, 61-63*
Tithing ministry funds, *199*
Token limitations, *10, 20, 176-77*
Trust savings account, *157*

U

Unitrust, *157*
Unrelated business income,
    Checklist, *34*
    Debt-financed income, *37*
    Exceptions, *37-38*
    General, *32-39*
    Rental income, *35*
    Reporting and filing requirements, *33, 36*
    Tax liability, *38*
Unemployment taxes, *2, 103, 105*
Unreasonable compensation, *55*

V

Vehicles,
    Donations, *176-75*
    Expense substantiation, *75-81*
    Lease valuation, *64-65*
    Personal use of employer-provided, *63-65*
Voluntary income tax withholding, *91-92*
Volunteers, *114, 197, 199*

W

Withholding, *89-93*
Worker classification, *2, 85-89*
Workers' Compensation, *2, 72*
Works for hire, *18-19*

10 Biggest Tax and Financial Mistakes Made by Churches and Nonprofits

1. Not setting up and adequately monitoring an accountable expense reimbursement plan for employees. Chapter 3.

2. Failure to comply with the Fair Labor Standards Act for churches and other nonprofits. Chapter 3.

3. Not reporting taxable fringe benefits and social security reimbursements as additional compensation to employees. Chapter 3.

4. Deducting FICA tax from the salary of qualified ministers, whether employed by a church or other nonprofit. Chapter 4.

5. Failing to file Form 1099-MISC for independent contractors. Chapter 5.

6. Weak controls over revenue, including failing to have offerings and other cash and checks controlled by two individuals until the funds are counted. Chapter 6.

7. Inadequate controls over disbursements leaving the ministry at risk for embezzlement. Chapter 6.

8. Failure to issue a proper receipt (including the fair market value of the goods or services provided) when a donor makes a payment of more than $75 and receives goods or services. Chapter 7.

9. Providing receipts for the donation of services and the rent-free use of property. Receipting contributions designated for individuals without proper discretion and control exercised by the donee organization. Placing values on noncash gifts. Chapter 7.

10. Accepting earmarked gifts with the charity exercising inadequate control when the gift is disbursed to another charity or benevolent recipient. Chapter 7.

10 Tax and Finance Questions Most Frequently Asked by Churches and Nonprofits

1. **Tax exempt status.** Should our church or nonprofit file for tax exemption with the Internal Revenue Service? Are we required to annually file Form 990? Chapter 2.

2. **Unrelated business income exposure.** Do we have any filing requirements for unrelated business income? If we have some unrelated business income, will we lose our tax-exempt status? Chapter 2.

3. **Public disclosure.** Is our organization required to disclose any documents to the public based on appropriate requests for them? If so, which documents? Chapter 2.

4. **Political activities.** Are the activities of our orgnaization consistent with the political activity law? Chapter 2.

5. **Housing allowance.** How do we determine whether a minister qualifies for a housing allowance designation? Are the rules for qualifying for the housing allowance identical for churches and other nonprofits? Chapter 3.

6. **Reporting compensation.** Which payments to employees are taxable and must be reported on the annual Form W-2? Chapter 4.

7. **Handling gifts.** What steps can we take to ensure the highest integrity in processing gifts, especially cash offerings, and providing acknowledgments to donors? Chapter 6.

8. **Internal auditing.** Should we have an audit, review, or compilation by an independent CPA? If not, how can we perform a valid internal audit of our financially related processes? Chapter 6.

8. **Noncash gifts.** How do we handle noncash gifts? What type of receipt should we provide? Should we ever place a value on a noncash gift, including gifts of services? Chapter 7.

10. **Donor-restricted gifts.** When a donor restricts a gift, how do we determine whether we should accept the gift and whether it qualifies as a charitable contribution? Chapter 7.

Leadership Library
Making Vision Stick

Andy Stanley

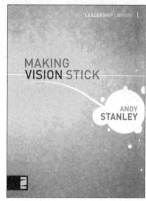

A vision. You as a leader may have it, but has your organization caught it? If a leader's vision is all about what could be and what should be, why are you buried under what is?

Noted author and pastor Andy Stanley points out that if followers don't get the vision, it's because the leaders haven't delivered it. He reveals the three reasons vision doesn't stick. And then he delivers three ways to make vision stick, to make you a leader worth following:

1. Cast vision strategically: defining your vision
2. Celebrate vision systematically: regularly rejoicing in the successes
3. Live your vision continuously: putting your vision into practice in your own life

With *Making Vision Stick,* you will learn how to propel you and your organization forward on the vision God has granted you.

Hardcover, Printed: 0-310-28305-1

Leadership Library
When Leadership and Discipleship Collide

Bill Hybels

Using stories from his own life and ministry, Bill Hybels shows how the laws for leadership success can sometimes crash headlong into another reality: an inner prompting of the Spirit showing you a different approach. The decisions you make at that point could affect not only you, but the ultimate destiny of those you lead.

Hardcover, Printed: 0-310-28306-x

The Leadership Network Innovation Series

Leadership from the Inside Out

Examining the Inner Life of a
Healthy Church Leader

Kevin Harney

You can serve God and his people for a lifetime and do it with passion and joy. You do not have to become another casualty in the growing number of leaders who have compromised their integrity, character, and ministry because they failed to lead an examined and accountable life.

The road forward is clearly marked. Leaders must make a decision to humbly and consistently examine their inner lives and identify areas of needed change and growth.

Also, wise leaders commit to listen to the voices of those who will love them enough to speak the truth and point out problems and potential pitfalls.

Kevin Harney writes, "The vision of this book is to assist leaders as they discover the health, wisdom, and joy of living an examined life. It is also to give practical tools for self-examination." Sharing stories and wisdom from his years in ministry, Harney shows you how to maintain the most powerful tool in your leadership toolbox: YOU. Your heart, so you can love well. Your mind, so you can continue to learn and grow. Your ears, your eyes, your mouth ... consider this your essential guide to conducting your own complete interior health exam, so you can spot and fix any problems, preserve the things that matter most, and grow as a source of vision, strength, and hope to others.

Softcover: 0-310-25943-6